Oxford Shakespeare Topics

# *Shakespeare and Classical Antiquity*

OXFORD SHAKESPEARE TOPICS

Published and Forthcoming Titles Include:

David Bevington, *Shakespeare and Biography*
Michael Caines, *Shakespeare and the Eighteenth Century*
Lawrence Danson, *Shakespeare's Dramatic Genres*
Janette Dillon, *Shakespeare and the Staging of English History*
Paul Edmondson and Stanley Wells, *Shakespeare's Sonnets*
Gabriel Egan, *Shakespeare and Marx*
Andrew Gurr and Mariko Ichikawa, *Staging in Shakespeare's Theatres*
Jonathan Gil Harris, *Shakespeare and Literary Theory*
Douglas Lanier, *Shakespeare and Modern Popular Culture*
Hester Lees-Jeffries, *Shakespeare and Memory*
Ania Loomba, *Shakespeare, Race, and Colonialism*
Raphael Lyne, *Shakespeare's Late Work*
Russ McDonald, *Shakespeare and the Arts of Language*
Steven Marx, *Shakespeare and the Bible*
Robert S. Miola, *Shakespeare's Reading*
Marianne Novy, *Shakespeare and Outsiders*
Phyllis Rackin, *Shakespeare and Women*
Catherine Richardson, *Shakespeare and Material Culture*
Bruce R. Smith, *Shakespeare and Masculinity*
Zdeněk Stříbrný, *Shakespeare and Eastern Europe*
Michael Taylor, *Shakespeare Criticism in the Twentieth Century*
Alden T. Vaughan and Virginia Mason Vaughan, *Shakespeare in America*
Stanley Wells, ed., *Shakespeare in the Theatre: An Anthology of Criticism*
Martin Wiggins, *Shakespeare and the Drama of his Time*

Oxford Shakespeare Topics

GENERAL EDITORS: PETER HOLLAND AND STANLEY WELLS

# *Shakespeare and Classical Antiquity*

COLIN BURROW

OXFORD
UNIVERSITY PRESS

Great Clarendon Street, Oxford, OX2 6DP,
United Kingdom

Oxford University Press is a department of the University of Oxford.
It furthers the University's objective of excellence in research, scholarship,
and education by publishing worldwide. Oxford is a registered trade mark of
Oxford University Press in the UK and in certain other countries



First Edition published in 2013

Impression: 2



British Library Cataloguing in Publication Data
Data available

ISBN 978–0–19–968479–3

Printed in Great Britain by
CPI Group (UK) Ltd, Croydon, CR0 4YY

*In memoriam Emrys Jones, 1931–2012*

# Preface

I am very grateful to all the many generations of scholars on whose work this book sometime builds but mostly rests. Without Baldwin, Miola, Martindale, and many others I would not know very much, and a lightly annotated book such as this one cannot adequately record the full extent of my debts. Pigmies and giants, that kind of thing. I have been very fortunate that several exceptionally perceptive readers have scrutinized much of it, notably John Kerrigan and Leah Whittington, as well as the series editors Stanley Wells and Peter Holland, to all of whom I am most grateful. What's still wrong in it remains my own, of course. I am also grateful to the Warden and Fellows of All Souls College, Oxford, for giving me the freedom to write it, as well as to Jacqueline Baker (and before her, Andrew McNeillie) for encouraging the work and tolerating my delays. Librarians in Oxford, Cambridge, and in particular at All Souls have been exceptionally helpful. Since so much of it is about how Shakespeare remembered his learning and teaching, I should also record my debts to my own teachers in the distant past, particularly to Derek Lucas, Anne Bowler, Roland Clare, and David Miller at Bristol Grammar School, John Casey and J. H. Prynne at Cambridge, and in particular to the supervisor of my D. Phil., Emrys Jones, whose *The Origins of Shakespeare* is one of the origins of my own interest in this topic, and whose sad and unexpected death occurred while I was finishing this book.

Quotations from Shakespeare follow William Shakespeare, *The Complete Works*, ed. S. Wells and G. Taylor 2nd edn (Oxford: Clarendon Press, 2005). Quotations from other early-modern sources are modernized in spelling and punctuation from early printed sources, or are taken from modernized editions. For ease of reference, quotations from classical texts are keyed to the relevant volumes in the *Loeb Classical Library*, although on occasions I have modified the text to bring it closer to that of editions printed in Shakespeare's lifetime. Translations are generally my own unless otherwise stated, though 'my own' here can sometimes mean 'a freshened-up version of the Loeb translation adapted to take account of what I want the text to mean for the purposes of my argument'.

# Contents

# *Illustrations*

# Introduction

Everybody knows that Shakespeare had 'small Latin and less Greek'. They know it because Ben Jonson said so in his elegy prefixed to the first Folio of Shakespeare's *Comedies, Histories and Tragedies* in 1623. It's worth reading the whole passage, though, to see if Jonson meant exactly what he is often thought to have said:

> For if I thought my judgement were of years
>   I should commit thee surely with thy peers,
> And tell how far thou didst our Lyly outshine,
>   Or sporting Kyd, or Marlowe's mighty line.
> And, though thou hadst small Latin and less Greek,
>   From thence to honour thee I would not seek
> For names, but call forth thundering Aeschylus,
>   Euripides and Sophocles to us,
> Pacuvius, Accius, him of Cordova dead,
>   To life again, to hear thy buskin tread
> And shake a stage; or, when thy socks were on
>   Leave thee alone for the comparison
> Of all that insolent Greece or haughty Rome
>   Sent forth, or since did from their ashes come. (27–40)[1]

Jonson was throughout his career keen to emphasize how far his classical learning outstripped that of his peers. His hard-earned reputation as a classicist has provided the usual framework for reading his elegy on Shakespeare as (in the words of John Dryden) 'an insolent, sparing, and invidious panegyric',[2] which claims that Shakespeare knew nothing or not much about classical literature.

Jonson, however, is not simply saying what he sounds as though he is saying.[3] The whole passage is hypothetical. It begins 'if I thought

I was mature enough to do so, I would say how superior you were to our contemporaries, and I would summon up an audience of classical dramatists to admire you . . . '. When Jonson moves on from considering Shakespeare's superiority to vernacular authors there is a shift of emphasis, and at this point a lot hangs on the single word 'though.' 'Though thou hadst small Latin and less Greek' could mean 'despite the fact that you only had a smattering of Latin and less Greek', as the orthodox reading suggests. It could alternatively mean 'even supposing (counterfactually) that you had only a little bit of Latin and even less Greek, the major classical dramatists would still admire you'. There is no way of finally knowing which of these alternatives Jonson meant, and probably he was praising Shakespeare in a double-edged way—he does manage, after all, to make it clear that it is *he* and not Shakespeare who is bringing the Greeks back to life, even if they are brought back to life in order to applaud Shakespeare's plays rather than Jonson's.

Shakespeare used to be represented as a natural artist, who warbled his native woodnotes wild, and is still routinely contrasted to the learned classicist Jonson. As the complexity of Jonson's tribute to Shakespeare suggests, that opposition is misleading. Shakespeare knew—from his grammar-school education and from his general reading—at least as much classical literature as many classics graduates today. He also knew enough to make his contemporaries think, just for a moment, that he might be a British equivalent to Euripides or Aeschylus, or, as Francis Meres described him in 1598, a reincarnation of the 'sweet witty soul of Ovid'.[4] The extent of that learning and the uses to which it was put will be the central concern of this book, which has three simple things to say.

1. Shakespeare knew quite a lot of classical literature. Given his education and the period in which he lived it would be surprising if he did not.

2. Shakespeare did interesting things with that classical learning, and understanding what he did with his knowledge, rather than just trying scrupulously to assess its exact extent, is central to an understanding of his work.

3. The ways Shakespeare used his classical learning changed throughout his career, in response to his contemporaries (including Ben Jonson), to new reading, and to the demands of different generic and theatrical settings.

Each chapter, five of which are for convenience devoted to Shakespeare's relationship to particular classical authors, explores these themes. Each chapter, though, and the book as a whole, tries to be a bit more than an introduction to what Shakespeare knew about the classics. It seeks to position Shakespeare within a larger narrative about changing understandings of classical antiquity in the late Elizabethan and Jacobean periods, and within a larger story about Renaissance attitudes to the classical past.

This is why the book is called *Shakespeare and Classical Antiquity* rather than, say, *Shakespeare and Classical Literature*. My title is, strictly speaking, anachronistic. 'Classical Antiquity' was not a phrase used in the late sixteenth and early seventeenth centuries. The phrase 'the classics', indeed, did not come to be used in England to mean 'classical authors' until the 1680s, more than half a century after Shakespeare's death. According to the *Oxford English Dictionary*, the adjective 'classical' was first used to mean 'belonging to the literature or art of Greek and Roman antiquity' in 1607, more than halfway through Shakespeare's theatrical career.

That's not a merely pedantic point about the history of a word. It tells us something about Shakespeare's historical position. Today most people would believe that the 'classical' world had its own religion, customs, political climates, and economy. This understanding of the classical past as a historically remote world is in part a legacy from what we call the 'Renaissance'—an extended period in which a whole range of different writers and scholars thought about works from ancient Rome and Greece, and in which the process of discovery, retrieval, and antiquarian investigation increasingly revealed quite how different the citizens of Greece and Rome were from each other and from those of the later world. Our present view of classical antiquity is also in part a legacy from eighteenth-century and nineteenth-century understandings of 'the Renaissance'. Again a glance at the dictionary can offer some pointers. The word 'Renaissance' was not used to describe 'The revival of the arts and high culture under the influence of classical models, which began in Italy in the 14th cent. and spread throughout most of Europe by the end of the 16th' until the 1830s. Even then, more than two centuries after Shakespeare's death, the word 'Renaissance' tends to be italicized by English authors to indicate that it was a recent importation from France. If Shakespeare was part of something we could call 'the Renaissance', he would not have known that he was.

He also probably would not have felt the longing for knowledge of the classical past which Johann Winckelmann, one of the great German classical scholars who inherited the idea of the 'Renaissance', described at the end of his *History of Ancient Art* (1764):

> I could not refrain from searching into the fate of works of art as far as my eye could reach; just as a maiden, standing on the shore of the ocean, follows with tearful eyes her departing lover with no hope of ever seeing him again, and fancies that in the distant sail she sees the image of her beloved. Like that loving maiden we too have, as it were, nothing but a shadowy outline left of the object of our wishes, but that very indistinctness awakes only a more earnest longing for what we have lost, and we study the copies of the originals more attentively than we should have done the originals themselves if we had been in full possession of them. In this particular we are very much like those who wish to have an interview with spirits, and who believe that they see them when there is nothing to be seen.[5]

Winckelmann both drew on and developed a form of romantic Hellenism which stressed the beauty of Greek art and its intimate relation to the liberty of Athens. He represented Roman sculpture and art as poor imitations of Greek originals. The notion that the 'classical' means pure lines, beautiful statues of beautiful (and often male) bodies, columns, and decorous admiration of the ancient Greeks would have meant almost nothing to late sixteenth-century English people. Before the mid eighteenth century it was unlikely that many English subjects had seen the Parthenon even in a picture. Greek statuary might have been known to a few through reputation, through sketches, or through engravings, but Greece certainly did not have associations with perfect beauty or with political freedom. Indeed, Shakespeare's plays set in Greece tend to emphasize the arbitrary and tyrannical nature of Greek laws. In *A Midsummer Night's Dream* the harsh law of Athens supports Egeus in his attempt to force his daughter Hermia to marry Demetrius. The wealthy and the well-born might travel to Rome, but in the sixteenth century, in the aftermath of Henry VIII's break with the Catholic church, 'Rome' meant not the forum or the statue of Laocoon, but Roman Catholicism, the whore of Babylon, over-ornamented worship, and morally and historically suspect traditions in Church government. The wonders of 'ancient' art and the 'modern' horrors of Rome were not fully separable. Greece was certainly not the ultimate object of historical desire.

For Shakespeare and his generation, reading and imitating classical literature were not activities only to be undertaken with reverence and awe, or with the trans-temporal longing described by Winckelmann. It was just what you did. At school you read Cicero and some Ovid and some Plautus alongside modern Latin authors like the humanist Desiderius Erasmus or the early sixteenth-century author of Latin eclogues known as 'Mantuan' (Baptista Spagnuoli Mantuanus, 1447–1516). As an adult you might read some Plutarch, perhaps even some Plato in translation, and if you were at university you would read some Aristotle too. These writers would inform you about how to live in the present and would provide material for your own writing. Many sixteenth-century readers encountered these texts in the spirit of 'What can this text do for me?' rather than of 'What culturally remote beauties can I discover here?' There were scholars who investigated how Cicero's ideas might relate to those of the Stoics, or what sources Plutarch used for his *Lives*, but these people, like many scholars today, were on the whole unpoetical souls. Shakespeare's encounters with 'classical antiquity' were more or less typical of what might be called practical humanism—that is, an engagement with Latin literature which was driven by need and use. It had only slight resemblances to the traditional picture of 'Renaissance' humanism, in which scholars and poets were driven by a desire to bridge the gulf between present and past, or to speak to the classical dead.

Slight resemblances, however, are not the same as no resemblance at all. As we shall see, there are several signs that Shakespeare did not *simply* think of classical texts as just another part of his reading which could be put to present use in the same way that he used Holinshed's *Chronicles* for his history plays or Arthur Brooke's *Tragical History of Romeus and Juliet* as a source for *Romeo and Juliet*. Sometimes passages of Ovid or Seneca do simply form part of the weave of his language. But at other times allusions to classical texts in his works are accompanied by a variety of effects which in one way or another flag them up for special attention. Displays of classical knowledge often provide delicate ways of differentiating between characters and their relative status, and can generate implied dialogues between characters onstage, as we shall see in Chapter 1. The 'Roman' cultural and ethical world described in Shakespeare's plays deriving from Plutarch, as Chapter 6 shows, often displays a distinct set of moral preoccupations, although Shakespeare was by no means trying to create a Roman world that was historically accurate. There are also occasions, particularly in the earlier part of his career, when he marks allusions to classical sources by a range of literary and stylistic effects that make them stand out from the surrounding works. This happens in a comic way in the Ovidian play put on by the rude mechanicals in *A Midsummer Night's Dream*, where Ovid becomes the foundation for a gloriously old-fashioned low-style drama (see below, pp. 119–23). The player's speech about Hecuba in *Hamlet* marks Shakespeare's longest and most explicit allusion to Virgil's epic poem the *Aeneid* (see below, pp. 62–71). It does so by a strange shift of style which is heralded by the prince's own attempts to recall what is clearly an old speech from his own past. In the narrative poem *Lucrece* the heroine sees part of the story related in Virgil's *Aeneid* in a picture which is also presented as old. In all these cases the classical texts suggest intense emotions, and they seem 'antiquated' in various senses.

These effects are curious and will be explored in detail in later chapters. They do in their various ways suggest that Shakespeare could associate works of 'classical antiquity' with 'oldness', and that in turn could be an indicator that Shakespeare regarded Latin literature as the product of a distinct cultural field called 'antiquity' which dated from centuries before his birth. They are not quite signs that he anticipated Winckelmann's 'earnest longing for what we have lost', since Shakespeare's tendency to associate classical texts and an 'old-fashioned' style early in his career was probably the result of several humdrum forces. He would have read Virgil at school, and by around 1600 he might have been labouring to recall the *Aeneid* just as much as Hamlet does when he prompts the player to recite the speech about Hecuba. By that date too, the majority of English verse translations of major classical poems and plays would have sounded stylistically antiquated to their English readers. Between the accession of Elizabeth I in 1558 and the death of Sir Philip Sidney in 1586, English poetry underwent more rapid transformations than in any other thirty-year period. Many of the major verse translations of Latin poetic and dramatic texts appeared in the very early stages of this process of literary transformation. Arthur Golding's translation of Ovid's *Metamorphoses* first appeared in 1565. Thomas Phaer's translation of Virgil's *Aeneid* was begun in the reign of Elizabeth's sister Mary, while the collected volume of translations of Seneca's ten tragedies that appeared in 1581 included translations that dated from the 1550s and 1560s. Shakespeare's early tendency to associate classical texts with an 'old' style does not necessarily show that he shared Winckelmann's sense of classical antiquity as a ghostly past realm. It may mean rather that he tended to associate classical texts with a slightly outmoded English verse style, and recognized that embedding such 'old' poems in his own plays was a clear way of establishing his sharpness and modernity by contrast. But these features of his engagement with classical writing had significant consequences. They mean that he can be connected to a larger story about the recovery of classical antiquity which leads on towards Winckelmann and beyond. Those stylistic effects in *Hamlet* and *A Midsummer Night's Dream* create the appearance of 'anachronism' and an effect of 'ancientness' in Shakespeare's treatments of classical texts, and the presence of these effects is part of what makes his response to classical antiquity so fascinating. They also, though, made Shakespeare's own responses to classical antiquity seem themselves to be a little out of fashion to his younger contemporaries such as Ben Jonson.

The word 'antiquity' in Shakespeare's lifetime had a rich and confusing range of senses. Shakespeare himself only ever uses the word to mean 'old', and usually does so in contexts which carry a suggestion of decrepitude. The speaker in the *Sonnets*, for example, describes himself as 'Beated and chapped with tanned antiquity' (62.10), like a piece of old wood or crinkled leather. During Shakespeare's lifetime, though, 'antiquity' had a rich range of other senses, and he was (unusually for him) rather old-fashioned in using the word as he did. Theologians defended contentious practices in the English Church by claiming that they dated back to 'antiquity', by which they might mean either Saxon times or the early Christian Church. The antiquity of books could also be taken as a token of their superior wisdom, as in the wonderful title of a volume which appeared in 1563: *This Book is called the Treasure of Gladness and seemeth by the copy, (being a very little manual, and written in vellum) to be made above two hundred years past at the least. Whereby it appeareth how God in old time, and not of late only, hath been truly confessed and honoured. The copy hereof is for the antiquity of it, preserved, and to be seen in the Printers' Hall.* Being old meant being a curiosity, but also being valuable, and being also a testament to truth. The 'old' language of the poet Gower in the prologues to *Pericles* has that force of 'antiquity' as meaning 'bygone but better'. As early as the 1580s, when Shakespeare was in his teens, the word could be used as it is today, of what we call 'classical' writing. A 1584 translation of the Greek historian Herodotus is called *The Famous History of Herodotus, containing the discourse of divers countries, the succession of their kings, the acts and exploits achieved by them, the laws and customs of every nation, with the true description and antiquity of the same.* 'Antiquity' there, we might note, goes along with curiosity about ancient customs: it is the chronological equivalent of physical distance, which makes the past resemble a strange country where 'laws and customs' might differ from those of the present.

Classical knowledge was also various, and was tied up in contemporary debates in a number of ways. Shakespeare wrote in an age which was acutely conscious of fashion, in clothing and consumer goods, and also in prose and verse style. He also wrote in a very competitive literary environment, in which relationships between modern and classical authors could be contentious. Fashion and competition both impinged on the ways in which classical literature was read and imitated during his lifetime. In 1598 (a year which was absolutely central for the development of Shakespeare's art and to the ways in which his career developed) Francis Meres's handbook of memorable comparisons called *Palladis Tamia* appeared, which presented Shakespeare as a reincarnation of the Augustan poet Ovid. It has often been suggested that the praise of Shakespeare in *Palladis Tamia* was a defining moment, which placed Shakespeare at the centre of the English literary scene and which influenced his sense of himself and his writing.[6] Meres recognized that there was a strong relationship between a large-scale ambition to revive and to emulate writers from classical antiquity and what now seems like a much more parochial ambition among English writers to outdo their contemporaries. Being listed by Meres as the English reincarnation of Ovid meant that Shakespeare was not just like Ovid, but that also he had outdone other contemporary poets who were seeking to emulate the eroticism and wit of Ovid—poets such as Christopher Marlowe or Arthur Golding.

Classical learning was charged with rivalry and could be highly topical. Through the later 1590s several high-profile literary quarrels were fought out through classical forms. In 1598–9 John Marston wrote satires, loosely based on Juvenal and Persius, which attacked the classically derived satires of Joseph Hall, and Hall responded in kind. On the stage through the last years of the sixteenth century and the early years of the seventeenth century several playwrights mocked their rivals by associating them with classical poets. John Marston tried to prick the bubble of Ben Jonson's classical pretensions in his *Histriomastix* (1599), which teases Jonson mercilessly. Thomas Dekker's *Satiromastix* (1601) also attacked Jonson through the character of the Roman poet and satirist Horace. Jonson duly replied with *Poetaster* (1601), which turns his enemies and rivals into the hack poets of Augustan Rome. Early in the seventeenth century too there was a wave of prestigious and high-profile prose translations of classical authors, often in expensive folio volumes. Philemon Holland translated Plutarch's *Moralia* as *The Moral Philosophy* in 1603. In the same year there was an augmented edition of Thomas North's translation of Plutarch's *Lives of the Noble Grecians and Romanes*, which presented a new printing of a text that had been available since 1579. Holland also translated Livy's *Roman History* in 1600. Tacitus's *End of Nero and the Beginning of Galba* had appeared in 1591, but it was augmented by a full translation of the *Annals* in 1598. Meanwhile George Chapman's translations of Homer began to appear from 1598, and Marlowe's close, sharp, and dense translations of Ovid's *Elegies* and the first book of Lucan's epic on the Roman civil wars had both found their way to the press by 1600. As we shall see, Shakespeare's treatment of classical texts underwent a number of changes in the new century. That was partly just because his drama was constantly evolving, but it was also because he was listening to the world around him.

Needless to say, Shakespeare put on a good show of knowing as much about classical literature as any other playwright in the period.

But there were various blind spots in his knowledge. Some of these were in areas about which few people knew at the time and so are of little significance. So it would have been impossible for anyone at this date to have known much about the Greek comedian Menander, for instance, because many of the fragments of his plays were not discovered until the 1960s. It would have been hard but not impossible for Shakespeare to have known much about the epicurean didactic poet Lucretius, whose long poem *De rerum natura* (On the nature of the universe) was not part of the curriculum of grammar schools, and the text of which, though it had been rediscovered in 1417 by Poggio Bracciolini and was a powerful influence on one of the most powerful influences on Shakespeare, Michel de Montaigne, remained difficult reading for someone with Shakespeare's background.[7]

But there are some kinds of classical learning which Shakespeare's rivals had, or which they were willing to show they had, which Shakespeare himself either did not have or did not choose to display. These can tell us something, by a negative image as it were, about the character of Shakespeare's classical knowledge. He shows almost no interest in Latin lyric. The elegists Propertius and Tibullus, although they were regularly printed along with Catullus in the sixteenth century, seem to have been outside his field of view.[8] Shakespeare also does not seem to have much interest in classical poems in complex stanzaic or metrical forms. Lines from Horace's odes are written out and wrapped around weapons in *Titus Andronicus*, but there is no sense that they belong within larger metrical and poetic structures: they are tags, with stinging applicability to their recipients (see below, pp. 24–5). This lack of interest in Latin lyric is not surprising in someone who mostly wrote for the stage. It's more or less impossible to register or represent lyric poetic structures—verse forms and metrical patterning—in a way that makes sense for a theatrical audience who are listening rather than reading. But several of Shakespeare's contemporaries did not share this blind spot. Samuel Daniel (born two years before Shakespeare) and Ben Jonson (born eight years after him) both wrote odes and Horatian verse epistles, as well as plays. Jonson experimented in his published and unpublished verse with stanza shape and line length in order to create equivalents for both Horatian odes and classical epithalamia, or marriage poems. Shakespeare's only attempt at a poem which he called an 'ode' was the love poem which Dumaine reads out in *Love's Labour's Lost* (4.3.99–118)—a poem which in the Quarto text of that play is comically called an 'Odo', as though there might be something a little odd, so far as the printer was concerned, about not just the form of the poem but even about its name. Dumaine's seven-syllable couplets are far removed from any of the stanzaic forms used in classical odes. As when the clown Costard, dressed as Pompey the Great, relentlessly declares: 'I Pompey am' (at 5.2.541, 542, and, yes, 545 too) and thereby makes it entirely obvious that he is not Pompey at all, there is in Dumaine's 'ode' or 'odo' a sense of classical garb not fitting its wearer at all comfortably.

The raunchy form of the classical epigram also had little direct influence on Shakespeare. There are plenty of 'epigrams', in the non-technical sense of sharp and pithy expressions, embedded in the *Sonnets* and in the plays, but the short, aggressive forms of Martial's *Epigrams*, which address a particular individual or describe a social event, seem just not to have suited Shakespeare's ear. Again this distinguishes him from several of the most notable poets in the 1590s. John Donne, Ben Jonson, Sir John Davies, John Weever, and John Marston all wrote epigrams grounded in classical models, and many of them also wrote (as Shakespeare did not) satires based on Horace and Juvenal. Significantly, each of these poets had connections among London lawyers, as Shakespeare did not. The classical epigram was associated with social and professional environments which were not Shakespeare's.

Shakespeare also seems not to have paid much attention to some of the larger debates about the relationship between English and classical poetry in the sixteenth century. Thomas Campion worked out elaborate metrical theories which were designed to enable English poets to adopt classical quantitative metres, which were based on notional duration of syllables rather than on patterns of stress.[9] These experiments in classical metre were partly aimed at eradicating 'gothic' elements (notably rhyme) from English poetry. The relatively few poets who followed Campion's example tended to be people who enjoyed experimenting with metrical and stanzaic forms, and who paid a close attention to the layout of printed poems on the page. Shakespeare was again not a poet in that vein, and his lack of interest in this learned tradition of classicizing lyric goes along with his lack of interest in shorter classical poems. It also reflects the particular nature of the lyrics that figure in his dramas. Shakespeare's songs are not only not classical; they tend to be explicitly English. The chorus of the song sung by Feste at the end of *Twelfth Night*, 'For the rain it raineth every day', is not a line a Roman poet would ever have been moved to compose, even though Rome does provide the odd day to make umbrella sellers rejoice. Shakespeare's songs can open up allusions to spaces outside or beyond the immediate action of the play ('Full fathom five thy father lies', *The Tempest*, 1.2.399), and these spaces are sometimes tinged with the exotic or the magical ('Those are pearls that were his eyes', *The Tempest*, 1.2.401; 'Lights that do mislead the dawn', *Measure for Measure*, 4.1.4). But there is not a single line in any of them which is clearly indebted to a classical source (and, incidentally, there are very few songs in the plays set in ancient Rome, which Shakespeare seems to have imagined as a largely unmusical place). When the Trojan Pandarus in *Troilus and Cressida* sings, he doesn't sound at all like a hero on the edges of the siege of Troy as celebrated by Homer and Virgil. He sings the song of a 'merry Greek', in the sixteenth-century sense of a sexually licensed pimp, rather than an evocation of classical song:

> These lovers cry 'O! O!', they die.
> Yet that which seems the wound to kill
> Doth turn 'O! O!' to 'ha ha he!'
> So dying love lives still.
> 'O! O!' a while, but 'ha ha ha!'
> 'O! O!' groans out for 'ha ha ha!' (3.1.117–22)

This almost aggressively keeps the classical world at bay, turning a Trojan hero into a downmarket balladeer. Samuel Daniel at the very start of the seventeenth century argued that introducing the conventions of classical poetic metres into English verse was a kind of slavery, and that 'we should not so soon yield our consents captive to the authority of antiquity'.[10] Daniel there uses 'antiquity' in the fashionable sense of 'ancient Roman example', a sense which Shakespeare never deployed. The kind of classicism Daniel was attacking, which sought to adapt English modes of versification to the principles and forms of Latin poetry, was absolutely not Shakespeare's kind of classicism.

What about Shakespeare's Greek? Even if we take Jonson's 'though thou hadst small Latin and less Greek' in the hypothetical sense ('even if...') there is no doubt that Shakespeare's knowledge of Greek was 'less' than his knowledge of Latin. That was true of every writer in the sixteenth century, including Ben Jonson himself, whose copy of a folio collection of the Greek poets survives. This volume has a Latin crib facing the Greek texts, and is in suspiciously good condition. Shakespeare and Jonson would have approached Greek literature through Latin. This was even true of their contemporary George Chapman, who made great boasts of his proficiency in Greek, but who actually struggled his way through the Greek texts of the *Iliad* and the *Odyssey* with the help of a Latin version on the facing page. Shakespeare, as well as most of his contemporaries, probably read no Greek tragedy in Greek, although he may have read some Euripides in Latin translation.[11] The stories of Orestes and of Oedipus were available to him through Latin sources and through English translations of those sources, as well as through dictionaries and mythographical handbooks. As the final chapter will suggest, Plutarch was a major source of Shakespeare's knowledge of at least some of the ethical thought implicit in Greek epic and tragedy, and had a profound influence on the way Shakespeare dramatized human character. Some Greek history might have been partially available to him in translation, but apart from the substantial counter-example of Plutarch's *Lives* (which he read in an English translation from a French version) there is little sign that he saw it as a major resource. Even in the case of Plutarch's *Parallel Lives of the Greeks and Romans* it was the lives of Roman heroes rather than those of their Greek parallels which principally caught Shakespeare's eye. The chief source of *Timon of Athens*—supposedly set in the Greece of the fifth century BC—is found in the life of the Roman Antony, though Shakespeare also took touches of the story from Plutarch's 'Life' of Alcibiades.

Despite the fact that Shakespeare probably didn't have a great deal of interest in Greek writing, there are a few pieces of Greek mood music in the canon, which imply at least an imaginative sense of what a 'Greek' atmosphere might be. The marvellous interstitial scene in which Cleomenes and Dion return from the oracle of Apollo at the start of Act 3 of *The Winter's Tale* brings a sudden Hellenic openness to the violent interiors which have dominated the play up to that point:

> The climate's delicate, the air most sweet;
> Fertile the isle, the temple much surpassing
> The common praise it bears.
> DION: I shall report,
> For most it caught me, the celestial habits—
> Methinks I so should term them—and the reverence
> Of the grave wearers. O, the sacrifice—
> How ceremonious, solemn, and unearthly
> It was i'th' off 'ring! (3.1.1–8)

There is magic here, and perhaps even a kind of Greek magic of ritual and oracle; but it is evoked by a persistent use of adjectives which deliberately avoid direct description of a Greek location or of Greek ritual. The island is 'delicate', 'sweet', and 'fertile' rather than, say, richly pastured or rocky or full of goats; the sacrifice is described through adjectives of unspecific numinosity ('celestial', 'grave', 'ceremonious', 'solemn', 'unearthly') rather than with detailed reference to tripods and smoking flesh. 'Habits' may suggest monastic robes, but it may simply be the priests' customs that are celestial. Combined with the fractured syntax of the two men, these features certainly evoke wonder, but they do not attempt to describe the Greek religious rituals which are the offstage and unimaginable cause of amazement. The scene may bring to mind oracles in Greek tragedy—in *Oedipus Rex*, or the sacred spaces of *Oedipus at Colonus*, perhaps—but there is no sign that Shakespeare looked at Greek material in order to evoke this environment. He follows his English source, Robert Greene's *Pandosto: The Triumph of Time* (1588) in conflating Delphi (the location of Apollo's oracle on mainland Greece) with Delphos, the island in the Aegean on which Apollo was supposed to have been born. Shakespeare then patched wonder into Greene's bald narrative, in which six lords of Bohemia briskly travel to the island 'where they were no sooner set on land, but with great devotion they went to the Temple of Apollo, and there offering sacrifice to the God, and gifts to the Priest, as the custom was, they humbly craved an answer of their demand'.[12] Shakespeare's 'Greek' vision in this scene is a kind of optical illusion brought about by brilliant use of numinously vague adjectives. It suggests that he was primed by his reading of translations and imitations of Greek prose romance to associate Greece with the oracular and the marvellous, but it does not mean that he knew much about Greek religion.

If the 'classical' is extended beyond words into painting, architecture, and sculpture we can see further blind spots in Shakespeare's knowledge. These are consequences of where he came from, where he worked, and who he knew. By the second decade of the seventeenth century there was an emerging 'classical' style in a range of media in England, but it was highly localized. This was particularly true of architecture. Walking around the streets of London in 1590 was not like walking around the canals of Venice, where the churches of Palladio would instantly evoke the architectural style of classical antiquity. Nor was London at all like Rome, in which the ruins of classical temples stood alongside elaborate classical and baroque buildings from the sixteenth century. The built world in which Shakespeare grew up was not very different in style from that experienced by Chaucer in the late fourteenth century. In Shakespeare's home town of Stratford-upon-Avon—which was a substantial but otherwise unremarkable provincial town—the chief civic centres were all gothic in style. Holy Trinity Church was begun in the thirteenth century. The guildhall (in the upper hall of which Shakespeare probably attended school), and the guild chapel were both fifteenth-century structures. Even in London the old gothic St Paul's Cathedral dominated the main area in which books were bought and sold: Christopher Wren's neoclassical dome was only built after the Great Fire of 1666 destroyed the original.

English architectural classicism in the second half of the sixteenth century tended to be ornamental rather than structural. At the royal palace of Nonsuch, for instance, European craftsmen provided what was called 'antique work' (ornamental classical features) for the interiors, but the crenellated façade of this Tudor palace, with its top-heavy, slightly Disneyesque towers, did not even aspire to look Roman. By the mid-sixteenth century there were a few visibly classical façades in London, notably Somerset House, and, by the later 1560s, Thomas Gresham's colonnaded Exchange. Apart from these few examples, and the odd great prodigy house built by Tudor magnates, 'classicism' tended to be superficial. Columns designed according to the classical orders might be used as door or fireplace surrounds within buildings which remained substantially gothic. Very few English architects before the early decades of the seventeenth century sought to show systematically that they were inspired by the theoretical writings of the Roman architectural theorist Vitruvius.

The theatre, curiously enough, had the potential to be one of the most visibly 'classical' locations in later sixteenth-century England. From the 1540s onwards the Revels workshop—where settings and backdrops for royal entertainments were constructed—was unusually rich in foreign workmen trained in classical styles.[13] Even the public theatres had some 'classical' aspirations. When James Burbage constructed the first successful purpose-built public theatre in England it now seems natural that it should have been called 'The Theatre'. In 1576 it was not so obvious: he used the anglicized form of the Latin word *theatrum* as an aspirational title, and deliberately avoided using the kind of name that might appear on an inn sign or shop—'The Turk's Head' or 'The Red Bull', or, indeed, 'The Globe'. The Theatre was probably not regarded by its audience as a replica of a classical amphitheatre, since it probably took more than hints for its design from the appearance of inn yards. Nor did the plays put on in it suddenly break free of native theatrical traditions: fools, vice figures, scenic structures from mystery and miracle plays, all fed the late Elizabethan stage, and may well have had more instant appeal for many playwrights and theatregoers than Plautus or Seneca (let alone Sophocles or Aeschylus). Yet the grammar-school- and university-educated men who made up the majority of those who wrote plays for the new fixed-site theatres certainly wanted to display and use their classical learning. For many of them it was their principal asset, and was part of what they had to sell to their audiences. Shakespeare began and ended his career in that environment.

But that environment changed, and in some respects it changed more rapidly than Shakespeare did. In particular, the places in which courtly entertainments were performed were radically transformed in the course of Shakespeare's professional life. In 1606—perhaps around the time Shakespeare was at work on his Roman play *Coriolanus*—James I demolished the wooden Elizabethan banqueting house. This had been a temporary structure in wood erected in 1581, decorated with hangings, royal insignia, and painted fruits, which was the main place in which plays were put on before the court. The new edifice, in brick, based on a Roman basilica, and sporting marbled Doric columns and an Ionic colonnade, survived for only thirteen years before it was destroyed by fire in January 1619. Its destruction enabled Inigo Jones—who had travelled to Rome in 1613–15, where he made sketches and measurements of Roman remains—to design an elaborately Palladian banqueting house to go in its place. Jones's Banqueting House had a ceiling painted by Rubens, which was so rich and ornate that it was decided in 1635 that it would not do to put on masques in the building because 'the smoke of many lights' would spoil the decor.[14] One of the main entertainment spaces of the court therefore underwent a gradual metamorphosis from what with only a little exaggeration could be described as a palatial garden shed with classicizing knobs on into a self-consciously classicizing, permanent structure. The most significant fact about this process so far as Shakespeare was concerned is that its most intense 'classicizing' phase occurred just after the end of his theatrical career.

It was, generally speaking, at state and public occasions in Elizabethan London that a 'classical' style was most visible. Here too fashions changed in the course of Shakespeare's life and Shakespeare responded to those changes. Triumphal arches were built by the guilds of London to welcome James I into the city on his accession in 1603, and these were consciously Roman in their design. Indeed, these makeshift ancient monuments even in a sense *spoke* Latin, since each was manned by allegorical personages who were primed to deliver Latin verses when the King passed by. The accession of James I was the point at which Shakespeare's company changed its title from the Lord Chamberlain's Men to the King's Men. This was also a moment when London presented itself to the world, Romanly, as Londinium. It is not at all surprising that a playwright, many of whose dramas were performed at court, should think about and use classical allusions in slightly new ways as the seventeenth century advanced. Some of the shifts of emphasis in Shakespeare's treatment of classical antiquity in his later career were without doubt connected to these larger changes in taste and fashion.

The built environments of London and Stratford were of course no more than the backgrounds, quite literally, of Shakespeare's career.

But the specific changes in English classicism highlighted here suggest a strong contrast between Shakespeare and Ben Jonson. Jonson actively engaged with all those currents in early seventeenth-century classicism which lay on or just outside the margins of Shakespeare's interests. Jonson wrote a handful of (not very good) Latin poems which served as dedicatory verses to editions of Latin texts compiled by his friends. In the early years of the seventeenth century he also undertook a wide range of close verbal translations of classical works, including Horace's *Ars Poetica.* He wrote Roman plays and court masques which included close translations of classical texts, as well as translating passages from the lyrics of Catullus for the songs in *Volpone.* In case his readers missed his classical allusions, Jonson was willing to draw attention to them in footnotes provided in the printed editions of some of his works. Jonson collaborated (albeit grumpily) with the classicizing architect Inigo Jones over court masques. Although he did not write English poems in classical metres, he boasted that he had written against both Campion and Daniel in the debate about the importation of classical quantitative metres. Jonson, by virtue of the circles in which he moved and in which he sought to make his mark, was far more closely connected than Shakespeare with the currents in English classicism which were shifting direction most rapidly in the early seventeenth century. Even if Shakespeare had visited the houses of the aristocrats with whom he is known to have had connections, he would have seen very splendid but largely gothic buildings. His early patron the Earl of Southampton had a house at Titchfield Abbey which was a gothic monastic foundation which had been converted into a crenellated and turreted Tudor residence. At Wilton House, home of the Earls of Pembroke (the first Folio of Shakespeare's works is dedicated to the third Earl), Shakespeare might have seen the 'Holbein Porch', a two-tier pile of classical columns. But if Shakespeare ever went to Wilton, no record remains of the visit, and the large-scale neoclassical remodelling of the house itself did not occur until the 1630s. By the 1620s Jonson's patrons were architecturally avant garde: in 1625 the Earl of Newcastle built a neoclassical stable block designed by the English classical architect John Smythson (son of the more famous Robert), and Jonson wrote a poem in praise of it. Jonson knew more than a little about the Roman architectural theorist Vitruvius. He also composed panegyrics for the classically ornate state entry of James I into the city of London.

All of these facts about Shakespeare's position within the wider currents of English classical culture give us pointers for interpreting Jonson's elegy, with which this introduction began. Jonson's reference to Shakespeare's 'small Latin and less Greek' is not a simple piece of testimony by a good mate of Shakespeare's, who wipes away his tears in order to lament that his dead colleague didn't put in a few more hours poring over Seneca by candlelight. Nor does it simply come from someone who was more learned than Shakespeare. Rather it was written by someone who used his classical learning in different ways from Shakespeare—probably, indeed, in ways which were designed to make him look different from Shakespeare—and whose classical learning brought connections with networks of scholars and patrons which were quite distinct from Shakespeare's milieu. Jonson was also writing just a few crucial years after Shakespeare's death, in the light of significant changes in the character of English classicism. What scorn there is in his elegy—and there is some—is a product of Jonson's very different understanding of what classical learning was, as well as of changes in attitudes towards classical antiquity during and immediately after Shakespeare's lifetime. In this respect Jonson's innocent-sounding disclaimer 'For if I thought my judgement were of years' is highly significant, and is far from innocent. It makes Jonson seem a mere boy or apprentice scholar in comparison with old Shakespeare. In fact, Jonson was over fifty when that line was printed. He wants to commend, but he also wants to make it sound as though he is rather more than eight years younger than his dead rival. And he wants to make it sound as though those eight years really matter. Jonson is in his own eyes that much more urban, that much more closely linked with innovations in classical learning and architecture, than the dead, and by 1623 just slightly unfashionable, Shakespeare. In his elegy Jonson was treading a very delicate line. He was not saying that Shakespeare was ignorant of the classics. Rather he was making it clear that his own kind of classicism was sharper and more modern than Shakespeare's. Shakespeare's engagement with classical antiquity was different (and in many respects generationally different) from Jonson's. That does not mean it did not exist or that it was not a significant part of his art. His knowledge of the classics was substantially that of an extremely clever Elizabethan grammar-school boy, as the following chapter will show. As it and the remaining chapters will indicate, that knowledge was used to brilliant effect.

# 1

# *Learning from the Past*

What did Shakespeare know about classical literature?

That question sounds very simple. It might imply that a learned critic could sift through Shakespeare's works and record all his indisputable allusions to classical poets, and conclude that Shakespeare 'knew', say, the first four books of Virgil's *Aeneid* pretty well, a number of comedies by Plautus and probably some by Terence, as well as a good number of Seneca's tragedies, possibly a dash of Homer, probably in translation, quite a lot of Ovid (the *Metamorphoses* and some of the *Fasti*, perhaps some *Tristia*, the *Heroides*, and the *Ars Amatoria*), possibly some plays of Euripides in Latin translation, maybe an ode or two of Horace, perhaps some of the satires of Juvenal and maybe a little Persius too, passages from Lucan's historical epic on the Roman civil wars, and quite a bit of Plutarch via Sir Thomas North's translation, as well as prose works by Cicero (the *De Officiis* in particular) and Seneca.

There's nothing much wrong with this particular list. But there is a general problem with lists of what authors 'knew'. They imply that knowledge is static, and that everything an author ever 'knows' is of the same kind and matters to the same degree. The extent of Shakespeare's knowledge of the classics became a matter of serious debate in the second half of the eighteenth century, when Shakespeare was becoming a symbol of English national literature, and when his works were being edited and annotated with scholarly care. Editors sought to identify his sources, and, being trained in classical literature themselves, they tended to find connections between Shakespeare's plays and the works which they themselves knew best. In 1767

Richard Farmer's *Essay on the Learning of Shakespeare* sought to blow this approach out of the water. Farmer argued that often what Shakespeare's editors thought were allusions to classical writing were in fact echoes of English translations of those works. Shakespeare, according to Farmer, 'remembered perhaps enough of his school-boy learning to put the *hig, hag, hog* into the mouth of Sir Hugh Evans... but his studies were most demonstratively confined to nature and his own language'.[1] Farmer was not just performing a neutral act of scholarly investigation. He wanted Shakespeare to embody a native 'English' genius. He, Master of Emmanuel College, Cambridge, was also quite willing to patronize both Shakespeare and his editors by showing that all of them knew less than most people thought, and certainly less than he did.

Things have changed since Farmer's day. The efforts of the indefatigable T. W. Baldwin to understand the curriculum of early-modern grammar schools, embodied in the two fat volumes called *William Shakspere's Small Latine and Lesse Greeke* (1944), have shown beyond reasonable doubt that Shakespeare read quite widely in Latin literature at school, and that more than '*Hig, hag, hog*' (which is Hugh Evans's Welsh version of 'hic, haec, hoc', the masculine, feminine, and neuter forms of 'this' in Latin) remained with him from school.

Baldwin made a big difference to our understanding of Shakespeare, but his approach had two significant weaknesses. The first was that he tended to overstate the rigour and the range of study at Elizabethan grammar schools, and to associate Shakespeare with the upper end of possible attainment. The evidence he used to reconstruct the curriculum at King Edward VI School, Stratford—which Shakespeare almost certainly attended, though the records of the school do not survive from the relevant period, so we cannot be quite certain that he did—were curricula and statutes of major metropolitan schools such as St Paul's and Westminster. The King's school in Stratford, with one master who was paid relatively well at around twenty pounds a year, was a decent provincial grammar school which was able to attract teachers who were university graduates. But it was not Westminster (the school which Ben Jonson attended). The second problem with Baldwin's approach, which has taken a long time to work itself out of the secondary literature on Shakespeare's classical learning, is that he believed Shakespeare's knowledge of the classics more or less ended with grammar school. Baldwin did not give much space to the possibility that Shakespeare forgot things which he learnt at school, or that he continued to read new works and to watch what was happening to classical learning around him throughout his life, or that he was a slightly resistant rather than a model pupil. Baldwin, like many earlier students of Shakespeare's classical learning, wanted to prove a case, and to prove men like Farmer wrong. He succeeded so well that he made Shakespeare's knowledge of the classics into something like a great database of memory derived from grammar school.

As this chapter will show, Shakespeare almost certainly read quite a lot of Latin literature at school. He also read a number of translations of classical texts at different periods in his life. But he also had other ways of acquiring what he would have thought of as knowledge of Latin literature. He came across classical quotations embedded in the *Essays* of Michel de Montaigne, in translations of Plutarch, and in other sources. He probably used a dictionary such as Thomas Cooper's *Thesaurus Linguae Romanae & Britannicae*, which includes an appendix of entries for classical characters and myths, as well as illustrative quotations from Latin authors to support many of its definitions. So Cooper's entry for 'Hecuba' says: 'The wife of Priamus king of Troy, daughter of Cysseus king of Thracia, a woman of noble courage, and most unhappy fortune. For having all her sons and husband slain, her fair daughter Polyxena killed upon the grave of Achilles, her other daughter Cassandra taken prisoner, beholding the noble city of Troy burned, herself in captivity, her youngest son Polydorus killed, she finally waxed mad, and did bite and strike all men that she met, wherefore she was called dog, and at the last was herself killed with stones by the Greeks.'[2] There's enough for a speech or a scene or even a whole play just in that dictionary entry.

Shakespeare might also have said that he knew things about classical texts which modern scholars would not regard as 'knowledge'. He probably read Virgil in editions or translations which included a final thirteenth book of the *Aeneid* by the fifteenth-century Italian humanist Maphaeus Vegius (1407–58), which concludes with Aeneas marrying Lavinia. He 'knew' about the Trojan war partly through translations and imitations of the supposed eye-witness accounts of the Trojan war attributed to Dares the Phrygian and

Dictys the Cretan. He may well have believed that versions of the Troy story deriving from these sources (which include Chaucer's *Troilus and Criseyde*) provided more reliable testimony of what happened than Homer did. A version of a classical myth in Chaucer or Spenser could colour his view of the same story in Ovid's *Metamorphoses*, and become an inseparable part of what he 'knew' about that classical work. By the late sixteenth century, humanist scholars had devoted much energy to dating and attributing spurious works from the classical period, and had laboured to edit and emend most of what are now regarded as the canonical classical texts. Shakespeare probably attached little weight to these scholarly developments.

Students in the sixteenth century were trained to record 'commonplaces', or memorable phrases from classical and modern works, in notebooks. These might have alphabetical headings for recording entries on particular topics ('Death' or 'Sunrises'), or they might be more like what we call diaries or albums, in which phrases or poems picked up in the course of a day could be recorded beside each other.[3] A writer in this period could in some sense 'know' a classical text—or look as though he had read it—as a result of having come across it as a tag or short quotation in a sermon, in the work of a learned historian or contemporary writer, or in a 'florilegium' or dictionary of phrases from the classics. This kind of memorable tag, or in the terminology of the period *sententia* (sententious saying), might be written down and remembered independently of its context in its original position within an ode by Horace, say; or it might be remembered as part of an essay by Montaigne. There are many texts which Shakespeare probably 'knew' in this sense, although he was well aware of how fragile and unreliable this kind of knowledge could be. In *Titus Andronicus* the hero sends the rapists Chiron and Demetrius weapons with lines of verse wrapped around them ('*Integer vitae, scelerisque purus, | Non eget Mauri iaculis, nec arcu*', 4.2.20–1: 'He who is whole in life and pure from crimes has no need of the spears of a Moor nor a bow'). Chiron correctly identifies this as a *sententia* from Horace (*Odes* 1.22.1–2), a passage which is twice cited in the elementary Latin grammar by William Lily, which was prescribed reading in schools: 'O, 'tis a verse in Horace, I know it well. | I read it in the grammar long ago' (4.2.22–3), he says. But as Aaron the Moor sardonically remarks in an aside, Chiron may be able to recognize the lines, but he is too much of a fool to realize that Titus has wrapped his weapons in this particular Horatian tag in order to threaten his daughter's rapists with retribution. Shakespeare knew very well that reading something in a grammar long ago does not necessarily mean that one understands it, nor that one grasps the force of a quotation when it is used in a new context.[4]

A more complex example of the various ways in which Shakespeare could 'know' about classical writing occurs in *Troilus and Cressida*. In Act 2 the Trojans debate whether or not to return Helen of Troy. Hector responds to the zeal of his younger brother Troilus by saying that he is 'not much | Unlike young men, whom Aristotle thought | Unfit to hear moral philosophy' (2.2. 164–6). Shakespeare, like every educated person in the sixteenth century, would have known something about Aristotle's ethics (at the very least that he defined virtue as a mean between two extremes) through popular handbooks and through paraphrases. But when he uses the name of Aristotle here (and the only other time he uses it, in *The Taming of the Shrew*, 1.1.32, is similarly approximate) he makes what would now be called an obvious anachronism as well as an error: Aristotle (who lived in the fourth century BC) was not dreamt of during the Bronze Age of the historical Trojan war. In his *Nicomachean Ethics* (1.3,1094b28–1095a11), Aristotle in fact says that politics, rather than ethics, is unsuitable for the young. A Richard Farmer would say that this 'mistake' shows that Shakespeare did not 'know' Aristotle. But Shakespeare's references to classical authorities are theatrically motivated performances rather than scholarly citations. Hector is playing the older, more learned brother to Troilus's impassioned youth, and Shakespeare wants his audience to remember that these are ancient Greeks, who of course read Aristotle because Aristotle was a Greek. The 'mistake' in which Aristotle's *Politics* is confused with his *Ethics* was very widespread. Erasmus says that his *Colloquies* aim to steal 'into the minds of young folk, who, as Aristotle truly writes, are unsuitable hearers of moral philosophy.'[5] Nicholas Grimald's translation of Cicero's *De Officiis* ends its preface with 'Now therefore (good reader) fare ye well, and remember how unfit (as Aristotle sayeth) and unprofitable hearers of moral science young men be, as long as either they follow their youthly affections, or do continue unskilful and rude in the deeds that of duty belong to a man's life.'[6]

There is one possible source for the mistake, however, which sets up some interesting possibilities, and which may help us to understand indirect and suggestive ways in which Shakespeare could allude to classical writing. This is Johannes Sturm's *Nobilitas Literata* (1549), which was translated in 1570 by Thomas Browne of Lincoln's Inn as *A Rich Storehouse or Treasure for Nobility and Gentlemen*. In his discussion of the imitation of texts from classical antiquity, Sturm writes: 'Therefore, as Aristotle did exclude young boys from his *Ethics*, so I also remove from this artificial practice [of imitation] not only children and boy, but also those men which know not the precepts of rhetoric.'[7] Sturm's *Storehouse* is just the kind of aspirational work which Shakespeare might have read.[8] It is a guide to acquiring gentility through the imitation of classical texts, and it was translated (as many classical works were in the second half of the sixteenth century) by a member of the social and educational elite at the Inns of Court, before whom, it is often thought, *Troilus and Cressida* was performed.

The context of Sturm's mistaken allusion to Aristotle is also highly suggestive. *Troilus* is a work which patches together a wide range of ancient and medieval sources about the Trojan war to create a play which continually raises questions about the moral stature of the heroes onstage. Sturm mentions Aristotle's beliefs about young men in a passage in which he is discussing the idea of literary imitation, or how one author adopts the style and adapts the content of an earlier one. Sturm is particularly interested in ways in which imitations may not come up to their classical originals, and argues that imitators should deliberately vary the shape and appearance of their originals:

> Neither is it to be doubted but the picture of Venus, which Apelles painted as rising out of the sea, appeared to be sprinkled with some foam of the sea, but yet in such sort as the same did make the form and beauty of the goddess more amiable and lovely. Wherefore as Apelles left some part of that picture rude and untrimmed, so likewise ought a writer and imitator to do, and to consider not how far a thing may be beautified and set forth, but how much polishing is meet therefor, the which being not considered the speech must needs be both swelling and puffed up, and also unapt and foolish. Therefore they give good advice, which will us to follow Minerva in Homer, who often changeth Ulysses into sundry forms, and sometimes maketh him a wrinkled, little, ill-favoured fellow... even thus must also an orator do, that he come

not always forth in a silken and precious garment, but oftentimes also in a worn coat, and common attire, and such as serveth for every day. (fol. 45v–46r)

Shakespeare's Ulysses is not a 'wrinkled, little, ill-favoured fellow', but many of the Greek and Trojan heroes are transformed in his play, whether by Minerva's magic or Shakespearian irony, into dim shadows of their counterparts in Homer, and the fear of 'puffed up' language runs through the drama. So does the notion of emulative imitation, or striving to be better than a rival, which is another major theme in Sturm's treatise.

So a reference to Aristotle does not mean that Shakespeare knew Aristotle. But it does not mean either that he simply culled phrases from here and there and laced them into his own writing indiscriminately. The 'mistaken' reference to Aristotle's *Politics* in *Troilus* could be a sign that Shakespeare had been thinking not about Aristotle but about the idea of imitating the voices of characters from antiquity. It may be that a phrase from a work about imitation came into his mind even as he sought to bring to life the voice of Hector as a patronizing older brother. A reference to the name of a classical author certainly does not indicate that Shakespeare had that author on his desk, or even that he read that author's works, but this example illustrates that what look like 'mistakes' or imperfect knowledge of classical writing can suggest what Shakespeare was reading and thinking about as he composed.

What classical texts might Shakespeare have actually owned? A professional writer would have possessed a relatively small library of favoured books, and would have kept most of these in a desk within a 'closet' or private study. Ben Jonson left behind a relatively large number of books which he marked with personal mottos and signatures. He also borrowed volumes from the antiquary Robert Cotton, some of which he did not return.[9] Jonson owned editions of the epigrammatist Martial and the satirist Persius by his friend John Bond. He proudly signed his name and motto 'tamquam explorator' (like an explorer) in a huge folio edition of Greek poetry with Latin translations on the facing page, which as we saw in the Introduction remains in remarkably good condition.[10] The clichéd opposition of learned Jonson and native happy-go-lucky Shakespeare does have at least this much to support it: Shakespeare appears not to have written his name in books, although forgers have sometimes tried to build him a library. A copy of Montaigne in the British Library was once believed to carry Shakespeare's signature, and a 1502 pocket-sized edition of Ovid's *Metamorphoses* in the Bodleian Library, equipped with a set of inscriptions that give it a suspiciously good provenance, bears the signature 'Wm Sh$^{e}$', which is almost certainly forged.[11]

The absence of signed books does not necessarily indicate that Shakespeare was less of a reader than Jonson. Many early-modern writers had occasional access to libraries which belonged to noblemen, or patrons, or friends. They might also spend time at bookstalls scanning over the latest titles and picking up snippets of information about new styles and fashions. Texts encountered in all these different ways—casually as a browser, formally as a favour from a nobleman, personally as a treasured or abusively read possession—might be expected to influence their readers in different ways. Then as now a writer was more likely to display his knowledge of a fashionable work which he had only glanced at on a bookstall than of one which he knew everyone else would have already read: there is (and was) kudos to be won from 'knowing', or at least showing that you know of, the latest thing.

Shakespeare also understood that reading was not simply a means of acquiring knowledge. Characters who read onstage in Shakespeare's plays are never simply learning things. They are always also performing an action that has significance to other characters onstage, as well as, often, to the audience offstage. The books that appear onstage as props in Shakespeare's plays are often not identified, and on the whole those which are turn out to be copies of Ovid, texts of whom appear onstage in *Titus Andronicus*, *The Taming of the Shrew*, and *Cymbeline*. In the early play *Titus Andronicus* (c.1593–4) a copy of Ovid's *Metamorphoses* is brought onstage to mark the play's persistent allusions to that work (discussed below, pp. 110–14). The physical presence of the book helps prompt the raped Lavinia to identify those who violated her. In later plays unnamed onstage volumes tend to function less as markers of the author's allusions to classical texts and more like props, or cues to a conversation between characters. In *Hamlet*, from around 1599, Polonius catches the prince reading a book. Hamlet says he is reading just 'words, words, words' in an unnamed and unidentifiable book by a 'satirical slave' who sounds a bit like the Roman satirist Juvenal (2.2.195–203). The satirical slave says 'that old men have grey beards, that their faces are wrinkled, their eyes purging thick amber or plum-tree gum, and that they have a plentiful lack of wit, together with most weak hams'. We have no way of knowing if these words are being 'read' by Hamlet, or are invented by him in order to insult Polonius. He could be providing an impromptu translation of Juvenal, or he could be using the book as a cover for saying what he wants to say to the interfering father of Ophelia.

In *Troilus and Cressida*, probably composed a few years after *Hamlet*, Ulysses is reading a similarly unidentifiable volume, which, by handy coincidence, tells Achilles exactly what Ulysses wants him to hear:

> A strange fellow here
> Writes me that man, how dearly ever parted,
> How much in having, or without or in,
> Cannot make boast to have that which he hath,
> Nor feels not what he owes, but by reflection. (3.3.90–4)

Achilles's reply is 'Nor doth the eye itself, | That most pure spirit of sense, behold itself, | Not going from itself' (3.3.100–102). This has sometimes been seen as a moment when Shakespeare shows off his classical learning. Scholars have sometimes identified the 'strange fellow' with Plato, who asks in the *First Alcibiades*, 133A: 'Then an eye viewing another eye, and looking at the most perfect part of it, the thing wherewith it sees, will thus see itself?' In Cicero's *Tusculan Disputations* there is another parallel of sorts: 'The soul is not able in this body to see himself. No more is the eye, which although he seeth all other things, yet (that which is one of the least) cannot discern his own shape.'[12] The strange feature of this 'classical' exchange, though, is that it's Achilles, who is not actually holding this 'classical' book, who picks up and develops the commonplace of classical and Renaissance ethics that the eye cannot see itself, rather than Ulysses, who actually has the book in his hand. Learning and knowledge spread around books in Shakespeare's mature plays, rather than being simply located in them—and he tends to give the authors of onstage books generic rather than specific names which reflect his interest in the effect rather than the exact origins of reading. They are identified as 'strange fellows' or 'satirical slaves' rather than as Plato or Juvenal.

That sounds like a tiny point, but it's actually very significant. In analysing Shakespeare's classicism it is necessary to be as sensitive to theatrical contexts as it is when analysing any other aspect of his plays. Classical sources tend to be adapted to their theatrical situations. The really big point that follows from these examples, indeed, is that for Shakespeare, 'knowledge' of the classics tended to be situational. That is, a particular scene or setting might recall some more or less dim memory of a classical text: a reference to 'Aristotle' could come to mind in a scene or a play about imitation if it was associated with literary imitation in the work in which Shakespeare came across it; a piece of pastiche 'Juvenal' might seem right for a scene in which a younger character is being rude to an older, partly because Juvenal is sometimes rude about the old, but also because Juvenal's name means 'juvenile'. Allusions to Lucan, who wrote an epic poem about Rome's civil wars, occur most frequently in historical works about England's civil wars, the Wars of the Roses. What Shakespeare 'knew' about classical literature is inseparable from the ways he used it, and he often used his knowledge in ways that create complex implied dialogues between characters onstage, and between his own writing and his reading. These effects all suggest that we should think of Shakespeare's knowledge of classical writing dynamically, as a changing and theatrically inflected resource rather than simply a static body of learning which he acquired during his teens and then used throughout his career.

## Shakespeare at School

Nonetheless Baldwin was quite right to draw attention to the role of the grammar-school curriculum in shaping Shakespeare's knowledge of the classics. What Shakespeare learnt at school did remain at the core of his knowledge of classical antiquity. But here too we should not think of 'knowledge' as a passive affair. When a sixteenth-century schoolboy sat at a desk in the hall of a grammar school he was not simply made to learn Latin grammar. Nor was he simply made to consign large sections of Ovid, Virgil, Cicero, and the playwright Terence to memory, although that was certainly part of his task. He was also supposed to be learning *how* to write like the people he read. He was as much learning technique as learning the words of an ancient author. Shakespeare learnt both content and method from ancient writers (and that fact will become particularly significant in the discussion of his relationship to classical comedians in Chapter 4).

We do not know what kind of schoolboy Shakespeare was, but there are two scenes in his plays which represent instruction in ancient literature. Both are from plays composed before 1600, and both associate education with social and sexual comedy. The first is sometimes taken as a representation of William Shakespeare's own education at King Edward VI School, Stratford-upon-Avon, where Thomas Jenkins (whose name suggests that he was Welsh, but who seems in fact to have been a Londoner) served as master from 1575 to 1579. In *The Merry Wives of Windsor* Shakespeare represents a boy called William receiving instruction from a Welsh schoolteacher called Evans. William is not a model pupil, and the lesson is a performance put on in public rather than just a drama enacted within the walls of a grammar-school hall. Among the onstage audience to William's Latin lesson is Mistress Quickly, who is a mistress of the malapropism:

> EVANS: What is your genitive case plural, William?
> WILLIAM: Genitive case?
> EVANS: Ay.
> WILLIAM: *Genitivo*: '*horum, harum, horum*'.
> MISTRESS QUICKLY: Vengeance of Jenny's Case! Fie on her!
> Never name her, child, if she be a whore. (4.1.52–7)

This is not simply a representation of the process of teaching, though the way young William buys time and prompts his memory by repeating his master's question is a trick most students in all ages would recognize. It is a representation of learning and teaching which is adapted to performance on the English public stage. Some of Shakespeare's audience would, like poor William in *The Merry Wives*, like Chiron in *Titus*, and like William Shakespeare himself, have ploughed their way through the Latin grammar of William Lily.

They would have learnt all the different 'cases' of the Latin pronouns (in Latin, nouns take on 'inflections' at their end to indicate whether they are the subject or the object of the verb; the 'genitive' is the possessive case). Master Evans's question would have instantly set up a rhythm in their minds, a pattern of expectations about what words would come next. Some members of Shakespeare's audience would not have been literate at all, or if literate would have little or no knowledge of Latin. The representation of teaching is therefore carefully tuned to appeal to an audience which itself contained several different perspectives. 'Horum' (the genitive plural form) combined with 'genitive' (which sounds as though it might have something to do with generation or genitals) invites 'schoolboy' giggles about whores. The aural surface of the classical language becomes opaque so as to suggest erotic English vernacular transformations. Add in the fact that 'case' in early-modern English could mean 'vagina' as well as a particular grammatical form of a noun or pronoun, and both the learned insiders and the Latinless outsiders have something to laugh about. The presence of Mistress Quickly as a form of onstage audience would also ensure that no one in the play's predominantly male audience would have felt that they were completely on the outside of the joke, since it's clear that she, a woman who is stuck with the vernacular, has got this Latin lesson indecently wrong, and is more on the outside than even the least literate member of the offstage audience.[13] Although a few schools did offer education to girls, and it seems that up to the age of around nine male and female pupils might be educated together, grammar schools were exclusively male.[14] Learning the language of antiquity in this scene of instruction is therefore closely connected with social differentiation and with gender differentiation. Women hear in an unruly and transformative vernacular. Young males might do so too (the boy William must be enjoying what Mistress Quickly is doing to his master's language), but schoolmasters are locked into an ancient tongue which everyone around them slightly misunderstands, and they seem to be missing the point and the fun of a classical education as a result.

The scene in *Merry Wives* suggests that classical learning, like many of the strongest forces in Shakespearian drama, is at least mildly unruly and at best packed with unpredictable energies. *The Taming of the Shrew* also contains a Latin lesson which also has an erotic charge.[15] This play was probably composed around 1590–2 when Shakespeare may have been himself in the process of learning his trade as a dramatist. The young men Lucentio and Hortensio disguise themselves so that they can be employed as tutors to the daughters of the merchant Baptista. Hortensio pretends to be a music master, while Lucentio takes on the role of Latin teacher, who whispers heated asides to his pupil while they pretend to 'construe' (translate) a bit of Ovid's *Heroides*:

> BIANCA: Where left we last?
> LUCENTIO: Here, madam.
> '*Hic ibat Simois, hic est Sigeia tellus,*
> *Hic steterat Priami regia celsa senis.*'
> BIANCA: Construe them.
> LUCENTIO: '*Hic ibat*', as I told you before—'*Simois*', I am Lucentio—'*hic est*', son unto Vincentio of Pisa—'*Sigeia tellus*', disguised thus to get your love—'*hic steterat*', and that Lucentio that comes a-wooing—'*Priami*', is my man Tranio—'*regia*' bearing my port—'*celsa senis*', that we might beguile the old pantaloon. (3.1.25–36)

It's not completely impossible that there is a whiff of autobiography to the classical pedagogy here: John Aubrey claimed in 1681 that Shakespeare was 'in his younger years a schoolmaster in the country', presumably in the narrow window between the end of his own schooling and his marriage to Anne Hathaway in 1582.[16] People new to teaching do often feel that they are frauds or playing a part, as Lucentio is doing explicitly here. More obviously and significantly this Latin lesson charges the process of learning the classics with a powerful strife-cum-collaboration between learner and teacher. The physical presence of the textbook onstage (and they must have only one copy between them for the scene to produce the required level of intimacy) is an excuse for the two of them to huddle together:

> BIANCA: Now let me see if I can construe it. '*Hic ibat Simois*', I know you not—'*hic est Sigeia tellus*', I trust you not—

> '*hic steterat Priami*', take heed he [that is Hortensio, who is tuning his lute in the corner] hear us not—'*regia*', presume not—'*celsa senis*', despair not.' (3.1.40–3)

The one thing that does not happen at all here, of course, is any translation of the passage from Ovid's *Heroides* which is the set text for the morning. That's its main joke. Another is the fact that the couple have only got thirty or so lines into the very first poem in the collection. They are slow learners. The meaning of the Latin text is entirely subordinated to the opportunities for intimacy afforded by the presence of the book, which Bianca firmly ('presume not') but gently ('despair not') resists.

The classical learning displayed here serves other purposes too. Many members of Shakespeare's audience would indeed have been able to 'construe', or translate, the passage, and some would have known it by heart, since Ovid's *Heroides* were a familiar starting point for learning classical poetry. They might see it as obliquely significant. The lines the lovers are quoting and pretending to translate are from the epistle from the faithful wife Penelope to her absent husband Ulysses. That choice of source is not accidental: *The Taming of the Shrew* is centrally concerned with a marriage between a powerful man and a talkative woman. Ovid's epistle from Penelope to Ulysses is partly about the ways in which texts and stories fail to be satisfactory substitutes for physical contact. Penelope begins by declaring '*nil mihi rescribas attinet: ipse veni*' ('writing back is no good to me: you must come in person', 1.2): she wants her husband back, and the stories she has heard about Troy are no substitute for his presence. In the passage which Hortensio and Bianca read out, Penelope describes a veteran of the fall of Troy mapping out a scene in wine on a tabletop ('Here the river Simois flowed, here is the land of Sigeia, here stood the high palaces of old King Priam'). For Penelope the end of Troy means that her husband might be on his way home, but if Troy really has fallen and other soldiers have come back to tell their tales, where is Ulysses? Typically of the heroines of the *Heroides*, the faithful Penelope is stuck with words and the aftershocks of events, rather than having a real husband beside her.

The context of the lines from Ovid therefore could send a cold breeze through the lovemaking of the modern students of Latin.

There is so much they don't hear in it: the anxiety that attends the fall of Troy, the unhappiness of living only with words and stories rather than with the physical intimacy which they temporarily share, the assymetries between male and female experiences of marriage. The whole scene, although it comes from the very start of Shakespeare's career, is characteristic of his way of positioning classical texts obliquely but allusively in relation to the main onstage action. Citation of classical literature can conjure up passions from the past which seem stronger and more awkward than those of the people who may be reading them or unwittingly re-enacting them. It also suggests there is nothing simple about the process of learning from the past: its lessons differ depending on where you sit. From Lucentio's seat next to Bianca, Ovid is sexy and warm, an excuse for snuggling up (the smaller the book, the closer he can get); from where Bianca sits Lucentio's Latin lesson seems presumptuously intimate, but more fun than irregular verbs; from one of the more expensive balcony seats in the theatre the quotation from Ovid might open up vast wastes of sea between Penelope and her Ulysses, and conjure up archetypes of faithful absent lovers who are stuck with words rather than bodily warmth.

The details of real-life early-modern grammar-school education are enough to make the most diligent of scholars wish for a Lucentio or a Bianca to lighten their burdens. It is no accident that Shakespeare's references to 'schoolboys' tend to go along with sighing, crying, or peevishness. Jacques, the malcontent in *As You Like It*, famously describes the 'whining schoolboy with his satchel' (2.7.145). Shakespeare also describes a lover who sighs 'like a schoolboy that had lost his ABC' (*The Two Gentlemen of Verona*, 2.1.21), and another that 'goes toward love as schoolboys from their books' (*Romeo and Juliet*, 2.1.201), since, obviously, getting away from books is what sixteenth-century boys desire most. It's not hard to see why. The life of an early-modern grammar-school boy, so far as it can be pieced together from curricula, textbooks, and memoirs, was hard. Early starts, long days, grumpy masters, and cold halls made the acquisition of learning a painful business. It's likely that young Shakespeare, between the ages of about seven and fourteen or so, dragged himself out of bed at around 5.30 am to study a curriculum that consisted almost exclusively of Latin, with perhaps a smattering of Greek in the higher forms. Maths, what we call science, even religious studies, were all secondary to the study of literature in sixteenth-century schools.[17]

Most grammar-school boys would have quickly mastered Lily's grammar, and then moved on to translate simple Latin phrases from a book known as *Cato's Distichs*, which consisted of two-line moral epigrams. To these were often added the sayings ascribed to the Seven Sages of Greece, which included sober precepts, such as (in the early seventeenth-century translation for schoolboys by the schoolmaster John Brinsley): 'Advise blamelessly. Neglect not yourself. Die for your country. Breed children of ingenuous women. Conceal a secret. Expect the opportunity. Give with profit.'[18] When Shakespeare's Polonius offers his quick-fire string of precepts to his son Laertes he would probably have struck many members of the early audiences of *Hamlet* as a man trying to sound like an eighth sage of Greece, a sort of ponderously didactic and ancient (in the sense of decrepit) reviver of old learning from the schoolroom: 'Neither a borrower nor a lender be, | For loan oft loses both itself and friend... This above all—to thine own self be true' (1.3.75–8).[19] After learning to translate these sober maxims, pupils might move on to passages from Cicero's letters, as well as, in many schools, dialogues and speeches from the work of Erasmus and other sixteenth-century humanists.

A number of students would go on to read Greek, though the level of attainment seems generally not to have been high. There is no reason to suppose that Shakespeare was not among this number.[20] The principal aim of grammar-school Greek was to read the New Testament in the original language. This is much easier than the language of Greek poets, and of course students would already know much of the New Testament in the vernacular from regular attendance at church services. If a crib was not already in his head, a schoolboy could have had a book next to him to help. John Brinsley says: 'Besides the Greek Testament I would have everyone to have his English Testament, or Latin, or both; and ever in the entrance before they learn a lesson to have read it over in the translation.'[21] Pupils might also read Greek versions of texts which they already knew well in Latin, since Erasmus's Greek translations of *Cato's Distichs* was a favourite starting point for the study of the more difficult classical language. This meant that for Tudor grammar-school boys Greek was subsequent rather than prior to Latin. That was, historically speaking, the wrong way round, since the majority of Greek literature predated its Latin imitations and offshoots by several centuries: Euripides wrote his tragedies in the fifth century BC, while Seneca read and imitated them, or intermediary versions of them, in the first century AD; Virgil imitated Homer centuries after the composition of the Homeric poems. But for early-modern students Latin came first. And Greek was not the language of Winckelmann's idealized ancient civilization. It was principally encountered as a language for understanding the founding texts of Christianity, rather than of pagan antiquity. A few poets in Shakespeare's generation regarded Greek as a great 'primary' source of literature: George Chapman insists in his translation that 'Homer's poems were writ from a free fury, an absolute and full soul; Virgil's out of a courtly, laborious, and altogether imitatory spirit.'[22] But it was more usual for pupils in Shakespeare's period to approach and experience Greek texts through their Latin imitations, of which the Greek texts might appear to be rougher and less sophisticated first drafts. Even Chapman, when he started his project of translating Homer, worked principally from a Latin version of the Greek which was, curiously enough, full of phrases drawn from Virgil's imitations of Homer, which were used to translate their original. This meant that even if a grammar-school boy did know Greek it would leave relatively little visible imprint on his writing, since competence in the Greek language would not significantly widen his reading beyond texts which he already knew in Latin or in English anyway. The slightly topsy-turvy relationship between the two languages may also have had some oblique influence on Shakespeare. His most 'Greek' play, *Troilus and Cressida*, the main place in which he may show some signs of interest in Homer, is steeped in parallel versions of the Troy story from different languages, from Chaucer and from Lydgate, and perhaps from Henryson, which all but blot out any lineaments of Homer. Is the Cressida we witness onstage in *Troilus and Cressida* the primary Cressida, the merry Greek original, who can escape her subsequent literary reputation as a jilt? Or is she a product of many different post-Homeric Cressidas? Troilus of course cries out when he sees her being unfaithful to him with Diomed: 'This is and is not Cressid' (5.2.149), and that cry is very much that of the play. Is she Chaucer's Cressida, Homer's Cressida, Shakespeare's Cressida, or Henryson's? Is Shakespeare's Achilles Homer's Achilles or an amalgam of later versions of that hero? Shakespeare's education may have tumbled together and confused the sequence of texts which we regard as 'primary' and 'secondary', and that may have left him with a creatively confused sense of literary chronology.

Although a Tudor grammar-school education was in theory grimly focused on language, and included what would be today regarded as a dismaying quantity of rote learning, it also offered a number of pleasures, many of which were only partially licit. Early on in their academic careers pupils would read Latin poets. Ovid was a favourite among schoolmasters, perhaps surprisingly given the eroticism of his writing. Passages from his great collection of mythical transformations, the *Metamorphoses*, as well as from Lucentio and Bianca's favoured verse epistles from unhappy heroines, the *Heroides*, would have filled long mornings and tiring afternoons for all early-modern grammar-school boys. Virgil's *Aeneid*, especially the fourth book, which relates the love of the Carthaginian queen Dido for the Trojan hero (and founder of the Roman people) Aeneas, and the second book (which relates the final destruction of Troy, and during which Dido falls in love with the narrator Aeneas), seems to have been a particular favourite. All of these texts are remarkable for the power with which they represent sexual desire and for the eloquence with which they endow their female characters. The early-modern grammar-school classroom was an exclusively male space, so much so that learning Latin has been seen as a kind of male puberty rite.[23] Yet in that male environment boys read many works which ascribed enormous rhetorical skill and power to women—a skill and power which were often provoked by suffering or mistreatment by men, and which frequently released all but uncontrollable emotions articulated in highly controlled rhetorical forms by male Latin poets. The homosocial environment in which Shakespeare and his contemporaries learnt to read Latin may have had long-term influence on his attitudes towards men.[24] Significantly perhaps, the Shakespearian classroom scenes which we have just encountered are not simply male preserves: they're charged with eroticism and innuendo by the presence of female characters. The supposedly male preserve of Latin learning was indeed for Shakespeare consistently feminized: young Lucius in *Titus Andronicus* is said to have been given his copy of Ovid by his mother (4.1.43) and to have had Latin literature read to him by his aunt.

The eloquence of Shakespeare's abandoned or mistreated women—from Lavinia in *Titus Andronicus* and his early narrative poem about Lucrece, through Viola in *Twelfth Night*, on to Cleopatra and the unnamed female speaker of *A Lover's Complaint*—are in part the product of a programme of classical reading which was supposed to make a man of him when he was a student in grammar school. In the *Sonnets* (printed in 1609) Shakespeare makes even more unorthodox use of his schooling. The speaker of the first seventeen poems in the sequence in which they are printed—adopting the persona of an 'antique', or old and wise, teacher instructing a young man on how to love—at several points echoes or adapts a speech by the great educationalist Desiderius Erasmus on the desirability of marriage. That exhortation to breed blends in with and perhaps even provokes the love the older poet feels for his younger addressee. The learned teacher, advising his charge to love, turns himself into a lover of his pupil.

All of the reading and translating of classical texts through which grammar-school boys slogged their way was intended ultimately to enable them not to display mastery in reading a dead language, but to write. Indeed, a two-word explanation of why the late sixteenth century produced more great dramatists than any other period in English history would be 'grammar schools'. Shakespeare, like Christopher Marlowe, Ben Jonson, and their slightly younger followers John Ford, John Webster, and Philip Massinger, spent years not just reading classical texts, but learning to write like those classical authors. Painstaking translation of Latin literature at school was not just an exercise in grammatical recall but a way of preparing for composition. Roger Ascham in his treatise on education called *The Schoolmaster* (printed in 1570) recommended that pupils should translate Latin texts into English, then have the original removed from them; then 'let the child translate his own English into Latin again'.[25] The aim of this process was not mechanical replication, although presumably people with very good memories for the original found it relatively easy to reproduce from their English translations the exact words of Cicero or whichever classical author was originally put before them. The aim was a reconstruction of classical literature which was both practical—that is, which was concerned with *doing* it rather than just absorbing it—and imaginative. Underlying the process was a requirement not to write Cicero's words again, like some demonic childish version of Jorge Luis Borges's Pierre Menard, who aims to reproduce the exact words of *Don Quixote*, but to internalize 'Cicero' as a principle of style. The boys were asked not 'How *did* Cicero write this letter and what words did he use?' but 'How *would* Cicero write this letter?' Ascham suggested that an ideal teacher would correct his pupil's efforts by saying 'Tully [that is, Marcus Tullius Cicero] would have used such a word, not this.'[26] This kindly advice implies that both master and pupil were accustomed to extrapolate from a body of writing by a past author a set of stylistic principles. It encouraged boys to think 'Cicero *would have* ended this sentence in this way,' rather than just binding themselves to the exact words of an earlier author. It also set up a relationship with an earlier author that could be charged with love: Johannes Sturm describes imitation as 'an ardent desire and love to attain to that in the oration and speech of another, [which] seemeth worthy of praise and admiration. And is nothing else but a means and way how to express in your own talk those manners and forms of speaking... which be commendable and beautiful in the talk of another.'[27] Reading and imitating classical texts were not mechanical processes: 'ardent desire and love' led to the replication of what was beautiful in another person's 'talk'—and the use of that word suggests that imitators were not just scrutinizing the texts of their models, but imagining those works as being spoken by real and lovable people who had distinctive ways of speaking, just like theatrical characters. Again this casts light on the speaker of the *Sonnets*, who is fascinated by procreation, and by the preservation and reproduction of a young man through verse: his love is a kind of reverse version of the eroticized desire to imitate the ancients that was taught in grammar schools. As we shall see in the Conclusion to this book, the narrator tries to make poems which seek to imitate, reproduce, and preserve a young man's beauty, rather than that of a classical author. Whether or not the 'young man' was a historical person, the speaker's relation to him was more or less constituted by the particular kind of education in the classics that Shakespeare received.

Creative imitation of classical authors might not necessarily be a loving relationship, though. It entailed grasping a set of more or less flexible rules about how those authors wrote. These rules could become generative and creative principles. The educationalist William Kempe (no relation of the clown of the same name) described the process of creative imitation rather drily as the extraction of rules which could then be turned into practice:

> Wherefore first the scholar shall learn the precepts: secondly he shall learn to note the examples of the precepts in unfolding other men's works: thirdly, to imitate the examples in some work of his own: fourthly and lastly, to make somewhat alone without an example.[28]

'Precept', that is the process of learning grammatical rules, has practice as its ultimate goal. Students should not just learn the grammatical and stylistic rules embodied in classical writing, but learn them so they could use them themselves in order to 'make [i.e. write] somewhat [i.e. something] alone without an example'.

As they sought to become like Cicero, but not slaves to Cicero, early-modern schoolboys would be required to write 'themes', in Latin, on particular topics. These might be on simple subjects ('Time') or based on adages, like 'Hurry slowly.' Themes might be set on open-ended questions, like that asked by Erasmus, and then in imitation of Erasmus by the speaker of Shakespeare's *Sonnets*, 'whether it is better to marry or remain single?' When Shakespeare uses the word 'themes' in his earlier writing he often evokes a whiff of the schoolroom. Venus attempts to woo Adonis by rehearsing familiar arguments in favour of marriage, and the young man puts down his mistress by telling her to 'leave this idle theme, this bootless chat'. Later he urges her not to fall again 'Into your idle, over-handled theme' (*Venus and Adonis*, lines 422 and 770). Adonis is sounding like a cheeky pupil who has seen it all: the goddess's persuasion to love is no more than a wearisome grammar-school exercise to him. Again, though, Shakespeare's memory of a classical schoolroom exercise brings with it a set of curious erotic reversals: the pupil, Adonis, knows it all already, while his teacher is not a man, like Master Evans in *The Merry Wives*, but an impassioned goddess, who takes over and charges good old Erasmus's arguments for marriage with erotic self-interest. School exercises in classical tongues were for Shakespeare surprisingly sexy.

Once he was well practised in composing 'themes', a pupil might go on to write orations which praised or dispraised an individual from history or a particular historical or mythical action—all in Latin. These exercises were designed to prepare early-modern grammar-school boys for careers in the law, or as clergymen. They were not intended to equip them to put speeches into the mouths of actors, let alone to put arguments in favour of sexual submission into the mouth of the goddess of love, as Shakespeare did in *Venus and Adonis*. But many of the skills practised in the early-modern classroom were transferable in gloriously unpredictable ways. Pupils in the higher forms of grammar school were encouraged to argue on both sides of a complex question. This was intended to provide training in how to marshal evidence and present a case. It had the secondary and unintended consequence of developing students' ability to engage in what would now be called imagining a different point of view. By arguing on either side of a question they would effectively be learning to dramatize the state of mind of people who are suspended between different and equally forceful arguments.[29] The sceptical Hamlet's meditation whether 'To be or not to be' is more or less a textbook piece of such classically inspired debate, in which he sets out both sides of the question with perfect crispness. This kind of debate was called a '*quaestio*', and of course Hamlet, a good student at Wittenberg, tells us that he knows just what he is doing: 'that is the question', he says, as though he is underlining the title of his rhetorical exercise. Beneath the English word 'question' he expects his audience to hear the Latin word *quaestio*: the greatest soliloquy in English has its origins in classically inspired debating techniques.

In the higher forms of grammar schools, students were sometimes told to write a speech in the persona of a particular character in a particular set of circumstances, known as a 'prosopopoeia'. They might write speeches in the persona of Helen of Troy, or of Queen Hecuba after the sack of Troy. The composition of speeches in the voice of Hecuba is specifically recommended in a volume called the *Progymnasmata* (that is, 'rhetorical training exercises'), which was composed by the fourth-century AD Greek rhetorician Aphthonius, and which was widely used in schools in a Latin translation by the humanist Rudolph Agricola.[30] Hamlet has of course been there and done all that too, as he shows when he struggles to remember an old speech about the sufferings of Queen Hecuba, which presumably he knew of old from his schooldays (2.2.453–521; see below, p. 71). Aphthonius also recommends the closely related exercise termed '*ethopoeia*', in which a student would evoke a particular person's '*mores*' (habits, or lexical mannerisms) in a speech. The skills of an early modern dramatist were multiple, but at their absolute centre lay the ability to put a case plausibly, to represent a debate from both sides, to mimic style and character, and to write as though from a particular character's situation and perspective. These were grammar-school skills which Shakespeare mastered in Latin and went on to use or abuse in the vernacular on the public stage.

All of this suggests why grammar-school training in the sixteenth century was such a potent literary resource, and why it provided Shakespeare with far more than just a body of passively acquired knowledge of the classics which he could deploy later in his career. The main value of early-modern education so far as a future dramatist was concerned, indeed, was that it didn't quite add up. Boys were supposed to learn at school how to sparkle in the male preserves of the Church and the Law, but they learnt these skills in oblique ways. How might imitating passages from Ovid written in the persona of women who had been abandoned or raped, or how might writing a speech in the persona of Hecuba, polish up the forensic skills of a lawyer? Sixteenth-century grammar-school boys did not have to have homoerotic inclinations to find that a curious and puzzling lesson in how men got on in the world. Boys were supposed to learn eloquence and virtue from their reading in the classics. That was fine when their studies were focused on sober old Cato stating that 'he that hath power to hurt, will be able to do good, that is to say, when time shall serve' or 'If thou be hurt of mighty men, dissemble as thou had no hurt;'[31] but what sort of virtue, and what sort of relationship between virtue and eloquence might they have learnt from reading Ovid's description of the goddess Venus trying to persuade the young boy Adonis to stay with her and lie with her rather than going off hunting the boar? Anyone with an ounce of perversity (intellectual or sexual) would have found in their education in the classics all kinds of potential that would have dismayed their teachers. Indeed, Shakespeare could even take the voice of old Cato himself and turn it into something dark and ambiguous:

> They that have power to hurt and will do none,
> That do not do the thing they most do show,
> Who moving others are themselves as stone,
> Unmovèd, cold, and to temptation slow—
> They rightly do inherit heaven's graces. (Sonnet 94.1–5)

Do people who live according to the chilly principles of *Cato's Distichs* really have virtue? This sonnet asks that sceptical question of what was almost certainly one of Shakespeare's very earliest encounters with classical writing. The deadpan ironic stress on 'rightly' here does not simply pose a question to the real or fictional addressee of the poem as to whether insensibility is a human good: it is a question posed to Cato, and to the whole notion that classical learning could instil virtue in its pupils. That questioning relationship to classical learning was a vital element in Shakespeare's intellectual make-up, and it was central to his writing.

The number of young men who received this training in classical eloquence in the second half of the sixteenth century exceeded to a significant extent the small number of suitable jobs in which eloquence and verbal skill could be used. If they lacked the family wealth or connections to train as lawyers, or to win an introduction to a bishop or nobleman whom they might serve as a secretary, these highly educated young men might find themselves without a clear role in life or any means of using their education. The emergence of the fixed-site theatres in London in the 1570s and 1580s was in this respect a godsend for grammar-school boys. The players and their impresarios needed eloquent writers to provide them with a stream of new plays so that their audiences would keep coming back for more. A whole generation of these men, of whom Shakespeare was one, used their classical learning to write poems and plays—plays rich with the tricks and tropes of rhetoric, full of persuasion, of open-ended debates, of women speaking with the voices of men, or of boys speaking in the voices of women who had the eloquence of men. Shakespeare the dramatist was effectively made by the collision of these two forces: his grammar-school education met the growing demand for plays on the public stage. His teachers would probably have been appalled to see what he did with the learning they gave him.

## Social Drama

Many of Shakespeare's contemporary professional playwrights were not just grammar-school boys. They also had university degrees. This entitled them to call themselves 'gentlemen', which was a significant mark of social status in this period. It also guaranteed that they were, as they were called by virtue of their degrees, Masters of Arts, people skilled in ancient tongues who were evidently learned. Shakespeare had no university degree, and in a society which was highly stratified, and in which learning was one of the means of social stratification, it was social death to display mere 'grammar-school' knowledge. Through the early 1590s the Cambridge scholar Gabriel Harvey had an extended pamphlet war with Thomas Nashe, who was a Cambridge graduate, but not a doctor. Harvey repeatedly mocks his adversary for displaying mere grammar-school learning, spiced up with a level of logic which a first-year undergraduate might display: 'He tossed his imagination a thousand ways, and I believe, searched every corner of his grammar-school wit, (for his margin is as deeply learned as *Fauste precor gelida*) to see if he could find any means to relieve his estate.'[32] Harvey is saying here that Nashe became a commercial writer who sought to exploit his minimal learning, his 'grammar-school wit', to make himself richer. He snidely alludes to the very first line of the Latin eclogues of Mantuan—one of the most popular grammar-school texts—to suggest that Nashe was an upstart know-nothing who proudly displays his humdrum learning as though he thinks it's something special which merits displaying in the margin, like a learned footnote.

This background of educational snobbery—and the row between Harvey and Nashe sparkled and rumbled through the early years of Shakespeare's theatrical career—was immensely important for Shakespeare. It had a profound influence on the ways he used his classical learning. He was a grammar-school boy, and not a Master of Arts, and he knew it. He knew the danger of displaying his classical knowledge in ways that could leave him open to mockery. As a result he tends to make fun of his characters' 'small Latin' in order to avoid being made fun of himself. The pageant of the nine worthies at the end of *Love's Labour's Lost*, for instance, is not about to take the risk of presenting a performance of classical antiquity with anything resembling a straight face. It is a comic turn in which pedants and amiably uneducated people fit themselves out to play classical heroes, and are laughed at for doing so. It is of a piece with the letter written by the aspirationally learned Don Armado to Jacquenetta (4.1) which quotes and then makes a meal of Julius Caesar's 'Veni, Vidi, Vici' (I came, I saw, I overcame). This famous phrase from Caesar is one of Shakespeare's favourite classical tags. He always uses it in deflationary ways, since he knew, and knew that his audience knew, that it was a completely commonplace piece of knowledge. Characters who use Caesar's saying seriously in Shakespeare tend to do so when they are inflating themselves and manipulating the truth. So Falstaff uses the parallel with Caesar to exaggerate his own heroism in *2 Henry IV* after Sir John Colville yielded to him in battle: 'I may justly say, with the hook-nosed fellow of Rome, "I came, saw, and overcame"' (4.2.40–1). In *Cymbeline* the evil Queen (following the British historian Geoffrey of Monmouth) denies that Caesar made an easy conquest of Britain, and declares 'A kind of conquest | Caesar made here, but made not here his brag | Of "came and saw and overcame"' (3.1.22–4). A more playful allusion to this piece of grammar-school learning is made when Rosalind in disguise in *As You Like It* describes how Celia and Oliver fell in love:

> There was never anything so sudden but the fight of two rams, and Caesar's thrasonical brag of 'I came, saw, and overcame', for your brother and my sister no sooner met but they looked; no sooner looked but they loved; no sooner loved but they sighed; no sooner sighed but they asked one another the reason; no sooner knew the reason but they sought the remedy; and in these degrees have they made a pair of stairs to marriage, which they will climb incontinent, or else be incontinent before marriage. (*As You Like It*, 5.2.28–38)

The humour here lies in taking a commonplace, then using it comically to inflate a description of a love affair into a mock heroic encounter, and then turning it into a little piece of extremely artful rhetoric. The point of the 'pair of stairs to marriage' with which

Rosalind concludes is that her whole speech is structured according to a rhetorical figure which was called a *gradatio* by classical rhetoricians, in which, in the words of Thomas Wilson, 'we rehearse the word that goeth next before, and bring another word thereupon that increaseth the matter, as though one should go up a pair of stairs and not leave till he came at the top'.[33] All of this shows that Rosalind (one of Shakespeare's super-articulate women) is far more than just a recycler of second-hand knowledge: she is one of those identified in the subtitle to Wilson's treatise as his target audience: 'such as are studious of eloquence'. The knowledge used here is grammar-school learning, but it is deployed as part of an intricate rhetorical and social drama.

The deflection, parodying, and channelling of cultural snobbery play a significant part in Shakespeare's response to classical antiquity. If he quotes a hackneyed phrase he tends deliberately to tag it as hackneyed. When he is fearful of displaying the level of understanding of Ovid that his contemporaries would expect from the son of a provincial artisan, he is very careful (as he does in the comic rewriting of Ovid's story of Pyramus and Thisbe in *A Midsummer Night's Dream*; see below, pp. 119–23) to put it into the mouths of rural artisans. A provincial grammar-school boy in this period was desperate to use the knowledge he had acquired at school, but had to do so in ways that did not make him sound like a provincial grammar-school boy. Grammar-school learning tends as a result in Shakespeare to be presented ironically. There is perhaps a further irony here. The fact that Shakespeare was so reluctant to display his classical knowledge in a completely straight form was one of the main reasons why later critics such as Richard Farmer thought that he did not have much of it.

Given the right audience and setting, however, Shakespeare could present unironized imitations of classical literature. This is particularly apparent in his plays which are either known or conjectured to have been performed at the Inns of Court. The Inns were effectively the law schools of Elizabethan England, which gathered together a large number of generally wealthy, high-born, and highly literate young men. For many of these young men, studying the law would have been secondary to displaying their wit, learning, wealth, and style.[34] They were stars well out of Shakespeare's sphere. The members of the Inns traditionally put on plays and revels during the Christmas season, and several of these were explicitly indebted to classical dramas. Two of Shakespeare's comedies, *The Comedy of Errors* and *Twelfth Night*, were certainly performed at the Inns, the former at Gray's Inn at the end of 1594 and the latter at the Middle Temple early in 1602. Both are based on plays by the Roman comedian Plautus, and their classical origins were meant to be noticed. In them Shakespeare was acutely conscious of having to get his learning right.

*The Comedy of Errors* is discussed in detail in Chapter 4 (pp. 143–51). It is a careful and explicitly classical fusion of several plays by Plautus. The later play *Twelfth Night*, which was performed at the Middle Temple at Candlemas (in February) 1602, gives some clues about the development of Shakespeare's relationship to classical drama later in his career. It has twin heroes, confusions of identity, and as John Manningham remarked in his diary is 'much like the comedy of errors, or Menaechmi in Plautus'.[35] Shakespeare's use of this broadly classical plot may have been a response to the elite forum in which this play was to be performed. Interestingly enough, however, the episodes in *Twelfth Night* which Manningham singled out for particular praise were extremely, even defiantly, unclassical. He was particularly taken with the love of Malvolio for Olivia: 'A good practice in it to make the steward believe his lady widow was in love with him.' No Roman comedy has a slave or freedman love a citizen woman, just as no Roman comedy would represent the manoeuvres which go on inside a household such as that of Viola, since it's a rigid convention that households in Roman comedy are represented entirely from the outside, by onstage doors, or by people coming and going through those doors (see below, pp. 145–8). In *Twelfth Night* Shakespeare takes us inside, to explore the inner workings of a household—indeed of two households, since the play moves between the houses of Orsino and of Olivia. This violation of a classical norm, and the correspondingly probing approach to social and erotic relationships, was what his classically informed audience particularly noticed about the play. Shakespeare would probably not have taken this kind of risk with classical convention a decade before when composing a play written for performance at the Inns.

*Twelfth Night* also illustrates another point. Shakespeare's relationship to antiquity is not simply two-way. It is not just a relationship between Shakespeare on the one hand and his sources on the other. It's also a relationship between Shakespeare and his audience. Classical allusions, that is, are part of the language of his drama, and part of his social language in particular. *Twelfth Night* carefully differentiates its characters according to the degree of classical knowledge that they possess. In the very first scene the Duke Orsino makes a not specially learned classical comparison with the Ovidian story of Actaeon, who while out hunting spied the goddess Diana naked and was transformed to a deer and pursued by his hounds as a punishment. Orsino says that when he saw Olivia, 'That instant was I turned into a hart, | And my desires, like fell and cruel hounds, | E'er since pursue me' (1.1.20–3). This has all the poeticism and involution which characterize Orsino: he knows the story of Actaeon from Ovid, and he knows that it was frequently read as an allegory of the way the passions tear apart a lover. In the next scene Viola and the sea captain locate themselves in a similar social register: the captain describes Sebastian, Viola's brother, during his shipwreck as having ridden the waves like 'Arion on the dolphin's back' (1.2.14). Arion was a mythical musician whose songs were sweet enough to enchant the waves and fishes, and the captain is delicately trying to suggest that a miracle could have happened, and Sebastian may have survived the shipwreck.

Strikingly, no other character in the play makes use of any similar classical comparison. Sir Toby Belch and his friends do not attempt similes of any kind, let alone classical ones. Their learning is instead limited to some wonderfully garbled wisdom given to them by the fool Feste: 'thou wast in very gracious fooling last night, when thou spokest of Pigrogromitus, of the Vapians passing the equinoctial of Queubus' (2.3.21–3). Editors have earnestly tried to decipher these impenetrable nonsense-names, but they probably originate in some learned fooling by Feste—who, as Viola says, can 'observe their mood on whom he jests, | The quality of persons, and the time' (3.1.61–2). He knows, that is, when to *sound* learned. When Viola gives Feste a coin he asks for another with 'I would play Lord Pandarus of Phrygia, sir, to bring a Cressida to this Troilus' (3.1.50–1)—that is, 'I'll play the go-between to make this coin breed.' He knows that Viola is the kind of person whose fancy can be tickled by a high literary allusion to ancient writing. Sir Toby Belch, on the other hand, is far less socially versatile. He has at best a drunkenly debauched grasp of the classics. At one point he defends staying up all night drinking with 'Not to be abed after midnight is to be up betimes, and *diliculo surgere*, thou knowest' (2.3.1–3). William Lily cited the proverb *diliculo surgere saluberrimum est* ('to rise at dawn is most healthy') in his grammar to show that an infinitive ('to rise') can be the subject of a verb. He certainly didn't mean it as a defence of all-night drinking bouts. The formidably dim Sir Andrew Aguecheek hasn't even got this far in this elementary textbook (the proverb is cited at the very start of Lily's Chapter 2, so you don't have to have gone far in your studies to have met it), and says he doesn't know what Toby is talking about. In *Cymbeline* the über-Clot Cloten also echoes the maxim, but in a clumsy vernacular vein ('I am glad I was up so late, for that's the reason I was up so early,' 2.3.31–2). Classical allusions and allusions to grammar-school learning are artfully and also socially inflected in Shakespeare's mature work. They are one of the many ways in which the plays distinguish between different groups, and by which they position characters in relation to others. They also create opportunities for that particularly Shakespearian trick of characters talking just past each other, in ways which build intimacy between the playwright and his audience even as it slightly detaches that audience from the onstage character. There is in *Twelfth Night* a quiet drama in literary and educational allusions, and that drama seems aimed at us. By 1602 the grammar-school boy from Stratford-upon-Avon could comfortably conduct conversations both between characters on his stage and between himself and his audience through classical allusions. Like his own Feste, he could 'observe their mood on whom he jests, | The quality of persons, and the time'. And his growing confidence in using his classical learning as part of a dialogue with his audience is apparent in his changing treatments of the work of the poet Virgil, to whom the next chapter turns.

# 2

# *Virgil*

Virgil was the most highly regarded, if not necessarily the most widely read, classical author in early-modern Europe. His status is apparent in how his works fared in print. In England, as on the continent, printers tended to produce editions of Virgil before they published texts of Ovid, but when it came to repeat editions Ovid stole the show.[1] This is more or less in line with Shakespeare's attitudes to the two poets. Virgil is often present in his works, and is often associated with high social or generic status, or with high emotional charge, but Ovid was the classical author of whom Shakespeare made the most extensive use. Charles Martindale suggested in 1990 that 'Shakespeare has little of the Virgilian sensibility',[2] and over a decade later stuck to his guns: 'I thus remain of the view that Shakespeare is not usefully to be described as a Virgilian poet. By that I mean that his reading of Virgil did not result in a profound modification of his sensibility and imagination.'[3] Martindale's scepticism has good foundations. None of Shakespeare's contemporaries ever compared him to Virgil, and none of his works could reasonably be described as 'Virgilian' in the way that his first narrative poem *Venus and Adonis* (1593) could be described as 'Ovidian'. And yet there is perhaps something slightly nineteenth-century about Martindale's judgement. It is as though writers are sensibilities, and where sensibilities are in harmony influence occurs. So, as it were, Shakespeare was a sceptical kind of a guy and Montaigne was a sceptical kind of a guy, and so when Shakespeare read Montaigne he could experience a 'profound modification of his sensibility and imagination'. But Shakespeare was not an imperial and melancholy kind of a guy, and so Virgil sat shallow in his mind.

This view of literary influence shouldn't be simply dismissed. Writers do have characters and characteristics, both innate and acquired, and some literary relationships do resemble friendships, elective affinities, amicable conversations, or even filial relationships. But literary influence does not operate only at the level of sensibility any more than it operates only at the levels of allusion and stylistic echo. As we have seen, Shakespeare read classical and contemporary works not just to plunder content (similes, *exempla*, phrases that could be put into plays) or narrative ideas (plots, subplots, scenes, gestures). He also read to learn a practice. The sixteenth-century German humanist and reformer Philip Melanchthon in his writing on literary imitation argued that 'imitatio specialis', or imitation of an individual writer, was chiefly a matter of emulating what he termed 'cohaerentia', or the various ways in which a writer puts his works together. So the imitator of Cicero should chiefly try to learn how to structure sentences and arguments in the way that Cicero did.[4] That is a clue to the fact that humanist readers read with an eye to the 'how' of what they read: they thought about the way a given author used rhetorical figures, how his sentences were structured, how his arguments or plots were constructed. Shakespeare was trained to read in this way. He also, of course, had a professional interest in the ways in which situated utterances work: as a dramatist he did not just have an ear for dialogue or monologue, but could imagine how particular words would sound to particular audiences.

This combination of his training and his profession means that Shakespeare can usefully be thought of as asking two questions of what he read. The schoolboy humanist in him might ask 'What can I learn from this text?' The playwright might wonder 'What are these words *doing* to their audience?' These questions lead to what is in two distinct senses a 'pragmatic' way of thinking about texts. A writer who asked them would have thought always about how he could use or learn from his reading. He also would have thought about how a particular remark or literary allusion might have performative force within a conversation between different people.

This may well explain why Virgil was never going to be quite as 'useful' to Shakespeare, or indeed to any other early-modern playwright, as Ovid was. Ovid's *Metamorphoses* provided a store of stories, and in relating those stories Ovid is continually aware of how his words work on both his actual readers and on the fictional listeners and audiences within his poem. That made him doubly appealing both to a humanist who wanted to imitate the 'how' of an author and to a dramatist who was always listening out for what an audience might hear in a speech: Ovid had a distinctive, rhetoricized and witty style. He also was continually interested in how words might sound to different audiences. Virgil was rather different. His works do include speeches, and he himself read and imitated Greek dramatic writers, as well as earlier Greek and Roman pastoral, didactic, and epic poets. But his works—the *Aeneid*, a twelve-book epic about the fall of Troy and the journey of a core of Trojan heroes to Italy, the ten densely crafted *Eclogues*, the four books of his poem on tillage, husbandry, beekeeping, and politics called the *Georgics*, plus a substantial gathering of shorter poems which were still widely ascribed to him in this period—could not instantly be assimilated into theatrical texts. Much of Virgil's artistry was put into establishing dialogues with earlier poets—with Homer, Theocritus, Callimachus, the early Roman philosophical poet Lucretius, or the early Roman epic poet Ennius—rather than with dialogue in a more literal sense. Indeed, interpersonal exchanges in Virgil's poems generally consist either of commands, requests for information, or narrations which require no answer from their audience.

Virgil was encountered by most serious readers in the sixteenth century in printed editions in which the words of the poet were physically surrounded, and almost crowded off the printed page, by annotations. Smaller quarto editions might devote roughly the same amount of space to pointing out literary allusions as they did to glossing difficult phrases. The title of the most popular English edition of Virgil in the sixteenth century was 'The Works of Virgil with Short Notes by Paulus Manutius in the Margin, along with the Main Places from Homer which Virgil Imitated'.[5] Virgil consequently appeared on the page as a writer who was part of an allusive literary system. This was true to varying degrees of all annotated classical texts, but for Virgil more than any other classical poet the editorial tradition harmonized with the kind of poetry he wrote. He tended to do things with the words of other poets—by allusion, quotation, transformation—rather than doing things with words in dialogue,[6] and his early-modern commentators made that instantly apparent to his readers.

None of this means that Shakespeare did not recite passages of the *Aeneid* to himself as his horse plodded dully home to Stratford, or that he didn't instantly recall a passage from the *Georgics* (3.75–94) when he saw an excitable stallion run after a mare in heat—as he seems to have done when describing Adonis's horse in *Venus and Adonis* (259–324). Nor does it mean that Virgil's identification of civilization with cultivation in the *Georgics* could not have influenced Shakespeare's understanding of history,[7] and neither, indeed, does it exactly mean that Shakespeare's sensibility was not 'Virgilian'. What it means is something much more simple: Virgil's kind of art was slightly out of step with a dramatist's kind of art.

Even this claim is easy to overstate. Virgil is often said to have included 'tragic' episodes within the *Aeneid*. When Aeneas arrives at Carthage and falls in love with and then abandons the Carthaginian queen Dido there are many echoes of tragic texts and sources. Virgil wanted his readers to notice these, and Book IV of the epic, which relates Aeneas's departure and Dido's suicide, has often been read as (and has often also been rewritten as) a kind of tragedy. It provided the foundations of a tragedy by Christopher Marlowe and (perhaps) Thomas Nashe in *Dido, Queen of Carthage*, which Shakespeare almost certainly knew. The extensive afterlife of the story of Dido and Aeneas in the operatic tradition is a significant indicator of the kind of tragic drama that might be expected to grow from Virgil's particular way of constructing action and speeches, however.[8] Virgilian orations translate naturally into arias, since they are carefully constructed performances in which the primary focus is on the emotions of the speaker rather than on those of a fictional audience or witnesses to the action.

Virgil was not, though, simply uninterested in the ways in which different characters respond to the same actions and events. He regularly 'focalizes' narrative through the experiences of a particular person (that is, he describes things in ways that correspond to the ways they would appear to one or more of his characters). But he wrote in genres which traditionally do not attach great significance to how people stand, physically or emotionally, in relation to each other. Even his *Eclogues*, several of which are presented as dialogues between different shepherds, tend to leave each participant at the end of the dialogue in much the same state as they were in at the poem's beginning (and *As You Like It*, the most eclogic of Shakespeare's plays, is also perhaps the play in which characters seem most consistently not actually to talk to each other). The dialogues in the *Eclogues* tend to be as much competitive performances as conversations, and running through them too is often an underlying dialogue, often also of a covertly competitive kind, between Virgil himself and his sources in Callimachus or Theocritus.

Early-modern English dramatists certainly recognized these aspects of Virgil. When Ben Jonson brought Virgil onstage in his *Poetaster* (1601), he presented him as the most elevated and serious of the Roman poets, who had the ear and indeed the chair of the emperor Augustus. But where Jonson's Ovid is shown sweating over poems and being told off by his father (Jonson had read Ovid's autobiographical poem *Tristia* 4.10 carefully), Virgil by contrast comes on to recite, at length, a translation of Book IV of the *Aeneid* about *Fama*, the goddess whose name means both 'fame' and 'rumour'. This is interrupted by the arrival of the poetasters who have (not coincidentally) damaged the *fama*, or reputation, of Jonson's alter ego in the play, Horace. While Virgil is reciting, the action on the stage simply stops, and there is no indicator of how his onstage listeners are reacting, though presumably they are standing in awestruck wonder. Victoria Moul has cleverly observed that the dialogue spoken by Jonson's Virgil is rich in borrowings from Horace's *Sermones* (the satires, or literally 'conversations'), which makes it appear that in order even to participate in a drama Virgil needs to ventriloquize the voice of another classical poet.[9] Shakespeare's attitudes to Virgil differed from Jonson's, as several studies have shown;[10] but Jonson here reveals a problem with using or representing Virgil onstage which was shared by all early-modern dramatists, including Shakespeare. Virgil belongs to a realm largely outside conversation. His idiom is that of the set-piece declamation, the performance of rhetorical artistry rather than of exchanges between people. In *Dido, Queen of Carthage* Marlowe has to give his Dido repeated interjections in order to punctuate Aeneas's story of the fall of Troy ('O end Aeneas, I can hear no more', 2.1.242).

What features of Virgil *were* useful for early-modern dramatists? Virgil's *Aeneid* is not concerned with the moment-by-moment effects of conversation, but it is profoundly concerned with the affective force of speech. Symptomatic of this is the long inset narrative which dominates Books II and III of the *Aeneid*, in which Aeneas relates the unutterable sorrows of the fall of Troy to Queen Dido.[11] The inset narrative was a conventional element of epic poetry, which enabled poets to encapsulate large amounts of history within a narrative that begins in the middle of things (Odysseus relates much of his history to the Phaeacian court in *Odyssey* 9–12). It serves partly as a generic marker ('this is epic'). Aeneas's tale to Dido also has a profound interpersonal effect, since after the hero has finished his narrative his words and his appearance are described as sticking fast within Dido's bosom ('haerent infixi pectore voltus | verbaque', 4.4–5), and she falls in love. That interpersonal effect is revealed all at once after the narrative has ended, like the sudden bursting of a wave. Along the way there are occasional moments where the narrative takes on the character of an interpersonal exchange, as when Aeneas asks (in the second person singular, as though directly to Dido) 'Perhaps you also want to know about the fate of Priam?' ('Forsitan et, Priami fuerint quae fata, requiras', 2.506), and there are repeated analogies between the stories Aeneas tells and the life of Dido.[12] But explicit indications as to how Dido is reacting to Aeneas while he relates his past and the history of the fall of Troy are very few indeed. Virgil presents instead the total and final response of Dido to Aeneas's narrative.

The first four books of the *Aeneid*, particularly Books II (in which Aeneas relates the fall of Troy to Dido) and IV (which relates the love affair of Dido and Aeneas and his departure at the command of Jove to found the Roman people), seem to have been more frequently read in Tudor grammar schools than any other passages from Virgil's epic, and Shakespeare would not have been unusual if there were sections within these books to which he devoted particular attention.[13] Those books provide models not of theatrical conversations but of what might be called situated affect. That is, they show the powerful influence of Aeneas's act of narrating on Dido. They also present the fall of Troy as being not just an event of great historical significance, but one which has enormous emotional power. The other thing that seems to have mattered about these books so far as Shakespeare was concerned is a curious one: there is no simple correlation between the emotion that results from the narrative and the events narrated. Dido does not respond to the tragic fall of Troy with sorrow. She falls uncontrollably in love with the narrator in a way that runs directly counter to the explicit force of the prophetic imperial narrative which Aeneas is trying to relate about himself. Affect spirals away beyond its narrative pretexts. This aspect of Virgil—the super-abundance of emotional affect over its narrative causes—was probably the single greatest thing that Shakespeare took from Virgil. It runs through Othello's description of his courtship of Desdemona:

> My story being done,
> She gave me for my pains a world of sighs:
> She swore in faith 'twas strange, 'twas passing strange,
> 'Twas pitiful, 'twas wondrous pitiful.
> She wished she had not heard it, yet she wished
> That heaven had made her such a man. She thankèd me,
> And bade me, if I had a friend that loved her,
> I should but teach him how to tell my story,
> And that would woo her. Upon this hint I spake.
> She loved me for the dangers I had passed,
> And I loved her that she did pity them. (1.3.157–67)[14]

This is not exactly an 'allusion' to Virgil, but it certainly draws on the powerful Virgilian association between storytelling and a huge, unpredictable, and perhaps also dangerous affective force.[15]

That was the big thing Shakespeare learnt from Virgil, and he learnt it very early. The narrative poem *Lucrece* (1594), the second printed work to which Shakespeare's name was attached, is based on a number of sources in Ovid's *Fasti* and in Livy's history of Rome. It relates how the rape of the chaste matron Lucretia by the son of King Tarquin led to the banishment of the kings from Rome. *Lucrece* is presumably the 'graver labour' promised the previous year in the dedication to the explicitly Ovidian *Venus and Adonis*, and grave it certainly is: rape, complaint, and the consequent transformation of the Roman monarchy into a republic give it not just a thematic gravity but also a clearly signalled generic gravity. Shakespeare never wrote an epic, and to judge by the complex near-mock-heroic idiom of *Troilus and Cressida* might never have felt comfortable doing so, but the Virgilian allusions in *Lucrece* suggest that this poem was, if not Shakespeare's attempt at epic, then his most sustained effort to write in narrative form about the origins of a particular political configuration in a way that had parallels to Virgil's epic of empire.

The principal Virgilian moment in the poem occurs after Lucrece has been raped by Tarquin. She complains at length, and then, 'Pausing for means to mourn some newer way' (1365), there comes into a her mind a 'piece of skilful painting', which represents the fall of Troy. Shakespeare describes the picture at length—and this kind of detailed description of a work of art, known in the rhetorical tradition as an 'ecphrasis', was highly fashionable in the 1590s. The painting gradually focuses on the betrayal of the Trojans by the traitor Sinon, and the subsequent fall of Troy:

> Here all enraged, such passion her assails
> That patience is quite beaten from her breast.
> She tears the senseless Sinon with her nails,
> Comparing him to that unhappy guest
> Whose deed hath made herself herself detest.
>   At last she smilingly with this gives o'er:
>   'Fool, fool', quoth she, 'his wounds will not be sore.'
>     (1562–8)

The whole passage is typical of Shakespeare's seldom explicitly Virgilian Virgilianism. It offers very little by way of precise verbal reminiscences of Virgil's poem. The fact that the end of Troy is described through a picture marks the whole passage as a separate episode, almost as though it is italicized for special attention, or 'framed' as an allusion. It shows that Shakespeare recognized the emotional function of epic narratives in Virgil, as well as that he understood the complex ways Virgil described the emotional effects of works of art. So when Aeneas arrives at Carthage in *Aeneid* I he sees the actions of the Trojan war represented on buildings in the new-rising city, and is overwhelmed with grief:

> constitit et lacrimans, 'quis iam locus,' inquit, 'Achate,
> quae regio in terris nostri non plena laboris?
> en Priamus! sunt hic etiam sua praemia laudi,
> sunt lacrimae rerum et mentem mortalia tangunt.

> solue metus; feret haec aliquam tibi fama salutem.'
> (*Aeneid*, 1.459–63)

He stopped and weeping said 'What place now, Achates, what area of the world, is not full of our labour? Look, here's Priam. Here too are the rewards of praise, here are the tears of things, and mortal events touch the mind. Set aside your fears. This fame will bring you some future well-being.'

This is in its way an imperial vision. The whole world is 'plena laboris', full of the deeds of Troy, as though the labours of the Trojans have spread through and conquered the world. But Virgil's description of Aeneas as he observes these images does not shy away from identifying that quasi-imperial vision of universal fame with self-absorption. The representation of Troy is described as a 'pictura inanis', an empty picture, over which Aeneas weeps at the representation of his own labours. Indeed, he sees the Trojan war in a way that is focalized to the point of egoism. He sees the body of Hector, then he sees Priam stretching out his hands in supplication, and then, finally, 'se quoque', himself too, mixed up among the foremost of the Greeks. This is not quite the final moment of the *ecphrasis* of the siege and sack of Troy witnessed by Virgil's hero Aeneas, however. It ends, significantly, with the woman-warrior Penthesilea leading the Amazons in to battle, and its final words are 'audetque viris concurrere virgo' ('A woman dares to fight against men', 1.493). The Latin word order ensures that the very last word used in the description of the picture is 'virgo', a virgin. That marks a shift in focalization from the man who looks at the representations of Troy towards the woman, Dido, Queen of Carthage, who ordered their construction. Epic is a literary form traditionally dominated by men, but in Virgil's epic gender dynamics do not always move in predictable ways. He does not simply associate males with fighting and females with emotion and contemplation. At the moment the imperial hero Aeneas is self-absorbedly zooming in on the parts of the image and the story of Troy that most concern his fate, Queen Dido enters from the hunt, like Diana bearing a quiver on her shoulder, or like the vigorous Amazon Penthesilea, bringing joy, delivering judgements, and 'instans operi regnisque futuris', driving on the work and the future kingdom.

That is a shocking reminder of how passive Aeneas has become, and in traditional terms how 'feminine' he is.

Shakespeare did not directly imitate the words of this passage from Virgil, but he did remember, from a distance, as it were, its affective force. And that became a central element in *Lucrece*. He also clearly learnt from its surprising reversals of expectations about the behaviour of different genders, since his equivalent of the emotional observer of the picture is not Aeneas but Lucrece, a woman who has endured rape. He also suggests that the representation of the sack of Troy might be a potentially specious form of consolation ('much imaginary work was there; | Conceit deceitful', 1422–3), just as that *pictura inanis* of Troy in Carthage is for Aeneas. But there is nonetheless one striking point of *dis*similarity between the two episodes. When Aeneas sees the representations of the Trojan war it is a recent event in his own life. The phrase *sunt lacrimae rerum* has often been treated as a generalized statement of the sorrow in human existence ('here are the tears that afflict mortality'). That is perhaps not quite what it means for Aeneas. He is seeing the sorrows of his own past. The word 'res' (which can mean 'affairs' or 'actions') in the phrase *lacrimae rerum* has perhaps something of the force it had in the title of the Emperor Augustus's relation of his own doings, the *Res Gestae Divi Augusti* ('Things done by divine Augustus'). It might suggest both 'public affairs' and a catalogue of actions by an individual. When Lucrece, an early Roman republican matron, sees the picture of the sack of Troy, on the other hand, there is a wide gulf of time between the moment she sees the representation and the action represented. Nothing in the picture directly represents her own experiences. She is seeking rather than simply seeing analogies between her own suffering and the fall of Troy. And that personal and historical distance between Lucrece and Aeneas adds an additional element to her misery. Aeneas sees a picture of his own life, which provides a sort of consolation for sorrow through fame. Lucrece sees a picture which provides a loose analogy for her woe. That has the effect not only of emphasizing her emotional isolation, but also of giving it a chronological dimension. Part of the sorrow of Lucrece is that the only vehicle she has through which to articulate her suffering is a representation of a set of events from the distant past at which she was not present.

Lucrece had originally been drawn to the picture because she recalled in it the figure of Hecuba, the wife of Priam, through whom writers in the tragic tradition often explored the horror of watching Troy fall. Hecuba in the painting is presented as a figure of immense antiquity—both in the sense of 'being immensely old' and perhaps also in the sense of being a figure from very long ago:

> In her the painter had anatomized
> Time's ruin, beauty's wreck, and grim care's reign.
> Her cheeks with chaps and wrinkles were disguised;
> Of what she was no semblance did remain.
> Her blue blood changed to black in every vein,
>   Wanting the spring that those shrunk pipes had fed,
>   Showed life imprisoned in a body dead.
>
> On this sad shadow Lucrece spends her eyes,
> And shapes her sorrow to the beldame's woes,
> Who nothing wants to answer her but cries
> And bitter words to ban her cruel foes. (1450–60)

Hecuba is 'Time's ruin', and 'Of what she was no semblance did remain'. Is this a portrait of an old woman, or is it a picture which is itself so old that it's fading before our eyes? The second of these two possible interpretations suggests a profound truth not just about Shakespeare's early responses to Virgil, but about his early classicism more generally. The picture of Hecuba and the fall of Troy in *Lucrece* shows, firstly, that Shakespeare responded strongly to Virgil's association between narratives, or artistic representations of narratives, and powerful emotions from the earliest stages of his literary career. What he remembered from Virgil were the outlines of stories and their affective consequences. This is exactly what you would expect from someone who read Virgil at grammar school, and who remembered a general scenario, a mood and a feel, rather than precise details of vocabulary. It is also the kind of response to Virgil that might be expected from a playwright, who thought about texts and stories theatrically, as the sources of emotional and affective meaning for particular people who stand in a particular relationship to those texts. But the painting of Troy in *Lucrece* suggests more about Shakespeare's early classicism than this. It is tagged in a range of different ways as *old*. Hecuba is old; the painting itself is tucked away at the back of

Lucrece's memory so distantly that she has to make a conscious effort to 'call to mind' where it hangs and to go and look at it anew. That could be read in a rather clunky biographical way as a sign that Shakespeare the grammar-school classicist is consciously trying to kick-start his own memory in order to retrieve an episode from the *Aeneid.* But it also raises a much larger question. Do the tremors of memory and age which surround Lucrece's picture of Troy mean that Shakespeare had an awareness of the gulf of time between the present and the past which, as we saw in the introduction, has traditionally been seen as one of the hallmarks of Renaissance humanism?

It's a good question to ask, but the answer to it is probably 'not quite' or 'not exactly'. The sense of 'antiquity' here is presented as a personal and indeed a biological matter. 'Antiquity' is (like the word 'antique' generally in Shakespeare's works) associated with age and with old things that are almost forgotten, rather than with a historically distinct cultural field. But this does not mean that the impression of chronological distance between Lucrece and the subject of the picture or the action related in Virgil's poem is not a significant element in the poem's overall effect. The gap between the experience of Aeneas and the experiences of Lucrece is used as a means of evoking and augmenting emotion. Lucrece's grief is made to seem worse than that of Aeneas. He has a representation of his own labours to look at, which will bring to him the consolation of fame. She, on the other hand, has an old picture of an old woman who bears no semblance to what she was, and a deceptive image of Sinon, a deceptive man who ruins Troy in a way that is loosely analogous to the way in which Tarquin has ruined her, and whose image she assaults in revenge, but who isn't really very like Tarquin at all, unless you are as overwhelmed by grief as she is. That is, part of the sufferings of Lucrece is that she cannot quite bring back to life the passions of the ancient world, or of Aeneas. The gulf of time becomes an emotional gulf, which has the effect of amplifying the affect released by the story of Troy in Virgil.

## Remembering Virgil in *Hamlet*

Reciting passages of Virgil from memory was quite an art, even a kind of party trick, in early-modern England. The diarist John

Manningham recorded that 'My cousin repeated *memoriter* [by memory] almost the very first book of Virg[ils] *Aeneids*. And this day he rehearsed without book very near the whole 2[n]d book of the *Aeneids*, viz. 630 verses without missing one word. A singular memory in a man of his age: 62.'[16] Not everyone had quite such a good memory as Manningham's aged cousin. Young Hamlet certainly did not. When the players come to Elsinore, the prince requests 'a passionate speech' which he had once heard. This again derives from Aeneas's moving narrative in *Aeneid II* about the fall of Troy, laced with some traces of Ovid.[17] Hamlet's memory stumbles as he begins to recall the speech, but he starts off the speech before he passes on the task of recollection and performance to a professional player:

One speech in it I chiefly loved, 'twas Aeneas' tale to Dido, and thereabout of it especially where he speaks of Priam's slaughter. If it live in your memory, begin at this line—let me see, let me see:

'The rugged Pyrrhus, like th' Hyrcanian beast—'

'tis not so. It begins with Pyrrhus—

'The rugged Pyrrhus, he whose sable arms,
Black as his purpose, did the night resemble
When he lay couchèd in the ominous horse,
Hath now this dread and black complexion smeared
With heraldry more dismal. Head to foot
Now is he total gules, horridly tricked
With blood of fathers, mothers, daughters, sons,
Baked and impasted with the parching streets,
That lend a tyrannous and damnèd light
To their vile murders. Roasted in wrath and fire,
And thus o'ersizèd with coagulate gore,
With eyes like carbuncles the hellish Pyrrhus
Old grandsire Priam seeks.'

So, proceed you. (2.2.448–68)

*Hamlet* and *Lucrece* were described by Gabriel Harvey as pleasing 'the wiser sort'—a remark which might well have pleased Shakespeare, had he heard it, because that same Harvey had been so scornful about the 'grammar-school' learning of Thomas Nashe.[18] Presumably

Harvey had registered that both *Lucrece* and *Hamlet* include large sections which mark themselves as being derived from Virgil. Certainly the player's speech on Hecuba that follows Hamlet's prompting of his memory is the most extended allusion to Virgil in the Shakespearian canon after *Lucrece*, and it has several features in common with the earlier poem. Shakespeare's interest in Hecuba in both passages may not simply have derived from reading the *Aeneid.* As we saw in the previous chapter, the Greek rhetorician Aphthonius encouraged students to try their hands at writing speeches that would 'show the commotion of the mind, like the words that Hecuba uttered after Troy was overturned'. In the English version of this school text, Richard Rainolde's *Foundation of Rhetoric*, there is a model speech called 'What lamentable oration Hecuba Queen of Troy might make, Troy being destroyed'.[19] Shakespeare's Virgil is so enmeshed in pedagogical practice that it often seems to have been reinvented through the practice of teaching and learning rather than directly imitated. But there are clear traces that Shakespeare was thinking of the Latin text here too. Hamlet first uses and then drops the epithet 'Hyrcanian', a word almost exclusively used of tigers in the sixteenth century, and taken in this usage directly from Virgil. This may hint that the learned Hamlet knows too much of Virgil's original poem to be able accurately to recall the vernacular theatrical version of it.[20] The context of the speech in Virgil is also played on with great canniness. As the first player takes over and describes Hecuba's grief at observing the death of her husband, he begins to weep. This discomforts Polonius, who bustles him off the stage with 'Look whe'er he has not turned his colour, and has tears in 's eyes. Prithee, no more' (2.2.522–3). Polonius interrupts the speech at just the moment when in Virgil Aeneas describes his own reaction to the death of Priam. At that moment Aeneas, like Hamlet a little earlier in the play, sees, or imagines he sees, his own father:

> At me tum primum saevus circumstetit horror.
> obstipui; subiit cari genitoris imago,
> ut regem aequaevum crudeli volnere vidi
> vitam exhalantem. (2.559–62)

And then first desperate horror engulfed me. I was struck dumb. There rose before me the image of my dear father, as I saw the king, who was of the same age as him, breathing out his life through a cruel wound.

The revival of the moment in which Aeneas relives the horror of the past, and in which an 'imago'—which can mean a mental image or even a ghost—of a father rises up in the hero's mind is prevented by Polonius. In the *Aeneid* Aeneas is goaded into vengeful fury by the sight of Priam's death. In *Hamlet* the pedantic Polonius ensures that the ghost of revenge remains buried. This interruption ties the speech in with some of the habitual rhythms of the play in which it appears. There is often a hiccup of aposiopesis (a figure of speech in which a sentence breaks off) in *Hamlet*, where a sentence gets going, runs on, and then loses itself in the intensity of emotion towards which it is leading. That rhetorical feature reflects and is reflected by the structure of the play, in which a hero who has a motive and a cue for passion and for action takes a famously long time to act, as though the emotions which in principle ought to drive an agent to act have become themselves barriers to action. Hamlet is also a character for whom the processes of remembering are central: he swears to remember the ghost rather than to avenge him.[21] The scene with the players rehearses, as it were, the structural hiccup of the play itself, in which remembering rather than revenging, or remembering *as* revenging, takes over the plot and leaves it sprawling, and then stops just short of reviving the vengeful passion of Aeneas.

Although this detail suggests how artfully the player's speech was woven into the texture of *Hamlet*, the style in which it is written is so different from that of the rest of the play that early critics, including John Dryden in the later seventeenth century, thought that Shakespeare could not have written it.[22] The epithets in the speech are remarkable, and are remarked upon within the play: when Hecuba is described as 'the mobbled queen' both Hamlet and Polonius pause over the word and savour it. Several words in the speech are found nowhere else in Shakespeare ('coagulate', 'fellies', 'repugnant', 'unnerved', and 'whiff') and several are not used elsewhere in the period ('impasted', 'mobbled', 'o'ersizèd', 'o'erteemèd', 'bisson'). It is very hard to assign these to a particular stylistic register. 'Baked and impasted' and 'o'ersizèd' in particular are curious, thick-textured words which seem to have been hoiked up into an epic narrative from a socially low sphere: they have artisanal origins, deriving from baking and from painting or plastering respectively, which are used to evoke the gore which covers Pyrrhus. The speech uses two adjectives with an 'over-' prefix ('o'ersizèd' and 'o'erteemèd'), which seem themselves deliberately oversize, aspiring to an epic massiveness that seems almost too heavy for its own good. Hamlet's grand and genuinely Virgilian epithet 'Hyrcanian'—which turns out to be a slip of the memory—is replaced in the player's section of the speech by a language that has vernacular roots, but which is aspiring towards a massive and gory heroic register. The metre, too, is stiffer, the interplay between sentence and line less flexible, than the norms for Shakespeare at this date.

These features were meant to make this 'classical' speech audibly different from the rest of the play. They serve the function, onstage, of quotation marks. And since Hamlet says he heard the speech long ago it's reasonable to assume that it is also meant to sound *old*. The speech has indeed sometimes been seen as a pastiche of earlier drama, and in particular as taking a swipe at Marlowe's *Dido, Queen of Carthage*, which includes a long narrative of the fall of Troy delivered by Aeneas to Dido.[23] But the resemblances to Marlowe's play are slight: both versions of the story have Priam knocked over by the air that rushes from Pyrrhus's sword ('Which he disdaining whisked his sword about, | And with the wind thereof the King fell down', 2.1.254–5), but there precise resemblances end. The speech sounds like it comes from old plays, or old versions of epic, but it's impossible to say which ones.

By the end of the sixteenth century the majority of English verse translations of major classical poems and plays were not only old but sounded old. Even the recent and self-proclaimedly original translation of the *Iliad* by George Chapman, the first instalment of which appeared in 1598, combined a dense syntax with the rhyming fourteen-syllable lines favoured by translators of the classics from the mid century onwards. This old-fashioned form had fallen so out of favour by the early seventeenth century that Chapman himself abandoned it in favour of decasyllabic couplets for his translation of the *Odyssey*. The main English translation of the *Aeneid* by Thomas Phaer, begun during the reign of Mary Tudor more than forty years before the composition of *Hamlet*, was also in fourteeners. Phaer's version was completed by Thomas Twyne in 1573 and continued to be reprinted until 1620 (with reprints right around the period in which *Hamlet* was composed, in 1596 and 1600). Phaer tended to combine Anglo-Saxon vocabulary with broadly Latinate word order (in which verbs are generally delayed to the end of sentences) in long rhyming lines. By 1600 this would have seemed notably unmodish. Hamlet's Pyrrhus moves in a more modern metrical form, but proceeds nonetheless according to Latin word order: he 'old grandsire Priam seeks', rather than 'seeks old grandsire Priam', and his persistent deferral of verbs may have a precedent in Phaer, who habitually slows action down in this way:[24]

> The fatal end of Priam now perhaps ye will require.
> When he the city taken saw and houses' tops on fire,
> And building broke, and round about so thick his foes to rage,
> His harness [armour] on his shoulders (long unworn till then)
>     for age
> All quaking, on (good man) he puts, to purpose small, and then
> His sword him girt, and into death and en'mies thick he ran.
> Amidst the court right underneath the naked skies in sight,
> An altar huge of size there stood, and by the same upright
> An ancient laurel tree did grow, that wide abroad was shed,
> And it, and all the carvèd gods with broad shade overspread.
> There Hecuba and her daughters all (poor souls) at the altar's side
> In heaps together afraid them drew, like doves when doth betide
> Some storm them headlong drive, and clipping fast their gods
>     did hold.[25]

Even in this passage of frantic action Phaer persistently delays verbs until the end of lines ('require', 'ran', 'was shed', 'overspread', 'drive'), of clauses ('he puts', 'there stood', 'did grow', 'them drew', 'did hold'), or of sentences. There is no direct verbal overlap with the player's speech on Hecuba, and indeed Phaer's adjectives are notably spare ('fatal', 'thick') where those of the 'Hecuba' speech are both prominent and unusual. But Shakespeare may well have taken some cues for his epic pastiche from the slow-motion lumber of Phaer's descriptions of battles in the *Aeneid*. In the player's speech the key moment when the wind of Pyrrhus's sword knocks Priam over, for instance, turns crisis into a moment of stillness and delay:

> Pyrrhus at Priam drives, in rage strikes wide;
> But with the whiff and wind of his fell sword
> Th'unnervèd father falls. Then senseless Ilium,
> Seeming to feel his blow, with flaming top
> Stoops to his base, and with a hideous crash
> Takes prisoner Pyrrhus' ear. For lo, his sword,
> Which was declining on the milky head
> Of reverend Priam, seemed i'th' air to stick. (2.2.475–82)

When Phaer translates the slow heavy violence of the ancient warrior Entellus as he does battle with his fists in the games in *Aeneid* 5.443–8, he too has a warrior stopping dead after the wind has whirled with his weapon—though here it's heavy boxing gloves rather than a sword:

> Entellus rousing then, his left hand bent on high did lift:
> He from the stroke that came, with good foresight, and body swift
> Avoiding shrank for fear, and from the dint thereof declined.
> Entellus missed his mark, and all his force he lost in wind,
> And over that, himself, with heavy peise [weighty crash] and heavy sound,
> All grovelling flat he fell, and with his limbs he spread the ground. (sig. H3r)

'Declined' here is not used in the unusual transitive form that the player deploys when he has Pyrrhus's sword 'declining' on Priam's head, but its appearance in such close proximity to the description of Entellus's weapon missing its mark and losing its force in 'wind' creates a highly suggestive parallel. Shakespeare certainly read Phaer, and he read him beyond Book IV. But he also read Virgil in Latin. In the episode as a whole Shakespeare is presenting a Virgil that is in dialogue between a humanist Hamlet, who knows the original ('Hyrcanian' could not have come from Phaer, who renders the Hyrcanian tigress of Book IV simply as 'Some Tigress', sig. F7r) and a vernacular translation which o'ersizes Virgil with gore, slows down its action to a walking pace, and milks the eyes of heaven for emotional effect.

Whatever its precise origins, the style of Shakespeare's speech is designed to emphasize one central fact. The player's Virgilian speech sounds 'older' than the nimble rhetorical artifice which prevails in Hamlet's Elsinore. Unlike Jonson, who brought Virgil himself on-stage in *Poetaster* to show-stopping effect, the grammar-school boy Shakespeare, who in 1592 had been accused by Robert Greene of beautifying himself with the feathers of his contemporaries,[26] presents a version of Virgil that sounds as though it dates from years before, and which sounds as though it has been hybridized with popular vernacular translations.

This is in part a self-defensive move: Shakespeare wants to incorporate an 'epic' register into the play, but he does so within quotation marks, as nervy pastiche. But the stylistic 'antiquity' of the player's Virgilian speech is not just modest. It o'ersizes its epic cake and eats it too, since it is one of the many ways in which Shakespeare establishes in *Hamlet* his own modernity. Like *The Murder of Gonzago*, the play put on before the guilty king Claudius, which deliberately pastiches earlier theatrical idioms, the speech about Hecuba has the effect of emphasizing the colloquial energy and modernity of the rest of the play. This again ties it in with Shakespeare's wider aims in writing *Hamlet*. This play reshapes in dazzlingly complex forms the 'old' idiom of earlier revenge tragedies from the later 1580s. It does so partly to emphasize the novelty of Shakespeare. The 'antiqued' voice of Virgilian tragic speechifying contributes in a modest way to that overall aim. From the stutters of memory, from the modest protestation that this is all old stuff written so long ago that a sharp university student like Hamlet can't properly call it to mind, comes a powerful suggestion: the play which includes this piece of 'antiquated' Virgil is so new that it makes everything else—earlier classical translations, earlier dramas on classical themes performed by boy players, earlier revenge tragedies—look old.

The speech also has a profound emotional effect within the play itself, which also in a rather different way emphasizes the modernity of the hero, and which also points back to the similarly 'Virgilian' passage in *Lucrece*. After the players depart Hamlet delivers one of his most famous soliloquies:

O, what a rogue and peasant slave am I!
Is it not monstrous that this player here,
But in a fiction, in a dream of passion,
Could force his soul so to his whole conceit
That from her working all his visage wanned,
Tears in his eyes, distraction in 's aspect,
A broken voice, and his whole function suiting
With forms to his conceit? And all for nothing.
For Hecuba!
What's Hecuba to him, or he to Hecuba,
That he should weep for her? (2.2.552–62)

Virgilian narratives, as we have seen, can generate uncontrollable emotions: Dido loves Aeneas not because of his intimate conversations with her but because of his speech and his story. Here that effect of emotional overcharge is redoubled: Hamlet does not simply rebuke the player for feeling emotion when he narrates Hecuba's sufferings. He rebukes himself for failing to feel a similar grief. That recoil upon himself is very much inspired by and kin to *Lucrece*, where the pathos of the heroine is augmented by her historical distance from the Virgilian scene onto which she projected her grief. Here Hamlet sounds as though he is not just 'modern', separated by gulfs of time from the emotions described in the *Aeneid*, but *tragically* modern. Part of his grief is his inability to feel grief, and part of his grief is a 'modern' incapacity to revive both the ancient woes of Troy and the passions of a heroic revenger.

This suggests several important things about Shakespeare's classicism up to around 1600—and indeed it may indicate why Shakespeare's classicism was such an important part of Shakespeare. His 'classical' moments tend in the earlier part of his career to be 'framed' in one way or another, either by being literally presented in a picture, as in the moment from *Lucrece*, or by being stylistically distinguished from the rest of the work in which they appear, as in *Hamlet*. This does not mean that Shakespeare had a 'humanistic' awareness of historical anachronism, or that he saw Virgil's Rome as historically distinct from his own times. It rather means that he had a pragmatic sense of the emotional and theatrical power that he could generate by creating the effect of distinct temporal and stylistic layers within his own works. Making classical passages sound 'old', and powerfully moving because they were old, could create strong emotional and theatrical effects. It could also be professionally useful. Shakespeare's modernity (as it would have appeared to his contemporaries) depended not so much on his having had an idea of 'classical antiquity', but on his ability both to mimic a style that sounds antique and to show that he himself belongs to a later age. The psychological vividness of his characters and their sufferings can also often be augmented by suggesting that they too are 'modern' in the sense of not being quite able to revive or relive the sufferings of Hecuba or Aeneas.

## Jacobean Virgil

Shakespeare's use of Virgil changes in his later writing, and, like every change in his theatrical practice, this was the result of a miscellany of causes—alterations in his company, reactions to his contemporaries, new reading, and perhaps a desire just to do something different.[27] After 1600 Shakespeare never quite associates Virgilian material with an 'antiquated' style in the way he does in the Hecuba speech, and he tends not to 'frame' his allusions to the *Aeneid* as he did in *Lucrece* and *Hamlet*. Robert Miola has argued that this change was largely a personal matter: Shakespeare changed and matured, and came to imitate Virgil more subtly, with the result that the *Aeneid* is insinuated less obviously into the texture of his later plays.[28] That's certainly part of the truth. But it's likely these changes resulted at least in part from causes which were beyond Shakespeare's immediate control. How to adapt classical authors to fit the modern world suddenly became a hot question in the London theatres at the very start of the seventeenth century. This was the period of what used to be called 'the war of the theatres', in which Ben Jonson, Thomas Dekker, and John Marston produced a string of plays (including Jonson's *Poetaster*, in which Virgil himself comes onstage) which satirically represented their fellow dramatists under the guise of Roman poets and poetasters, and which turned the literary rivalries of late Elizabethan England into versions of those at ancient Rome.[29] Shakespeare's relationship to this 'war' has been much debated. *Troilus and Cressida*, with its armed prologue and its satirical representation of the Trojan war, its heavy epithets, and its unsteady aspirations to an 'epic' style, is probably some sort of response to this battle between individual authors and between theatrical companies, whether or not that play contains, as was alleged by the character Will Kempe in the undergraduate play *The Return from Parnassus*, a satirical representation of Ben Jonson under the character of lumbering Ajax. Within a couple of years Ben Jonson also wrote his Roman historical drama *Sejanus* (1603), and began to lay claim to a reputation as the most learned and classically correct dramatist of his age. He did so not by tagging allusions to classical works as 'antique' through curious diction, or by 'framing' them as pictures in the way Shakespeare did in *Lucrece*. He did so by bringing the syntax and structure of classical sentences and speeches together with a contemporary vocabulary.

Shakespeare was unlikely to have been simply scared off making explicit allusions to Virgil by these developments, but he is very likely to have done some sustained rethinking in the course of these crucial years about the way he made use of classical literature. The strategy of linking 'Virgilian' subject matter with archaic or outré diction could easily backfire: it could make Shakespeare look like a grammar-school boy who didn't have a very good recall of classical texts or a good ear for Englishing them. In the much longer term the undervaluation of Shakespeare's classical learning by the critical tradition may partly, indeed, have arisen from his tendency in his early career to allow the seams to show between 'classical' and 'native' writing. The archaic 'Virgilian' speech in *Hamlet* in particular could suggest that Shakespeare did not feel entirely at home with Virgil, or, worse still, that his response to Virgil was *actually* old-fashioned rather than artfully so.

There were other changes in the early seventeenth century which influenced attitudes to Virgil in particular and to the classical world more generally. Some were very simple. The 1606 Act to Restrain Abuses of Players was not good news for playwrights, who could no longer take the name of the Lord in vain; but it was very good news for the classical pantheon, since the monosyllable 'Jove' neatly replaced the banned monosyllable 'God'. A clampdown in the summer of 1599 on dramas on English historical themes may also have encouraged playwrights to think with some urgency about how to locate their dramas in the classical rather than the more recent past. The accession of James VI of Scotland to the English throne in 1603 had further and quite particular consequences for British attitudes towards Virgil's *Aeneid*. James was often associated by his panegyrists with a Virgilian empire without end ('imperium sine fine', *Aeneid* 1.279), and with a willingness to spare the conquered and subdue the proud ('parcere subiectis et debellare superbos', *Aeneid* 6.853). These Virgilian themes were blazoned from the rooftops at the new king's state entry into the city of London, which, as a result of the plague of 1603, was postponed until the following year.[30] The poems and speeches written by Ben Jonson to accompany the elaborate neoclassical triumphal arches built for this occasion make deep and sustained allusions to Virgil, tags from whose works were presented in a grand mélange along with phrases from other classical and post-classical poets (Martial, Ovid, Horace, Statius, Seneca, Claudian, Silius Italicus). Jonson's panegyrics presented the new king as fulfilling the prophecies associated with the emperor Augustus: he closes the doors of Janus and brings an end to war (*Aeneid* 1.293–6), and brings back the age of Saturn (*Eclogues* 4.6). James's son Henry is directly addressed as 'the springing glory of thy godly race', making him the English equivalent to Aeneas's son Ascanius ('Ascanium surgentem et spes heredis Iuli', *Aeneid* 4.274). Jonson's allusions to Virgil are quite deliberately taken from all over the *Aeneid*, rather than just the grammar-school boy's favoured early books, and they make ostentatious use of the up-to-the-minute 1599 edition by Jacobus Pontanus. They were meant to be noticed, and were meant to be more sophisticated than the classicism of any of his fellow dramatists.

Jonson's full-dress classicism on this most public of occasions clearly irritated at least one of his rivals in the war of the theatres. Thomas Dekker composed a vernacular account of the royal entertainments for readers who needed to have their Latin translated, which complained that 'to make a false flourish here with the borrowed weapons of all the old Masters of the noble science of poetry, and to keep a tyrannical coil [fuss, racket], in anatomizing *Genius*, from head to foot, (only to show how nimbly we can carve up the whole mess of the poets) were to play the executioner, and to lay our city's household God on the rack, to make him confess how many pair of Latin sheets we have shaken and cut into shreds to make him a garment'.[31] In other words, according to Jonson's enemies, his excessive and unnecessary display of learning on this occasion killed the city's celebrations stone dead.

Shakespeare must have witnessed this display of classical sophistication, and must have heard too these early Jacobean prophecies of a new era of *pax Britannica*. No resident in London, let alone a sharer in a company which was shortly to become the King's Men, could have missed them. The affective, rhetoricized, impassioned Virgil of Shakespeare's schooling and of his earlier writing would have seemed not just out of fashion but out of place in this new landscape. Sonnet 123, which may have been prompted by the seventy-foot high pyramids (no less!) which were erected in the Strand as part of Jonson's celebration of the royal entry, is notably defiant in its reaction to vulgar architectural innovations:

> No, time, thou shalt not boast that I do change!
> Thy pyramids built up with newer might
> To me are nothing novel, nothing strange,
> They are but dressings of a former sight. (123.1–4)

Despite the protestation that the speaker of the Sonnets will remain the same, changes in Shakespeare's ways of presenting his classical learning did accelerate in the new reign.

These changes, like many literary changes, were in dialogue with political events but were not simply caused by them. Genre also played a part. Virgil's *Aeneid*, although it is now regarded as the archetypical epic poem, includes within it elements from many genres, and has the potential to provide materials for imitators at work in almost any literary kind. The shipwrecks and adventures of Aeneas in particular could provide the foundation for a providential comedy. So at the start of *The Comedy of Errors* (1.1.31–139), Egeon describes his shipwreck in ways that echo Aeneas's narrative (*Aeneid* 2.1–267, 1.88–91). That play was performed in 1594, and is largely based on Plautus (see below, pp. 143–51), but brings to its major source the seascapes and lost children of Greek prose romances. Sixteenth-century readers tended to be very aware of the magical, illusory, and potentially comic (in the generic and structural rather than simply humorous sense) elements in the earlier books of the *Aeneid*. Virgil's poem had been thoroughly assimilated by the magical and unruly Italian romances written in the early part of the century. The first six books are deeply indebted to the prototypical romance wanderings of Ulysses related in Homer's *Odyssey*. Aeneas's shipwreck, his encounter with the disguised goddess Venus his mother, his fabulous meeting with the harpies, all recall the actions of Odysseus. Many of those narrative topoi had in turn been assimilated into the Greek prose romances of Heliodorus and Achilles Tatius. Those associations gave to Virgil's imperial epic a lustre of magic and of comedy. The Greek prose romances, most of which were translated into English in the last third of the sixteenth century, came to have an enormous though usually indirect influence on dramatic plot structures by the end of the first decade of the seventeenth century.

That fashion brought with it the possibility of staging Virgil's epic as a kind of romance. In Shakespeare's later romances there are no more tragic Virgilian tableaux which evoke uncontrollable emotions. There tend instead to be glancing allusions to the actions and narrative of the *Aeneid*, which can be used to suggest an under-plot or even a counter-plot to the main narratives. This was not something entirely new to the Shakespeare of the Jacobean period, since a slight reference to a well-known classical text could be used to highlight the difference between the onstage action and that in the earlier work even in his very early dramas. *Titus Andronicus* has a heroine called Lavinia, who is raped and mutilated in a fictional but notionally 'late' period in the Roman empire, in which the Goths are not just at the gates of Rome but one of them is married to the emperor. Lavinia's name is chosen in order to make a savage contrast to the blushingly chaste Lavinia who is Aeneas's destined bride in the *Aeneid* at the very foundation of Rome's imperial history.[32] *Titus* also makes much tortured play with the idea of *pietas*, the characterizing virtue of Virgil's hero. This becomes not the emotional-cum-ethical sense of obligation to family and to the gods that it tends to denote in Virgil, but a kind of savage piety, a motive for child murder, revenge, and cannibalism.[33] Virgil as a result sounds like a distant, strangled voice in the play, and the *Aeneid* might be regarded as a work which represents an alternative kind of Roman empire to the one presented on the stage.

The later plays are less overt than *Titus*, but they too can invoke Virgil to suggest a counter-narrative to the main plot. The main action of *Antony and Cleopatra* (*c.*1606), in which Antony leaves Cleopatra, then returns, then leaves, then dies because he follows her, is constructed as a kind of reversal of the Dido and Aeneas story, in which the Roman hero (like the heroes of many Italian epic romances) simply cannot leave Cleopatra, the equivalent of the exotic queen Dido.[34] This counterpoint between the epic and the play is not forced on an audience, but is effected by providing little glimpses of Virgil from oblique angles. So when Antony is attempting to kill himself in the mistaken belief that Cleopatra is already dead, he declares:

> Eros!—I come, my queen.—Eros!—Stay for me.
> Where souls do couch on flowers, we'll hand in hand,
> And with our sprightly port make the ghosts gaze:
> Dido and her Aeneas shall want troops,
> And all the haunt be ours. Come, Eros, Eros! (4.15.50–4)

When Aeneas sees Dido in the underworld (*Aeneid*, 6.450–76), she turns her back on him and walks away to her husband Sychaeus. Antony's transformation of that moment is not easy to interpret. Is the alternative plot which he imagines, with Dido and Aeneas together forever in the Elysian fields, just wishful thinking on his part? Is it an explicit marker that *Antony and Cleopatra* rewrites the love plot in the *Aeneid* and reverses its emotional priorities? Or is it just one of Shakespeare's mistakes? It's probably best thought of as something more delicate than any of these things. Antony's reference to Dido and Aeneas invites an audience to think about the plot of the *Aeneid*, and to allow Virgilian epic to provide an undertow to the action onstage. That could be a deliberate effect, or it could just be an effect of a misfiring memory and an inspired pen. But it's indicative of a general tendency in the way Shakespeare touches on Virgil in his later plays. As we saw in Chapter 1, classical allusions within Shakespeare's plays often mean slightly different things to different characters. In the later plays that multiplicity of perspectives tends to migrate upwards and outwards to encompass the audience, who are presented with possible allusions to or transformations of classical texts, and are then given the task of working out how they might function and what their theatrical and moral valence might be. Little touches of Virgil can in this environment be used to make an audience ask questions about how the action before them is unfolding, and how what they are seeing might or might not relate to other stories with which they are familiar. Is Antony a wilful misreader of the *Aeneid*? Or does he just wishfully transform it? Those are questions which are raised, but which are not simply answered.

*The Tempest* (*c.*1610) is scattered with references to the *Aeneid*, the effects of which are extremely hard to pin down.[35] The initial shipwreck and the dispersal of the royal party have points in common with the first book of the *Aeneid*, in which Aeneas is separated from his companions and then meets his mother Venus in disguise. But the storm with which the play opens seems to have turned the *Aeneid* upside-down along with the world of the mariners. So when Ferdinand first sees Miranda he describes her as 'Most sure the goddess | On whom these airs attend' (1.2.424–5). 'Most sure the goddess' is a literal translation of 'o dea certe' ('oh goddess, surely that's what you are', *Aeneid* 1.328), which Aeneas says of and to his mother Venus, who comes to him in disguise. This does not imply a simple equation between Ferdinand and Aeneas, or if it does it's a topsy-turvy transformation in which Aeneas's supportive but disguised mother is turned into the potential lover of Ferdinand. The phrase 'Most sure the goddess' also does not mark a sudden recognition of a deity as it does in Virgil. Either it's a piece of flattery (modern editors mark it as an aside: there is no such marking in the Folio text, in which it could be a piece of courtly flirtation directed by the sophisticated Ferdinand to the innocent Miranda) or it's a forgivable mistake: Miranda, though lovely, is not literally a goddess. Virgil's Venus actually is one.

Many of the other allusions to the *Aeneid* in *The Tempest* raise similar possibilities for interpreting the action of the play, and most do so in very oblique ways. The dialogue between the loyal old Gonzalo and the flash aspiring courtiers Sebastian and Antonio about 'Widow Dido' is the most notorious example:

> Gonzalo (*to Adrian*): Methinks our garments are now as fresh as when we put them on first in Afric, at the marriage of the King's fair daughter Claribel to the King of Tunis.
>
> Sebastian: 'Twas a sweet marriage, and we prosper well in our return.
>
> Adrian: Tunis was never graced before with such a paragon to their queen.
>
> Gonzalo: Not since widow Dido's time.

ANTONIO (*to Sebastian*): Widow! A pox o' that! How came that 'widow' in? Widow Dido!

SEBASTIAN: What if he had said 'widower Aeneas' too? Good Lord, how you take it!

ADRIAN (*to Gonzalo*): 'Widow Dido' said you? You make me study of that: she was of Carthage, not of Tunis.

GONZALO: This Tunis, sir, was Carthage.

ADRIAN: Carthage?

GONZALO: I assure you, Carthage.

ANTONIO (*to Sebastian*): His word is more than the miraculous harp.

SEBASTIAN: He hath raised the wall, and houses too.

ANTONIO: What impossible matter will he make easy next?

SEBASTIAN: I think he will carry this island home in his pocket and give it his son for an apple.

ANTONIO: And, sowing the kernels of it in the sea, bring forth more islands.

GONZALO (*to Adrian*): Ay.

ANTONIO (*to Sebastian*): Why, in good time.

GONZALO (*to Alonso*): Sir, we were talking that our garments seem now as fresh as when we were at Tunis, at the marriage of your daughter, who is now queen.

ANTONIO: And the rarest that e'er came there.

SEBASTIAN: Bate, I beseech you, widow Dido.

ANTONIO: O, widow Dido? Ay, widow Dido. (2.1.73–106)

It's easy to see that this is very different kind of reference to the *Aeneid* from the highly rhetoricized and pathos-filled allusions to the matter of Troy in *Lucrece* or *Hamlet*. But that's where the easiness ends.[36] Gonzalo's parallel between the voyage home from a marriage and the wanderings of Aeneas is an attempt to console Duke Alonso for the loss of his son. Alonso is locked away in grief at the apparent loss of Ferdinand, and Gonzalo is trying to find a higher purpose to the journey and to the shipwreck, and so uses a comparison with Virgil's epic history to suggest that the whole story of the play could turn out to be a providential romance, and perhaps a piece of empire-building too. Sebastian and Antonio refuse to see it like that, and even Adrian wonders if the parallel between Tunis and Carthage is at all helpful. The comparison between the action of the play and that of the *Aeneid* works in different ways for different characters, some of whom do not think there is any parallel at all. Sebastian and Antonio have fun making 'Dido' (in which the 'i' is long) rhyme with 'widow', and (presumably) get the giggles over this mispronunciation of the name of Virgil's tragic heroine which is required to make her suit Gonzalo's low-register word 'widow'. There might even be a further layer of allusion here too, in which Virgil is embedded in a specific British and colonial context. In the section of Holinshed's *Chronicles* about Ireland there occurs one of the surprisingly infrequent references in sixteenth-century England to Dido as a 'widow'. This section of Holinshed also had Virgilian associations, since it was written by Richard Stanyhurst, who in 1582 had published a translation of the first four books of the *Aeneid* into highly eccentric English verse, which adopted the metrical system of classical Latin. Stanyhurst's account of the early settlement of Ireland includes a grandiose comparison between the nation-founding activities of (widow) Dido and an episode in which a widow called Rose builds walls around the city of Rosse:

In which consultation a famous Dido, a chaste widow, a politic dame, a bountiful gentlewoman, called Rose, who representing in sincerity of life the sweetness of that herb whose name she bare, unfolded the device, how any such future mischance should be prevented: and withal opened her coffers liberally to have it furthered... Her device was, that the town should incontinently be enclosed with walls, and therewithal promised to discharge the charges, so that they would not stick to find out labourers... Some were tasked to delve, others appointed with mattocks to dig, divers allotted to the un-heaping of rubbish, many bestowed to the carriage of stones, sundry occupied in tempering of mortar, the better sort busied in overseeing the workmen, each one according to his vocation employed, as though the civity of Carthage were afresh in building, as it is featly verified by the golden poet Virgil, and neatly Englished by master Doctor Phaer:

> The Moors with courage went to work, some under burdens
> groans:
> Some at the walls and tow'rs with hands were tumbling up
> the stones.[37]

The references to the raising of walls, combined with a long quotation (abbreviated here) from Phaer's translation of Virgil, may well indicate that this passage, which implicitly equates the early history

**Illustration 1.** A storm blows a very medieval-looking Aeneas towards the Strophades.

Codrington Library, All Souls College, Oxford, shelf mark a.7.2: *P. Virgilii Maronis Poetarum Principis Opera*, ed. Jodocus Badius et al. (Venice, 1533), fol. 69r. Reproduced by kind permission of the Warden and Fellows of All Souls College, Oxford.

of Ireland with the building of a new civilization at Carthage, played some part in the genesis of Shakespeare's play. But where Stanyhurst elevates an episode in early Irish history to an epic scale, Shakespeare makes a parallel with the story of the *Aeneid* become dialectical to an unsettling degree. *Is* there any viable comparison between the shipwreck in *The Tempest* and that in the *Aeneid*, or is it just a piece of banter to fill in time? Is there an imperial or colonial narrative going on in the background here? The *Aeneid* seems so diffracted by the variety of perspectives on the stage that it seems barely to have a direct connection with the play.

The relationship between the *Aeneid* and *The Tempest* is indirect, but that does not mean it is insignificant. Allusions to Virgil often add shadows (sometimes dark ones) and depths to the action onstage.

That is in part a consequence of the genre of the play. It is also a consequence of an even simpler fact. *The Tempest* is a play rather than a narrative poem. Taking inspiration from the early books of the *Aeneid* is natural enough, but turning the marvels witnessed by Aeneas into a theatrical performance was a major technical challenge. So in Book III of the *Aeneid* the Trojan wanderers come to land on the Strophades islands (see Illustration 1). There they find a feast, which is snatched from them and defiled by winged harpies (*Aeneid*, 3.219–57). As related by Aeneas, the story of the harpies' intrusion is a dire event (they are called 'dire birds' and they predict 'dira fames', dire hunger, *Aeneid*, 3.256). It also has a major significance within his larger narrative, since the harpies bring an accurate prophecy not just of the Trojans' arrival in Italy but of their future hunger and misery. Presenting this episode onstage would almost necessarily press at the boundaries of theatrical representation and illusion. A *stage* harpy requires feathers and wires and more than a little faith from your audience: a mangy theatrical set of wings might completely destroy the terror and the prophetic power of Virgil's violent and dangerous birds. That practical difficulty, of translating an epic poem to the stage, Shakespeare relished and used, and in turn it casts further shadows over allusions to the *Aeneid* in *The Tempest*. Shakespeare does not simply have harpies appear: he has Ariel *act* a harpy in order to rebuke the courtiers for the usurpation of Prospero's dukedom. As a result of this overt theatricality Virgil's harpy episode becomes in *The Tempest* much more morally ambiguous than its original. Ariel's harpy-show is an illusion put on in order to elicit fear and repentance, in which part of what Ariel says is not only not untrue but is known to be untrue by the audience. Ariel claims to be a 'minister of fate'. He is not. Ariel claims that Ferdinand is dead. He is not. The Virgilian episode also again becomes a way of differentiating between the different ways different characters have of viewing the world. The frozen amazement of the 'men of sin' (3.3.53) who hear Ariel's speech makes it impossible either to know how they react to the performance or even to assume that all of them hear Ariel utter the same words. It's not clear, for example, that Gonzalo has heard the voice of the harpy at all. He says 'why stand you | In this strange stare?' (3.3.93–4) to Alonso, as though he can't understand what the Duke has just witnessed. He is an onstage audience who seems to be looking at Alonso's reaction rather than listening himself to the voice of the supposed harpy, and who seems as a result to be occupying a reality which is slightly out of kilter with that of the other characters onstage. Shakespeare turns Virgil into an illusion, and then makes different characters see different aspects of that illusion depending on their characteristics and their moral nature. Some hear a voice of doom. Some hear a distant roar. And perhaps some hear nothing at all.

All of this means that the *Aeneid* is not exactly 'central' to *The Tempest*, nor that it is peripheral to it either. The *Aeneid* shimmers across the work rather than shaping it, repeatedly providing options and possibilities for a larger understanding of the story. These tend then, like the harpies' feast, to be snatched away. It is possible, like Gonzalo, to see yourself as a character in a providential epic narrative. It is also possible not to. It is possible to see Ariel the harpy as a piece of magical illusion and manipulation which is designed to produce powerful passion ('why stand you | In this strange stare?'). Or it is possible to see him as a minister of vengeance and retribution. Romance wanderings and desires are among the many possible kinds of plot registered within the story of Aeneas; conversely an imperial narrative and a tale of retribution are possibilities registered within *The Tempest*. Which of these stories you see depends partly on what you want to see, and partly on the angle from which you look at them.

Critics have often said that the oblique and diffracted manner of invoking Virgil in *The Tempest* has political implications. The play's treatment of Virgil, in which the imperial plot of the *Aeneid* seems to have been broken up and reassembled into a string of shadowy resemblances to the action onstage, has often been said to imply unease with or opposition to Jacobean absolutism.[38] The way that Prospero turns elements in the *Aeneid* which have divine origins into illusions or theatrical performances might also generate unease about the nature of Prospero's power, or about theatrical illusions, or about the *Aeneid*, or about colonialist readings of the *Aeneid*. It is very difficult to arbitrate between these possibilities because Shakespeare so carefully allows belief in Virgilian fictions to be simultaneously contingent (the plot of the play *can* be seen as a version of an imperial narrative, but it doesn't have to be seen that way) and morally desirable. And their moral desirability is often also slightly absurd.

Gonzalo may get a bit muddled in his geography by comparing Tunis to Carthage, and Alonso may not want to hear his consoling quasi-epic fictions, but Gonzalo's Virgilian fantasy is a well-meant effort by an old (even antiquated) man to console his master. Ariel's performance as harpy may be a show, but it is a show which powerfully influences its intended audience, and which may make them recognize that usurpation is not the best way in which to acquire a dukedom. There is no simple dismantling in this play of Jacobean analogies between an imperial future in the new world and the unfolding empire promised to Virgil's Aeneas. Nor is there a simple endorsement of those analogies either. Virgilian tales present possible fictions on the stage, stories in which you can either choose to believe or not, and by which you can either choose to be moved or not.

*Cymbeline* (which was probably also composed around 1610) has an even more oblique relationship to Virgil. It is Shakespeare's most complex Romano-British drama, in which shadows of Virgil—sometimes very distant shadows—play a small but significant part. The play is set in an imaginary Britain during the reign of Virgil's emperor Augustus. The British king Cymbeline refuses to pay the tribute demanded by Rome as a result of the conquest of his nation by Julius Caesar. These events are connected to Virgil's *Aeneid* partly by a thin thread of genealogy. Geoffrey of Monmouth had claimed in his twelfth-century *History of Britain* that the British kings derived their lineage from Brutus, who was a descendant of Aeneas. This provided a convenient justification for British historians and panegyrists to claim that Britain's empire was lineally descended from that of Rome, and that its kings ultimately derived from the hero of Virgil's *Aeneid.* The humanistic historian Polydore Vergil printed in 1534 a history of Britain which was sceptical about this suspiciously upmarket imperial lineage for Britain. Nonetheless, poets and historians continued to draw on the imaginative comfort provided by a belief in a westward movement of empire from Troy, to Rome, and thence to Britain.[39] William Camden's *Britannia* (1586), which was translated into English in 1610, mounted a new attack on Geoffrey's imperial genealogy of the British kings. It did so principally on the authority of Roman and Greek historians (Caesar, Tacitus, Diodorus Siculus). Britain as presented in Roman history and poetry was an island separated from the rest of the world, which was heroically conquered by Julius Caesar. Camden was diplomatic in the way he debunked native British history and historians. When discussing the supposed descent of Britain from the line of Aeneas, he declared: 'Let antiquity herein be pardoned, if by intermingling falsities and truths, human matters and divine together, it make the first beginnings of nations and cities more noble, sacred, and of greater majesty.'[40] He also celebrated the union of Britons and Romans: 'meet it is we should believe, that the Britons and Romans in so many ages, by a blessed and joyful mutual engrafting, as it were, have grown in one stock and nation'.[41] *Cymbeline* is a response to this historiographical moment, in which new-style, fashionable, and Roman-inspired historians were cutting the dynastic links between Britain and Aeneas, and yet were also happy to allow for 'intermingling falsities and truths', as well as the intermingling of Roman and British history and peoples.

In his selection of names for characters in *Cymbeline*, Shakespeare seems almost deliberately to have made his British world at once both closer to and further away from ancient Rome than any historian would have allowed. In particular he makes his characters seem both near to and far from the hero Aeneas. In Holinshed's *Chronicle*, Innogen is the wife of Brutus, who is described in turn as the great-grandson of Aeneas. In Shakespeare she is the daughter of King Cymbeline. Posthumus is in the chronicle sources the son of Aeneas (and hence the grandfather of Brutus), so belongs to an earlier generation, and yet Shakespeare uses that name for the husband of Innogen (and that form of the name is used in the chronicles: the Folio's 'Imogen' is almost certainly a typographical error).[42] The play's relationship with the *Aeneid* is similarly unsettling and hybridized. Innogen compares her husband Posthumus to 'false Aeneas' (3.4.58) after he has abandoned her. This draws on the tradition of the perfidious Aeneas, which derives more from Ovid's *Heroides* than from the *Aeneid* itself. The scene in which Innogen awakes in Wales next to the headless body of Cloten also provides a strange visual echo of Virgil's description of Priam's body lying headless on the shore ('iacet ingens litore truncus, | avolsumque umeris caput et sine nomine corpus', 'the huge trunk lies on the shore, the head torn from its shoulders and the corpse left with no name', *Aeneid* 2.557–8). The moment when Priam dies is a disaster for Troy, and comes at the climax of Aeneas's narrative of Troy's fall in Shakespeare's favourite

Book II of the *Aeneid*. There it is followed (like so many passages from Virgil which lived in Shakespeare's memory) by a wave of ever-so-slightly incongruous emotion in Aeneas: 'then first dreadful horror enfolded me' ('At me tum primum saeuus circumstetit horror'), and then the image of his own dear father ('cari genitoris imago', 2.559) comes into his mind. Innogen's vision of this headless substitute for Priam prompts a similar vast and sounding grief—in which, as in the allusion to the same moment in the history of Troy in *Hamlet*, Priam's wife Hecuba plays a part. Innogen laments:

> A headless man? The garments of Posthumus?
> I know the shape of 's leg; this is his hand,
> His foot Mercurial, his Martial thigh,
> The brawns of Hercules; but his Jovial face—
> Murder in heaven! How? 'Tis gone. Pisanio,
> All curses madded Hecuba gave the Greeks,
> And mine to boot, be darted on thee! (4.2.310–16)

Posthumus is in Innogen's imagination almost too Roman to be true. With his foot like that of the fleet-footed Mercury and his thigh resembling the martial god Mars, his death seems to bring down the entire classical pantheon. The audience of the play knows, however, that neither Posthumus nor Priam, let alone a battery of Roman deities, are here lying headless on the shore, but the brutally British Cloten. That frames Innogen's stagey grief as a highly emotional consequence of perceptual error. The allusion to Hecuba also points back to Shakespeare's own earlier explorations of Virgilian passions: we have already seen how the 'ancient' griefs of Priam's wife sat just slightly askew from the modern miseries of Lucrece and Hamlet. *Cymbeline* blurs many chronologies. It even seems here to glance back at the idiosyncratic classicism of Shakespeare's own earlier career.

Ben Jonson, as we have seen, tapped Virgilian veins of imperial prophecy in the public performances to mark James I's accession. In *Cymbeline* Shakespeare also draws on the prophetic and imperial elements of Virgil. But once again this Romano-British play takes those Virgilian elements and contaminates them with other sources. At the end of the play Posthumus has a prophetic dream vision. Posthumus's father and his mother (who are described in the stage direction as respectively 'attired like a warrior' and 'an ancient matron') appeal to Jupiter to help their son. These ancient Romans even sound 'antique', since they speak in the fourteen-syllable couplets favoured by early sixteenth-century translators of classical epic poetry. They urge Jupiter to 'Peep through thy marble mansion. Help, or we poor ghosts will cry | To th' shining synod of the rest against thy deity' (5.5.180–4, relineated). Shakespeare rarely used fourteeners, and it has been suggested that by doing so here he locates the ghosts stylistically in a 'different, more primitive universe' which harks back to the popular romances of the earlier Elizabethan stage.[43] This may indeed be part of the effect of the 'old'-style couplets spoken by the ghosts, although there remained a strong association between fourteeners and the translation of classical poetry even in the early seventeenth century. Philemon Holland's translation of Camden's *Britannia* regularly uses fourteeners to translate quotations from verse, as does Thomas North's translation of Plutarch's *Lives*.[44] The poetic form in which these ancient Romans speak, that is, matches their antique garb: it is itself 'ancient'.

The 'antique' style of Posthumus's parents is matched by the architectural setting in which the 'classical' prophecy occurs. Jupiter descends from his 'marble mansion', and when he disappears 'the marble pavement closes' (5.5.214). As we saw in the introduction, Jacobean court masques were performed in physical settings that drew richly on fashionable classical architectural styles. Here Shakespeare seems to be imagining a grand marble edifice around his god, as though he is straining to be 'classical' in his architecture as well as 'antique' in his style. When Jupiter arrives to respond to Posthumus's parents he puts on a theatrical display even grander and more amazing than Ariel's performance as a harpy: he 'descends in thunder and lightning, sitting upon an eagle'. His speech, however, contrasts with that of the ancient Roman parents of Posthumus by using trim and authoritative decasyllabic quatrains:

> No more, you petty spirits of region low,
> Offend our hearing. Hush! How dare you ghosts
> Accuse the thunderer, whose bolt, you know,
> Sky-planted, batters all rebelling coasts?
> Poor shadows of Elysium, hence, and rest
> Upon your never-withering banks of flowers.
> Be not with mortal accidents oppressed;
> No care of yours it is; you know 'tis ours.

Whom best I love, I cross, to make my gift,
  The more delayed, delighted. Be content.
Your low-laid son our godhead will uplift. (*Cymbeline*,
    5.5.187–97)

This speech is not rich in words of Latin origin, but it is nonetheless aspiring to make Jupiter speak a kind of English that sounds both more elevated and more like classical Latin than the 'ancient' speech of the ghosts. He favours compound adjectives ('sky-planted', 'never-withering', 'low-laid'), and replicates the compression of past participles in Latin ('The more delayed, delighted'). Shakespeare is here attempting to create in English an idiom which would sound suitable for a classical deity: austere, peremptory, rich in epithets, and disciplined in form. In the scene as a whole he uses almost every resource he had—stage effects, scenic description, stylistic variation—to indicate that this is a great ancient Roman scene.

It is tempting as a result to take Posthumus's dream vision as simply Roman. The entire scene could be seen as Shakespeare's greatest attempt to stage the visions that Aeneas receives from his father Anchises in the underworld in Book VI of the *Aeneid*, in which the hero is given a vision of the dynasty of rulers which will emerge to rule Rome. But Shakespeare's 'Roman' scene is not quite that simple. Like Innogen's lament over the body of Cloten, which multiplies classical gods in order to amplify her grief, Posthumus's Roman dream vision seems to use just too many different ways of marking itself as 'classical' and 'ancient' actually to succeed in doing so. And the content of the prophecy with which Jupiter leaves Posthumus also marks the scene as not being in any simple sense a Virgilian one. Jupiter does not in fact give Posthumus a vision of an imperial future which is analogous to the prophecies received by Aeneas in the underworld. Instead he leaves him with a prophecy in English:

> Whenas a lion's whelp shall, to himself unknown, without seeking find, and be embraced by a piece of tender air; and when from a stately cedar shall be lopped branches which, being dead many years, shall after revive, be jointed to the old stock, and freshly grow; then shall Posthumus end his miseries, Britain be fortunate and flourish in peace and plenty. (5.5.232–8)

The riddling style here is similar to the British prophecies of Merlin, which were solemnly recorded by Geoffrey of Monmouth and printed in Holinshed. These related the future events of the realm of Albion in dark and ambiguous language. Jove's prophecy also has some resemblances to the oracles and dream visions which run through Greek prose romances and their Elizabethan offshoots, from Sidney's *Arcadia* to Robert Greene's *Pandosto*.[45] Jupiter strikingly fails to offer Posthumus empire without end, *imperium sine fine*, as Jupiter does in *Aeneid* 1.279. His prophecy is not simply Roman. It is rather distinctively Romano-British: it fuses together the prophetic style of the native British wizard Merlin with imperial overtones from the *Aeneid*. It also depends on a series of interlinguistic puns between English and Latin. A Roman soothsayer in Act 5 (5.6.447–53) is needed to decode 'tender heir' into a pun on the Latin word 'mulier' (woman or wife), which was popularly derived from 'mollis aer' or 'soft air'. The 'lion's whelp' is of course Posthumus Leonatus, lion-born. The play leaves us with a polyglot prophecy that depends on Romano-British cooperation to reveal its significance. It is a practical representation of what Camden described as a 'blessed and joyful mutual engrafting' of Romans and Britons. And because of that the prophecy prepares for the end of the play, in which Cymbeline defeats the Roman forces and yet voluntarily decides to pay tribute to the emperor anyway: Rome and Britain are represented in this play as nations and civilizations which need to collaborate.

Nonetheless, *Cymbeline* pointedly does not conclude with a vision of a British imperial dynasty which extends in a single line from Aeneas, through Posthumus, to the crack of doom. Indeed, with the rediscovery in Wales of the lost sons of Cymbeline (the 'lopped branches' of the prophecy), Innogen ceases to be the most likely heir to the crown, and Posthumus is able to look forward to a future not as a progenitor of future kings, like a new Aeneas or a new Brutus, but as a happily married minor royal. The 'Virgilian' prophecy turns the character most closely associated in the play with Aeneas into a side shoot from the line of British kings.

What are we to make of this? The Virgilian elements in *Cymbeline* have, like those in *The Tempest*, given rise to a number of political interpretations. Patricia Parker, who brought them to critical attention, saw the play more or less as an endorsement of James I's rule. She argued that *Cymbeline* overlays British, modern Italian, and Roman imperial ideals in a deliberately anachronistic manner so as to suggest a *translatio imperii*, the movement of Roman political and cultural authority northwards and westwards towards Britain. Heather James presents a more oppositional reading of the play and the role of Virgilian allusions within it, seeing in *Cymbeline* a programmatic scepticism about Jacobean imperial ambitions: 'Through its unstable "mingle-mangle" of sources and historical periods, *Cymbeline* threatens to dissolve rather than ratify the emergent British nation along with its Jacobean political iconography.'[46] There is a further alternative. Shakespeare was in this play trying to create a Romano-British romance, in which he worked together his recent reading in Camden's *Britannia* with his much longer-standing knowledge of Holinshed's *Chronicles*, as well as with his even longer-standing reading of Virgil. This play explores what it might mean for Britain and British writing to derive from a wide range of classical sources, and yet also to be itself. Britain in this play owes tribute to Rome both literally and literarily, but is still an autonomous nation. In presenting Britain in this way Shakespeare may also have been seeking, very delicately, to distance himself from the full-on Romanizing style of Ben Jonson—and it was particularly neat that in doing so he was taking a few cues from Jonson's own former schoolmaster William Camden. He resisted the potentially rather flat-footed use of Virgil's *Aeneid* as a source of simple panegyrics for James I, and instead offered his own style of 'antiquity': gods who speak in a Latinizing idiom, 'ancient' Romans who use slightly old-fashioned poetic forms, fusions of ancient British and ancient Roman sources. This was a political act in its effects, since Shakespeare's play clearly did not slavishly adopt the public association between Virgilian *imperium* and Jacobean rule which had been established early in James's reign. But the motives behind it may have been as much personal and professional as political. Shakespeare wanted still to speak in his own distinctive, slightly archaic, classical voice.

*Cymbeline* also illustrates the three most important truths about Shakespeare's ways of alluding to classical texts. The first is that Shakespeare tended to think about what texts and utterances might mean to particular people and how they might be interpreted in the light of their preoccupations. That made his classicism deeply, and increasingly, perspectival—and perhaps also intrinsically prone to be associated with perspectives that look 'devolved' in relation to any single or central political ideal. Innogen's glimpse of Cloten-as-Priam is a momentary thing, and is just one perspective among many. So are the equally fleeting presentations of Posthumus as both a faithless Aeneas and an imperial hero. A single classical text will never provide a road map for the interpretation of a whole play. The second major feature of Shakespeare's way of alluding to classical texts is that he tended to hybridize sources and styles. This was probably not a conscious process with clear objectives. It was just what he did. He had no particular reason to keep the outlines of a Virgilian dynasty clear, or to keep it separate from a dash of Geoffrey of Monmouth or a little bit of Greek-style oracular prophecy: the 'joyful mutual engrafting' of Roman and British elements was what he liked to do. The third crucial fact about Shakespeare's ways of alluding to classical texts is that they are always inflected by the genre in which he was working. In a romance, a Virgilian prospect of empire without end is likely to be just one possibility among others, rather than a single and controlling destiny.

Combine all these tendencies together and we are in a position to see the distinctive shape which Virgil came to assume within Shakespeare's later plays. A perspective of Virgilian empire-building is available to some characters some of the time, but it is never simply presented as the main point of the play. Gonzalo sees his shipwreck as an episode in a larger and ideally providential dynastic narrative. Posthumus hears in the voices of the ancient gods a prophecy that promises 'then shall Posthumus end his miseries, Britain be fortunate and flourish in peace and plenty' (*Cymbeline*, 5.5.237–8). But those 'Virgilian' ways of perceiving the action of the play are not firm indicators of political truths, nor are they even entirely sound guides to the way in which the plot will unfold.

The larger story told in this chapter about Shakespeare's changing relationship to Virgil is representative of wider changes in his relationship to classical antiquity more generally in the course of his career. References to the *Aeneid* and to the Troy story in his works up to about 1600 tend to be held up for special attention, almost as though in quotation marks, as old, or stylistically separate from the works in which they appear. They also often bring with them intense emotions, which might sit in a slightly uneasy relationship to their literal narrative pretext. Virgilian allusions in Shakespeare's later romances function in rather different, but not absolutely different, ways. Virgil continues to be associated with moments of unfathomable emotion (as when Gonzalo says to Alonso 'why stand you | In this strange stare?', or when Innogen wails at the apparent death of Posthumus). But the ways of making and marking allusions, as well as the function of those allusions, have changed. These changes were not simply a matter of Shakespeare moving on from overt allusion to more insinuating forms of imitation, or of Shakespeare growing up as a dramatist. Allusions to the *Aeneid* in the later plays often provide reference points that could be either misleading or consoling both for characters within the drama and for the audience of the plays. A Virgilian imperial narrative might be one possible structure which could at times be seen behind the action of the play, but which at other times could just vanish. These changes in his treatment of Virgil came about for a variety of reasons: rival playwrights, historical events, changing tastes in historiography, as well as shifts in genre and theatrical fashion all play their part. But the next chapter will suggest that there was a broadly similar shape to the story of Shakespeare's treatment of Ovid.

# 3

# *Ovid*

Writers don't become influential by accident. They have to mean something to the people who read them, and usually that results from affinities which they and their writings appear to have with their readers or with their interests. Sometimes these affinities are real, sometimes imagined, and often it's hard to tell the difference between the two. Titus Ovidius Naso (43 BC–17/18 AD) was certainly the Latin poet who had the greatest influence on Shakespeare. If one wanted to construct a league table of the classical poets who meant most to all English writers in the sixteenth century, then his name would come at the top. Shakespeare would without doubt have read and learned by heart relatively large sections of Ovid at school. He wrote in a way that was ideally suited to the priorities of early-modern teaching and learning. Masters could isolate, underline, and analyse the rhetorical tropes and figures in every line of Ovid's writing, and instruct their pupils to emulate them. Meanwhile the eroticism and narrative energy of all of Ovid's writing might have put a slight spring into the step of even the most snail-like of whining schoolboys 'with his satchel | And shining morning face' (*As You Like It*, 2.7.145–6) as he crept unwillingly to school.

Ovid was by far the sexiest poet from antiquity in the late sixteenth century. This was partly because, more than any other Roman author, he seemed like a contemporary. His *Elegies*, in which lovers tempestuously yearn for their mistresses, hide from their rivals, or joke over their own eagerness, were perfectly adapted to suit the poetic and erotic sensibilities of young urban poets writing after, and under the influence of, Petrarch's love poems. Ovid's ingenious lover-persona—

slightly ironized but erotically successful, acutely self-conscious of literary effect while also being capable of bribing a mistress's maid or hiding to avoid a rival—was a natural vehicle for poetic innovation and imitation among poets in the London of the 1590s. Christopher Marlowe, who belongs right up there with Ovid on the league table of Shakespeare's biggest influences, translated all of Ovid's *Elegies* with urgent literalism at some point probably early in his career, although the translations did not appear in print until 1599. In the late 1590s and the very early seventeenth-century John Donne adapted the bedroom milieu and the impassioned self-ironizing voice of Ovid for several of his early elegies and for a number of his 'Songs and Sonnets' too. Marlowe's *Hero and Leander*, as well as narrative poems by Thomas Lodge, by Shakespeare himself, and by Francis Beaumont, all sought to emulate the quick-moving, catch-me-before-I-wink-at-you-and-vanish vividness of individual tales from Ovid's *Metamorphoses*.

Ovid also stood out among classical authors in the sixteenth century because enough was known about his life to make him seem like a person. An ancient biography of Virgil by Aelius Donatus was regularly printed in editions of Virgil's works. For Ovid, however, Renaissance readers could respond to a biographical and literary persona created by the poet himself. In *Tristia* 4.10, where he addresses posterity as though in an epitaph ('So that you know who I was, the playful poet of tender loves, receive what you're reading, oh posterity'), Ovid relates most of the known facts of his life.[1] He describes how he was banished from Rome to Tomi on the Black Sea (modern Costanta) in 8 AD, for, as he later puts it, 'carmen et error'—a poem and a mistake (*Tristia*, 2.1.207). The 'poem' that caused his banishment was his libertine *Ars Amatoria* ('The Art of Love'). It was generally believed in the sixteenth century that the 'error' was an affair with the Emperor Augustus's daughter Julia. This belief resulted from confusing the emperor's daughter with his grand-daughter of the same name, who was indeed exiled at roughly the same time as Ovid. This became part of the mythology of the poet's life, which in turn became a subject for dramatic representations. In Jonson's *Poetaster* (1601) the young Ovid is represented as a bright youth about town who makes the mistake of defying his father's ambition that he should become a lawyer. He appears in a play along with Augustus's daughter Julia which louchely represents the gods. This leads to his exile. In George Chapman's *Ovid's Banquet of Sense* (1595) Ovid is represented as a philosophical sensualist, spying on Julia as she bathes whilst philosophizing about the feast she offers to his senses. Ovid in exile became a stock example of an ultra-civilized person who was stuck among barbarians. This added to his appeal among younger poets in the 1590s, who, in the way of younger poets, felt their degree of culture warranted rather more rewards than the barbarians around them seemed to want to offer them. Shakespeare's one direct allusion to Ovid's exile is in *As You Like It*, when Touchstone, who is the play's fool, uses Ovid's exile to describe his own separation in the forest from the world of courtly cultivation:

> TOUCHSTONE: I am here with thee and thy goats as the most capricious poet honest Ovid was among the Goths.
> JACQUES: O knowledge ill-inhabited; worse than Jove in a thatched house. (3.3.5–8)

This is a highly *theatrical* reference to Ovid's exile. It illustrates how aware Shakespeare was that Ovid could appeal to different types of reader in differing ways. Touchstone has by his lights been learned: 'capricious' derives from the Latin for goat, *caper*, and so produces a pun on 'goats' and 'Goths' (which could be pronounced with a hard final consonant, so sounded like 'Goats'). Jacques, who is a lord, deliberately outflanks Touchstone by alluding not just to received wisdom about Ovid's life, but to an episode in one of Ovid's poems: in Book VIII of the *Metamorphoses* Jove visits the mortal couple Baucis and Philemon in their thatched house. Ovid was, far more than Virgil or Horace, both a poet and a life story in the sixteenth century. Here even the less educated character Touchstone can refer to Ovid's life, while the melancholy learned Jacques can allude to the poems. Shakespeare can do both.

Ovid's exile poetry played a significant part in his reputation in the sixteenth century, although the influence of this aspect of his work on Shakespeare is usually oblique.[2] In the *Tristia* Ovid longed for his past life in Rome and complained that he was surrounded by barbarians. To make the point he revisited his own earlier epistolary and erotic poetry, and transformed its sexual longing into a desire for spatial and temporal return to his homeland.[3] That longing to return to Rome could have a particular resonance for Ovid's Renaissance readers, since his literal, geographical exile could be transposed into the temporal and metaphorical 'exile' of early-modern writers from the sources of Roman learning and inspiration in the classical world. If Ovid was geographically distant from Rome at the end of his life, his Renaissance imitators were temporally removed from this great cultural centre from the very beginning, with even less hope of return. This aspect of Ovid's influence chiefly came to England filtered through sixteenth-century French poetry. The sonnet collections called the *Les Regrets* and the *Antiquitez de Rome* (1558) by Joachim du Bellay (1522–60) draw prominently on Ovid's exile poetry to explore the ruination of contemporary Rome, in which du Bellay spent a period as secretary to his kinsman Cardinal Jean du Bellay.[4] Du Bellay's sonnets became popular in England partly because they made the exiled Ovid sound like a Protestant Englishman deploring the decline of Rome into Roman Catholic decadence. The young Edmund Spenser translated eleven sonnets from the *Antiquitez*. This was a sign that Ovid could speak to a generation for whom Rome was in literal ruins and was alienated from its imperial past and virtue as a result of its Catholicism. Traces of this preoccupation with exile and ruin (Ovid trickled through Renaissance France and then through Spenser) run through Shakespeare's *Sonnets*.[5] Their 'bare ruined choirs' and their background of decaying pomp ('Ruin hath taught me thus to ruminate', 64.11) register faint traces of the poetry of Roman ruination and exile which was one element in the early-modern reception of Ovid. That was one example of just how rich a resource this poet might be, and how 'modern' he might sound.

Indeed, if Ovid had not existed then Renaissance Europe would have had to invent him. His *Heroides* seem even better suited than the exile poetry to be read by an age that saw the communication between the present and the classical past as only sporadically a two-way process. The *Heroides* are dramatized epistles from lovelorn and (frequently) abandoned heroines to the men who have left them behind. Ovid was therefore both a love poet and post-love poet, who could represent the hot frustration of a male lover in the elegies and the subsequent misery suffered by the object of his desire. The *Heroides*, like the exile poetry, are also by their nature well suited to echo in the minds of later readers, since they repeatedly dramatize the distance between their fictional authors and their imagined addressees: as Phyllis complains to her lover Demophoon, 'I complain that you are absent' ('abesse queror', 2.2). Ovid's heroines seem to speak through time as well as through space to their generally unreceptive male addressees. The *Heroides* can often seem as a result like letters to the future, dramatizing the anxieties intrinsic to writing in time: they raise questions about where, how, and when they might be received, and even how they might go astray.[6] The *Heroides* are again a significant but indirect influence on Shakespeare: they are at the root of the tradition of female complaint to which both *Lucrece* and *A Lover's Complaint* contribute, but neither poem explicitly alludes to them. In the plays they serve more down-to-earth purposes: as we saw (above, pp. 32–5), Lucentio and Bianca struggle through the *Heroides* in their Latin lesson, which gets stuck a mere thirty lines into the first epistle. They talk closely while the lovers of whom they read are separated by space and (from their readers) by time.

Ovid wrote works from which all kinds of unexpected lessons could be drawn—even practical ones for lovers. The *Ars Amatoria* tells more or less everything both women and men need to know about how to behave: how to pick up a girl at the theatre (1.89–134), how to win her with eloquence and classical learning (2.121–42), and the value of simultaneous orgasm (2.683–92, 2.727–8). This poem was often printed in editions along with the *Heroides* and Ovid's other elegiac verse, so it was one of the most readily obtainable pieces of erotica in the sixteenth century. In 1582 the Privy Council ordered that Christopher Ocland's neo-Latin poem *Anglorum proelia* (The Battles of the English) should be taught in schools rather than 'such lascivious poets as are commonly read and taught in the said grammar schools' and in place of 'some of the heathen poets now read among them, as *Ovid de Arte Amandi*, *De Tristibus*, or such like'.[7] That injunction is vague ('or such like') and probably expresses a general concern for the morals of the young and a dim sense that Ovid was a naughty unchristian poet rather than marking a clampdown on a mass outbreak of pornographic Ovidianism in the schoolroom. However, it was not impossible that at least some schoolmasters were venturing into the more risqué parts of the Ovidian canon, or were teaching Ovid from editions which included the more sexually explicit texts. Lucentio proceeds from his Latin lesson in the *Heroides* to claim that he is reading *The Art to Love* (*The Taming of the Shrew*, 4.2.8). This is not just a hint to his mistress that he hopes to proceed in his affair: it suggests he is progressing through an actual volume of Ovid, since the *Ars Amatoria* was often found in the same volume as the *Heroides*. Indeed, the printer and publisher of Shakespeare's *Venus and Adonis* and *Lucrece*, Richard Field and John Harrison, produced in 1594 an edition of Ovid which started with the *Heroides* and the *Amores* and went on to include an unexpurgated text of what was then called the *De Arte Amandi*. Ovid's simultaneous orgasms appear on folio 155r of this edition: the original owner of the copy now in the Huntington Library has marked the relevant lines (in ink, I hasten to add) for future reference.

A potential reader with hot tastes and reasonable Latin could therefore pick up Shakespeare's two narrative poems along with a copy of Ovid's naughtiest work at the same bookstall, at the sign of the white greyhound in St Paul's Churchyard. If they did so they might think that the muscly Venus in *Venus and Adonis* (1593) sounded very like Ovid the *praeceptor amoris*, the teacher of love (2.497), as she urges her lover to get on with it.[8] Venus says to the reluctant Adonis: 'Make use of time; let not advantage slip. | Beauty within itself should not be wasted. |Fair flowers that are not gathered in their prime | Rot, and consume themselves in little time' (129–32). Ovid's worldly lover declares to those whom he is instructing in the arts of love: 'Violets do not bloom for ever, nor lilies open-mouthed; when the rose is perished, the hard thorn is left behind. And to you, lovely boy, will soon come white hairs and wrinkles that will plough furrows in your body' ('Nec violae semper nec hiantia lilia florent, | Et riget amissa spina relicta rosa. | Et tibi iam venient cani, formose, capilli, | Iam venient rugae, quae tibi corpus arent', 2.115–18). Shakespeare's *Sonnets* also show traces of the raunchy *Ars Amatoria*. I have translated the Latin 'formose' rather freely as 'lovely boy' in order to make the point. This phrase is used of the addressee of Shakespeare's sonnets in what has been traditionally regarded as the final poem addressed to him (126.1). The voice of Ovid in the *Ars Amatoria*, a seasoned male lover who urges a younger male to fight off the furrows of age by having sex, is certainly one of the shaping influences on Shakespeare's poems to the young man, as well as on his bossily erotic Venus.

It was, however, Ovid's vast mythological poem the *Metamorphoses* which mattered most to authors in the sixteenth century, and to Shakespeare in particular. The *Metamorphoses* deals with myths, passions, changes of shape, divine lust, the origins of the world. Its imaginary realm covers the span from the very beginning of time to the geographical and chronological points at which the sway of the Roman empire ends. It incorporates many apparently didactic and philosophical elements, but those elements are always qualified by Ovid's continual—and highly theatrical—awareness that the force of words is changed by the nature of the speaker and by an audience's attitudes to that speaker. The final book includes a discourse of the philosopher Pythagoras, who seems almost to be articulating the philosophy of the whole poem when he explains about the doctrine of metempsychosis (the transmigration of souls) and the permanent flux of the universe. But Pythagoras is also something of a wild-eyed vegetarian crank, whose philosophy can scarcely be taken straight—and indeed references to Pythagoras and metempsychosis in Shakespeare are almost always jokes.[9] The last part of the poem also offers a narrative about the age of heroism, which is a more or less ironical commentary on the more orthodox versions of the doings of ancient heroes in Homer and Virgil. Ovid's sidelong glances at the doings of Homer's and Virgil's heroes probably had a distant influence on the unorthodox presentations of those figures in *Troilus and Cressida.* Indeed, throughout Shakespeare's career, references to characters in Virgil are often shadowed by allusions to the often less than simply heroical versions of them in Ovid: so Ovid's version in the *Heroides* of the departure of Aeneas from Dido, which dominates Virgil's *Aeneid* IV, presents Aeneas as a betrayer and Dido as a heroine. When Lorenzo in *The Merchant of Venice* says 'In such a night | Stood Dido with a willow in her hand' (5.1.9–10), he is probably thinking not of Virgil's Dido but of Ovid's heroine, as well as of Ovid's Ariadne in *Heroides* 10.41. Ovid's suggestion that all histories might have another alternative version of that history running alongside them goes right through the *Metamorphoses* until its conclusion. The poem ends with a prophecy of its own immortality which seems simultaneously to be a prophecy that Rome itself is a transient thing, which may die while the poetic corpus—which means both the literal body and a 'corpus' of verse—of Ovid will live:[10]

> Iamque opus exegi, quod nec Iovis ira nec ignis
> nec poterit ferrum nec edax abolere vetustas.
> cum volet, illa dies, quae nil nisi corporis huius
> ius habet, incerti spatium mihi finiat aevi:
> parte tamen meliore mei super alta perennis
> astra ferar, nomenque erit indelebile nostrum,
> quaque patet domitis Romana potentia terris,
> ore legar populi, perque omnia saecula fama,
> siquid habent veri vatum praesagia, vivam. (15.871–9)

> Now have I brought a work to end which neither Jove's fierce wrath
> Nor sword, nor fire, nor fretting age with all the force it hath
> Are able to abolish quite. Let come that fatal hour
> Which, saving of this brittle flesh, hath over me no power
> And at his pleasure make an end of mine uncertain time.
> Yet shall the better part of me assurèd be to climb
> Aloft above the starry sky; and all the world shall never
> Be able for to quench my name. For look how far so ever
> The Roman empire by the right of conquest shall extend,
> So far shall all folk read this work. And time without all end
> (If poets as by prophecy about the truth may aim)
> My life shall everlastingly be lengthened still by fame.[11]

These lines were written while Rome ruled much of the known world. To read them *after* the fall of the Roman empire, in Britain, a nation once included in its very northern edge, would be to experience the force of their prophecy in a very different way from Ovid's contemporaries. And the passage itself seems to allow for the possibility that it could be read at a temporal and geographical remove from ancient Rome. Even if the ancient world has ended, Ovid suggests, the poem, and with it the poetic *corpus* of the poet, lives on. That sense of the physical permanence of writing and the fragility of the bodies and the civilizations which give rise to it is a recurrent element in Shakespeare's *Sonnets*, which frequently return to images and thoughts from the more philosophical sections of the *Metamorphoses*:

> Not marble nor the gilded monuments
> Of princes shall outlive this powerful rhyme,
> But you shall shine more bright in these contents

Than unswept stone besmeared with sluttish time.
When wasteful war shall statues overturn,
And broils root out the work of masonry,
Nor Mars his sword nor war's quick fire shall burn
The living record of your memory.
'Gainst death and all oblivious enmity
Shall you pace forth; your praise shall still find room
Even in the eyes of all posterity
That wear this world out to the ending doom.
  So, till the judgement that yourself arise,
  You live in this, and dwell in lovers' eyes. (55)

The sonnets' blend of interests—the frailty of life, the possibilities of rebirth, the hope for poetic immortality—as well as the way in which those themes are threaded through with a dense weave of irony and uncertainty—are all profoundly Ovidian. There is even perhaps a buried pun on Ovid's reference to the sway of Rome in the line 'your praise shall still find room' from Sonnet 55, since in Shakespeare's English the word 'Rome' was pronounced to rhyme with 'room'. The sonnet suggests that the young man shall still find a Rome, a society which can praise him and give him immortality, even after the ruin of the world. It was from the supposedly playful Ovid that Shakespeare derived some of his most philosophically serious writing.

The *Metamorphoses* is a highly self-conscious poem. Ovid's rhetorical skill has often been noted and deplored by his readers. The Roman rhetorician Quintilian (35–100 AD) declared that the poet was 'too much in love with his own wit' (10.1.88) and later readers have often echoed his view. But the *Metamorphoses* is also (and was read in the sixteenth century as) a compilation of myths and stories, many of which are violent, bloody, and potentially tragic. The poem seems as a result a jarring combination of 'ancient' mythological matter with a sharp and stylish rhetorical surface. This makes the experience of reading it unsteadying: its rhetorical sophistication seems often deliberately to pull in a different direction from the emotional weighting of the narrative. Some of the most vivid examples of this aspect of the poem are found in Book X, which was the epicentre of the poem so far as Shakespeare was concerned. That book encapsulates the two features of Ovid that captivated the early Shakespeare: his ability to write tragedies in a style that is unsettlingly over-polished, and his ability to mine seductively into the sexuality of his readers. The whole of Book X is narrated by Orpheus, who, as both Ovid and his Renaissance readers knew, was by reputation one of the first and the greatest poets, who almost managed to bring Eurydice back from the underworld by his art.[12] Ovid presents Orpheus in a deliberately unorthodox way, as a poet who gives up on girls after he has finally lost Eurydice, and who takes up the love of boys instead. The series of stories related by Orpheus begins with 'I would sing of boys beloved by gods, and maidens inflamed by unnatural love' (10.152–3). His stories weave the homoeroticism of the narrator and the heteroeroticism of the stories themselves into an intricate dance of sexual confusion. Among the tales he relates is the story of Pygmalion, who is presented as an artist who shares a loathing of women with his narrator Orpheus. Pygmalion makes a statue of an ideal woman with whom he falls in love, becoming like Ovid himself 'too much in love with his own wit'. Ovid's own artistry speaks through the description of the statue, and through the artistry of both Pygmalion and Orpheus:

> virginis est verae facies, quam vivere credas,
> et, si non obstet reverentia, velle moveri:
> ars adeo latet arte sua. miratur et haurit
> pectore Pygmalion simulati corporis ignes.
> saepe manus operi temptantes admovet, an sit
> corpus an illud ebur, nec adhuc ebur esse fatetur.
> oscula dat reddique putat loquiturque tenetque
> et credit tactis digitos insidere membris
> et metuit, pressos veniat ne livor in artus. (10.250–8)

> The look of it was right a maiden's look,
> And such a one as that ye would believe had life and that
> Would movèd be, if womanhood and reverence letted [prevented] not:
> So artificial was the work. He wond'reth at his art
> And of his counterfeited corse [body] conceiveth love in heart.
> He often touched it, feeling if the work that he had made
> Were very flesh or ivory still. Yet could he not persuade
> Himself to think it ivory. For he oftentimes it kissed
> And thought it kissèd him again. He held it by the fist,
> And talkèd to it. He believed his fingers made a dint

> Upon her flesh, and fearèd lest some black or bruisèd print
> Should come by touching overhard. (p. 303)

This tale offers at least two different and potentially incompatible things. It presents a story that can be remembered independently of the particular way in which it is presented. Man makes statue; loves it; believes it lives. It lives. This myth potentially has a life which is independent of the way in which Ovid (and Orpheus) narrate it: it could be regarded as a myth about the power of art to create, or (as in George Bernard Shaw's *Pygmalion*) an allegory of male efforts to transform the object of their desire into what they want it to be rather than what it actually is. It could also be treated as a more or less adaptable myth about the animating power of passion, or of creative energy, or as a study of how observers help to construct a work of art. But Orpheus (and over his shoulder Ovid too) elicits, solicits even, the desires of his readers in his particular way of relating the story: *you* would believe it lived, he says—and then, with a flutter of indirect speech which leaves it uncertain whose thoughts are whose—you would believe that it wanted to move, or to be moved, if it weren't for *reverentia*—that is, its own chastity, or perhaps the reader's own reverence for a work of art, or Pygmalion's fear of turning a material object into an object of lust.[13] The myth is over-layered with a flickering surface of erotic confusion.

Ovid's retelling of this myth is characteristically radical. He was probably the first person to have made Pygmalion himself into the artist who makes the statue. He also makes this story of an artificer in love with his own artistry live on through much of the rest of Book X. The helpful goddess Venus brings Pygmalion's stony girl to life. The veins pulse under his fingers, and the artist marries his statue. From the union of this woman-fearing artist and his own artefact there is born a child called Cinyras, who in turn has a daughter called Myrrha. She falls in love with her father and tricks him into an incestuous union, and is turned, weeping, into a myrrh tree before her father can have his revenge. From this incestuous desire felt by the granddaughter of a statue for the son of the same statue springs the lovely boy Adonis, who to be born bursts painfully through his mother's bark after her metamorphosis. And at this stage Orpheus, Ovid's pederastic narrator of Book X, exacts his revenge on Venus—

the goddess of heterosexual passion. He relates how she falls in love with the self-regarding Adonis, whose only interest is in hunting. To keep Adonis with her, Venus herself turns narrator (so by this stage of the book we have three narrators: Ovid, Orpheus, and Venus) and tells Adonis the story of Atalanta. Atalanta is yet another of Orpheus's phutophobes, or sex-haters. She is warned that if she marries it will be the death of her. So she insists her suitors run against her in a race, at which she is unbeatable. When Venus describes this virago Atalanta being looked at by her lover Hippomanes, Ovid's art of queering the vision reaches a climax:

> ut faciem et posito corpus velamine vidit,
> quale meum, vel quale tuum, si femina fias,
> obstipuit tollensque manus 'ignoscite', dixit
> 'quos modo culpavi!' (10.578–81)

> But when
> He saw her face and body bare (for why the lady then
> Did strip her to the naked skin) the which was like to mine,
> Or rather, if that thou wert made a woman, like to thine,
> He was amazed. And holding up his hands to heaven, he saith,
> 'Forgive me, you with whom I found such fault even now.' (p. 314)

The layer of different erotic perspectives here is dazzling and deliberately bewildering. The two literal narrators, plus their master Ovid, are all working overtime. The homosexual Orpheus describes the heterosexual Venus describing a boyish girl in a way that is designed to appeal to the reluctant Adonis. Venus creates an erotic hermaphrodite, which is at once like Venus herself ('Imagine me naked,' she says) and like the youthful Adonis, if he were to become a woman ('I'm imagining you naked,' she implies). The second-person mode of address, in which the goddess of love speaks directly to Adonis ('fias' means 'if you were to become', almost as if she's threatening to metamorphose his sex) almost invites the reader (as Francis Beaumont put it in the dedication to his erotic narrative on the story of Salmacis and Hermaphroditus) to 'turn half-maid with reading it'.[14]

That is the part of the *Metamorphoses* from which Shakespeare learnt most. His *Venus and Adonis* comes directly from the illusionistic, sexually polymorphous series of tales told by Orpheus—and right at the end of his career, in the conclusion to *The Winter's Tale*, he returns, as we shall see, to the story of Pygmalion. *Venus and Adonis* was printed in 1593, by the same Richard Field who was a year later to print Ovid's *Ars Amatoria*. Field was a high-status literary printer, and he was the closest thing to an Ovidian printer in early modern London, since he had inherited the business of Thomas Vautrollier, who had been granted the exclusive right to print editions of Ovid. *Venus and Adonis* was, in its highly patterned rhetorical surface, in its subject matter, and in its printer, Shakespeare's most Ovidian work. It was designed to appeal to young, educated males with money to spare, and it may well have been designed to be bought alongside texts of Ovid's erotic poems. It became Shakespeare's most successful printed work by a wide margin, going through at least ten editions before his death in 1616. The poem cuts out Ovid's (or Venus's) inset story of Atalanta and Hippomanes altogether, and puts in its place the voice of Ovid the *praeceptor amoris*, teacher of love, in the *Ars Amatoria*, as Venus cajoles the reluctant Adonis (at length) to stay with her and lie with her. The gender-bending delights of Book X of the *Metamorphoses* are registered in the poem's reversal of expected roles: Venus chides, chivvies, and persuades Adonis to stay with her. She sounds for all the world like a man persuading a woman to love him. Adonis is, however, true to his genealogy in Ovid. Since he is simultaneously the grandchild and great-grandchild of a statue and the son of a tree, he does not respond:

> 'Fie, lifeless picture, cold and senseless stone,
> Well painted idol, image dull and dead,
> Statue contenting but the eye alone,
> Thing like a man, but of no woman bred:
>   Thou art no man, though of a man's complexion,
>   For men will kiss even by their own direction.' (211–16)

Venus persuades, persuades, persuades. But even when she falls on top of her resistant lover she achieves only the kind of imaginary sex which Ovid had so teasingly offered his erotically inclined readers in the story of Pygmalion, the (great-)grandfather of Adonis:

> Now is she in the very lists of love,
> Her champion mounted for the hot encounter.
> All is imaginary she doth prove.

He will not manage her, although he mount her,
  That worse than Tantalus' is her annoy,
  To clip Elysium, and to lack her joy.

Even so poor birds, deceived with painted grapes,
Do surfeit by the eye, and pine the maw;
Even so she languisheth in her mishaps
As those poor birds that helpless berries saw.
  The warm effects which she in him finds missing
  She seeks to kindle with continual kissing. (595–606)

Ovid's Venus made Pygmalion's statue come to life. Shakespeare's is stuck like a gullible bird pecking at painted grapes, mocked with art.

## Rape and Tragedy

*Venus and Adonis* established Shakespeare as one of the cleverest, most rhetorically skilled, erotically confusing writers in late sixteenth-century England. This poem was the principal reason that Francis Meres in 1598 said 'as the soul of Euphorbus was thought to live in Pythagoras, so the sweet witty soul of Ovid lives in mellifluous and honey-tongued Shakespeare'—and that comparison may well have been one reason why later in his career Shakespeare was so keen to make jokes about Pythagorean beliefs in the transmigration of souls.[15] The relationship between Shakespeare's narrative poems and his plays has often been sidelined in the past because of the low critical valuation of the poems. But there is no doubt that Shakespeare's growing reputation as an Ovidian poet in the 1590s fed back into his stage career, and perhaps vice versa. *Titus Andronicus* may just predate the narrative poems, which were probably composed during a period in which the public theatres were closed as a result of the plague in 1592–4, but it certainly belongs to a larger story about Shakespeare's relation to Ovid in which both the narrative poems and the stage plays have a part. *Titus* is showily Ovidian, even to the extent of bringing young Lucius, a Roman schoolboy, onstage with a copy of the *Metamorphoses* which he says he was given by his mother. Ovid's story of the rape of Philomela provides the inspiration for the rape of Lavinia, both for the author of the play and for characters within it: she is violated by the evil sons of the Gothic empress of Rome, Chiron and Demetrius, who deliberately attempt to go beyond

Ovid. Philomela in the *Metamorphoses* was raped by the Thracian king Tereus and had her tongue cut out when she threatened to reveal his crime, but she could still use her hands to weave a tapestry which depicted her violation. Having read this story, presumably at school, Chiron and Demetrius cut off Lavinia's hands as well as her tongue.[16] She is left—in a highly literary, post-Ovidian way—unable to express herself except by gesture, and is taught how to identify her rapists by using the schoolboy's copy of Ovid to show what happened to her, after which her uncle teaches her how to write the names of her attackers in the sand by holding a stick with her stumps.

The Ovidian grotesquerie of *Titus* continues through its climax, in which Titus makes the empress eat her children in a pie, and did not endear the play to earlier generations of critics. Nonetheless, the play is a powerful theatrical response to one central feature of the *Metamorphoses*.[17] Again and again Ovid takes human characters through violent experiences which are at the limits of human endurance. Repeatedly his clear-edged style is used to describe realms of experience and of pain which are too great for human words: Myrrha, turned to a tree, bursts open in order to give birth to her son Adonis, who splits her bark asunder while it weeps odorous gums and balms. Repeatedly the changed forms of Ovid's characters seem to function in two contradictory ways: transformation into trees or stones seems to give fixity and a final form to the suffering of the characters concerned, but the transformation can also be represented as a kind of prison which takes them beyond any possibility of expressing their suffering. And to that prison Ovid's sharply self-aware rhetoric can add an additional bar and lock: he shows his mastery over eloquence in virtuoso descriptions of his characters as they lose all ability to speak. These features of the *Metamorphoses* make it seem repeatedly to pose a question which had a particular resonance for an early-modern dramatist trained in the art of rhetoric: how does artfully patterned and self-consciously rhetorical language function as a means for representing extremes of suffering? Can it be as much a barrier to the communication of raw suffering as a means of enabling it?

And that in turn relates to perhaps the deepest problem with which Ovid relentlessly plays in the *Metamorphoses*: how does a rhetorically sophisticated civilization like that of Augustan Rome relate and respond to ancient and barbarous mythological fictions? The story

**Illustration 2.** *Metamorphoses*, Book VI: Tereus attacks Philomela in the top-right background.

Codrington Library, All Souls College, Oxford, shelf mark b. infra.1.22: *Ovid's Metamorphosis Englished, Mythologized, and Represented in Figures*, trans. George Sandys (London, 1632), facing p. 201. Reproduced by kind permission of the Warden and Fellows of All Souls College, Oxford.

of Philomela is perhaps the episode in the *Metamorphoses* which most directly addresses these questions, and Shakespeare read that tale not just with great intelligence, but in the light of his education, which had immersed him in a rhetorical and literary culture that enabled him to appreciate the full force of both the tale and of the way that Ovid tells it. The story is partly about the relationship between a civilization founded on eloquence and barbarism, and seems indeed at times to anticipate the fate of Ovid, exiled among the supposed barbarians at Tomi. Tereus, the king of Thrace, marries Procne, the daughter of the king of the ultra-civilized Athens. He is consistently called 'barbarus' (6.515, 532)—a word which was even in the ancient world etymologically associated with inarticulacy ('barbaroi' are those whose language sounds like 'babababable'), and which was defined in Thomas Cooper's Latin Dictionary (the most popular aid in translating Latin into English in the sixteenth century) as 'churlish, without eloquence, uncivil'.[18] His wife Procne retains a pious love of her family (with which her Roman readers would immediately identify: *pietas* is the defining virtue of Virgil's Aeneas), and asks to see her sister. When Tereus goes to Athens he is so struck by his sister-in-law Philomela's beauty that he is made eloquent by love for her (6.469). Being a barbarous tyrant, however, he takes her home and rapes her (see Illustration 2). In Ovid's tale, contact between the virtuous women from Athens, the very origin of classical eloquence, and the barbarous Thracian king has a painfully transformative effect on eloquence. It is channelled into violence. When Philomela threatens to publish Tereus's villainy to the world he cuts out her tongue (her '*lingua*'—the same word is used in Latin of tongue and of language). And this is the climax of the super-articulate Ovid's tragedy of inarticulacy:

> ille indignantem et nomen patris usque vocantem
> luctantemque loqui conprensam forcipe linguam
> abstulit ense fero. radix micat ultima linguae,
> ipsa iacet terraeque tremens inmurmurat atrae,
> utque salire solet mutilatae cauda colubrae,
> palpitat et moriens dominae vestigia quaerit. (6.555–60)

> But as she yearned and callèd aye upon her father's name,
> And strivèd to have spoken still, the cruel tyrant came

> And with a pair of pinsons[19] fast did catch her by the tongue,
> And with his sword did cut it off. The stump whereon it hung
> Did patter still. The tip fell down and, quivering on the ground,
> As though that it had murmurèd it made a certain sound.
> And as an adder's tail cut off doth skip a while, even so
> The tip of Philomela's tongue did wriggle to and fro
> And nearer to her mistress-ward in dying still did go. (p. 195)

Struggling to speak, the tongue becomes a thing, a dying snake. It is a mini-metamorphosis of eloquence into a bubbling hiss of barbarism. And the concern with making the barbarian speak continues as Philomela, deprived of language, takes up a Thracian fabric, which is described as 'barbarica' (6.576), and weaves on it the story of her rape, which she sends to her sister. When Procne learns from the tapestry what has happened she experiences a speechless grief which parallels the forced silence of her sister. Silence becomes a miracle of pain:

> et (mirum potuisse) silet: dolor ora repressit,
> verbaque quaerenti satis indignantia linguae
> defuerunt. (6.583–5)

> She held her peace. A wondrous thing it is she should so do,
> But sorrow tied her tongue and words agreeable unto
> Her great displeasure were not at commandment at that stound [moment].
> And weep she could not. Right and wrong she reckoneth to confound,
> And on revengement of the deed her heart doth wholly ground. (p. 196)

The rape forces both women towards extremes of suffering that stifle their speech. It also transforms civilized virtues into their proximate vices, bringing barbarism, as it were, so far into the language of Athens that its eloquent tongue is curbed. And the eloquence of Athens in this tale serves as a proxy for the civilized eloquence of Rome. Throughout the *Metamorphoses* Ovid repeatedly distorts and contorts the great Virgilian virtue of *pietas*—which covers a range of attitudes through 'family feeling, love for friends' to 'duty'. The story about the incestuous love of Myrrha (the mother of Adonis) for her father Cinyras plays on the word *pietas* insistently, metamorphosing dutiful affection for a father into sexual passion. The confrontation between civility and barbarism in the tale of Philomela and Tereus puts that Roman virtue of *pietas* under an even greater strain. The love that Procne feels for her and Tereus's son Itys is called *pietas* (6.629). When she kills Itys and serves him up to her husband to eat, her infanticide is prompted by the thought that *pietas* towards a husband such as Tereus is a crime (6.635). The apparently barbarous act of killing her son and cooking him up for her husband becomes a perverse transformation of good old-fashioned Roman piety.

Ovid in this story and elsewhere creates an acute split between what we might call carnal reading, which imagines the physical pain and the mental suffering of the characters in the poem, and rhetorical reading, which focuses on Ovid's brilliant manipulations of words, on his skill in representing the unimaginable and the unbearably painful. The polish and skill with which he puns on the words *lingua* (tongue/ language) in the mutilation of Philomela and on *pietas* throughout the tale pose in acute form two questions that are asked repeatedly throughout the *Metamorphoses*: what is the relationship between physical or emotional suffering and rhetorically skilled expression? What kinds of pressure does pain put not just on virtue but on the language of virtue?

These questions lie at the heart of *Titus Andronicus*, and give to this play something far more than Elizabethan bad taste, or early Shakespearian tonal instability. The play is continually pressing at boundaries between what I have termed carnal and rhetorical readings of Ovid. Those two ways of responding to the *Metamorphoses* are both heightened to the point where the cracks between the two don't simply show, but positively scream. Lavinia is raped, has her tongue cut off, and (in super-Ovidian excess) has her hands cut off too. She was, we learn, responsible for reading to her cousin Lucius: like Philomela and Procne she is associated with eloquent civility. When Lavinia's uncle Marcus comes across her mutilated and muted body in the forest an audience sees physical horror—Lavinia is pouring blood from her mouth and arms, and has been raped—and hears, well, this:

> Speak, gentle niece, what stern ungentle hands
> Hath lopped and hewed and made thy body bare

Of her two branches, those sweet ornaments
Whose circling shadows kings have sought to sleep in,
And might not gain so great a happiness
As half thy love. Why dost not speak to me?
Alas, a crimson river of warm blood,
Like to a bubbling fountain stirred with wind,
Doth rise and fall between thy rosèd lips,
Coming and going with thy honey breath.
But sure some Tereus hath deflowered thee,
And, lest thou shouldst detect him, cut thy tongue.
Ah, now thou turn'st away thy face for shame,
And, notwithstanding all this loss of blood,
As from a conduit with three issuing spouts,
Yet do thy cheeks look red as Titan's face
Blushing to be encountered with a cloud.
Shall I speak for thee? Shall I say 'tis so?
O that I knew thy heart, and knew the beast,
That I might rail at him, to ease my mind!
Sorrow concealèd, like an oven stopped,
Doth burn the heart to cinders where it is.
Fair Philomel, why she but lost her tongue
And in a tedious sampler sewed her mind.
But, lovely niece, that mean is cut from thee.
A craftier Tereus, cousin, hast thou met,
And he hath cut those pretty fingers off,
That could have better sewed than Philomel. (2.4.16–43)

Critical responses to Marcus's speech vary. Some find it typical of 'immature' Shakespeare to have a character discoursing eloquently of bubbling fountains and of Ovid while his niece suffers and bleeds in front of him.[20] Some readers have highlighted the gender relations in the scene: an eloquent, humanistically trained male says 'Shall I speak for thee?' in the presence of a woman who has had the power of speech taken from her by male violence, and have asked how far Shakespeare is complicit in this brutal form of ventriloquism, and how far the men in the play are in fact able to translate Lavinia's suffering into terms which they can understand.[21] It is indeed a moment which it is hard to discuss without feeling in one way or another compromised, since Marcus is attempting to use his classically derived rhetorical education to describe raw pain of a kind that is beyond both his and the audience's comprehension. The result is an acute shortfall between the language that Marcus uses and the pain that he and the audience of the play both see before their eyes. Both violence and eloquence are separately intensified to the point at which they seem mutually incommensurable. Lavinia's suffering is so great that Marcus can only produce an approximate version of it, in a story he once read in Ovid, which serves as an analogy for the raw pain he is presently witnessing. Like the description of the sack of Troy in *Lucrece* (above, pp. 57–62) this is a classical speech in which there is tragic lack of connection between the words used and the pain felt by a violated woman.

It seems wrong simply to see the inadequacy or inappropriateness of this speech as a satirical reflection on Marcus, or on the inadequacies of his classical education, or to see the whole speech as showing the tonal insecurity produced by an inexperienced playwright. It could certainly be related to the experiences of the Elizabethan schoolroom, in which, as we saw in Chapter 1, male pupils spent surprising amounts of their time studying texts which ventriloquized female suffering. But the speech seems to probe much deeper than this. It is partly responding to that repeated dilemma which runs through many episodes of Ovid's *Metamorphoses*: does rhetorical skill inevitably part company with extreme pain? It does not shy away from extending that question into regions that are discomforting: is part of the *pleasure* of writing about pain getting to the point where this separation between language and emotion occurs? Can there be a rhetoric of suffering which does not end up drawing attention to itself at the expense of the suffering to which it supposedly testifies? And can intense pain finally be evoked in language only by enacting some kind of break between the physical experiences of the sufferer and its rhetorically fashioned expression? It also suggests a further set of higher-level thoughts about the effects of witnessing tragic suffering. Maybe someone, like Marcus, who witnesses extreme pain of a kind which he can never experience *can only* respond to it in a way that is inadequate, or by approximation, by remembering an old text and hoping that it roughly fits what he sees. Perhaps this is a bit like Ovid, he suggests, knowing that it is more and worse than an old narrative, and that this Tereus, the modern decadent Tereus, is 'craftier' than the original.

*Titus Andronicus* was very probably written in collaboration with George Peele, who was eight years older than Shakespeare and had a university degree, of which he was not above boasting on title pages to his works. It seems likely that Peele wrote the first act of the play.[22] The older and more experienced playwright may well have been briefed with establishing the historical setting, and created in Act 1 a Rome full of ceremonial entries and state burials. This section of the play contains a number of exotic 'Roman' words to establish a historical mood: the words 'Pantheon', 'candidatus', and 'palliament' appear in the first act of *Titus* and in Peele's works, but nowhere else in the canon of Shakespearian plays. The 'historical' setting established in Act 1 is actually a fictional period in the late Roman empire. Rome is suffering from both internal battles over the rival merits of hereditary or elective monarchy and external battles with the Goths. When the old emperor's eldest and least deserving son Saturninus becomes the new ruler of Rome, his name suggests a collapse into barbarism: the age of Saturn was in Roman mythology (and in Ovid) the earliest and most savage period of the world. When Saturninus marries the Goth Tamora we enter a nightmare Rome which is at once thrown back to the mythically early barbaric reign of Saturn and projected forward to a period of its late decline, when barbarian and Gothic hordes threaten to overturn it. The opening act established a setting which gave Shakespeare a chance, as it were, to present an Ovidian narrative among the Goths, a representation of barbarian Rome which is in exile from itself.

It's likely that Shakespeare was tasked with writing the sections of the play which derive more directly from the *Metamorphoses*. There are signs that the two writers did not simply work on their own, disconnectedly, but had a common set of concerns. Both sections of the play make much of relations between *pietas*, Roman duty, and pity. Both repeatedly use the word 'barbarous', which occurs seven times in *Titus*, far more frequently than in any other Shakespearian play. The concern of both playwrights with barbarism and piety certainly suggests that both authors (if there were indeed two of them) had been thinking about Ovid's tale of Philomela in similar terms, as a work which juxtaposed the 'barbarian' king Tereus and his pious wife Procne in ways that put 'Roman' virtues under extreme pressure. We can press this a little harder. Shakespeare seems to have learned a great deal both about Ovid and about how to represent Rome from *Titus*, and from the part of the play which was probably written by Peele in particular. The play as a whole creates oblique and indirect connections between the political debates presented in the early scenes and the Ovidian rape and tragedy of its core. These in turn raise questions about the causal relationships between the two. How do rape and barbarism relate to the political disturbances represented in the first part of the play? The breakdown of eloquence in the face of violence that dominates the Shakespearian sections seems in the context of the whole drama to have a constitutional edge: it occurs as Rome turns away from elective monarchy towards tyranny. Rape seems to become a metaphor for, as well as a consequence of, political decline. And by the end of the play Shakespeare seems to be pushing his own drama towards the kind of historical learning displayed in the first act. He makes comparisons between Lucius, the exile who returns to liberate Rome, and Coriolanus (4.4.68), about whom he was to write a play well over a decade later (see below, pp. 226–39).

The date of *Titus* is not known with certainty, and the play was revised at some point. It is very likely that this early collaborative work set Shakespeare thinking in roughly the period 1592–4 about the relationship between Ovidian tales of violence and larger historical and political narratives about Rome. In the dedication to *Venus and Adonis* he had promised the Earl of Southampton a 'graver labour'. When the narrative poem *Lucrece* appeared in 1594 it was certainly 'graver' than the earlier poem of Ovidian eroticism. Its subject is the rape of Lucretia by one of the sons of Tarquinius Superbus, and the banishment of the kings from Rome that followed. The new poem drew much of its plot from the story of Lucretia as related in Ovid's *Fasti*, an unfinished poem which associates a range of myths with different periods in the Roman calendar. Much of the atmosphere of the earlier part of the poem—the heated deliberation of Tarquin, his description after the rape as a 'captive victor that hath lost in gain' (730)—comes from Ovid's poem ('quid, victor, gaudes? haec te victoria perdet'—why do you rejoice as a victor: this victory will undo you, 2.811); but Shakespeare widens out from the close erotic drama evoked in the *Fasti* to include Lucrece's lengthy complaint after her rape, which is compared to but which seems much more present and real than the grief of the ancient Hecuba (above, pp. 57–62). A prose 'Argument' (narrative summary) prefixed to the poem emphasizes the effects of the rape on the constitution of Rome: 'Brutus acquainted the people with the doer and manner of the vile deed, with a bitter invective against the tyranny of the King; wherewith the people were so moved that with one consent and a general acclamation the Tarquins were all exiled and the state government changed from kings to consuls.' In the Roman historian Livy's prose history of Rome, the rape of Lucretia directly leads to the banishment of the Tarquins from Rome and the establishment of what the republican Livy calls 'the good fruit of liberty' (2.1.6). Ovid—writing with some care late in the reign of the emperor Augustus—is aware of the association of Lucretia with the *regifugium*, the flight of the kings, but his poetic version of the story just concludes with dry brevity 'that was the last day of kingly rule' (*Fasti*, 2.852). Within Shakespeare's poem, however, the relationship between the rape and the political changes which it indirectly causes is strongly suggested, but is left suggestively blurred.[23] So far as Lucrece is concerned, the poem is about woe (a word which appears an astonishing thirty-four times), her own 'never-ending woes' (935), 'Troy's painted woes' (1492), and the fact that 'In me more woes than words are now depending' (1615). Inarticulable Ovidian grief is for her the centre of the poem, while its margins—its prose argument, its rapid conclusion—suggest that from the perspective of masculine Roman history the exile of the Tarquins carries a political rather than an emotional significance. That combination—unutterable grief plus a larger, semi-detachable political narrative—partly results from the range of sources which Shakespeare used in writing the poem. He may well have read Ovid's *Fasti* in an edition which included the commentary by Paulus Marsus (Paolo Marsi, 1440–84).[24] This edition, which was frequently reprinted, includes in its notes to the Lucretia story (which festoon the margins of Ovid's poem) quotations from Livy's version of the story, as well as translations of speeches from the Greek historian Dionysius of Halicarnassus (see Illustration 3). Shakespeare therefore probably came to the tale as one in which the historical changes brought about by the rape of Lucretia were quite literally marginal to the sufferings of the heroine, but in which the consequence of her tragedy for both male eloquence and political life at Rome were also highly visible on the page.[25]

LIBER SECVNDVS XLI

¶Interpretationes Secundi Fastoꝝ libri Per Anto. de Fano: & Paulũ Marsum Poetas clarissimos & Rhe.
Anus hẽt fi. cum car. cre. & an. Vtilis exornatio siue color rhetoricus Græci metabasin: latini ANT.
trãslationẽ uocãt. Oñdit.n. breuiter qđ dictũ est ac ꝓponit breui qd cõsequat: ut Hasten⁹ ar. FAN.
uoꝝ cul. & si cœli nũc te Bac. canã. Annũ aũt naturalẽ accipe ex quo magni cõstabat ciuiles
noiati q̃ eos ppl̃i siue gẽtes ꝑ arbitrio sibi statuerẽt: ut is q trieteris dr̃ duob⁹ ãnis uertẽtib⁹ cõ Annus
stãs q̃uis sic ꝓprie dicteris. Sir & is q olympias q̃ttuor ãnos amplexus: uñ qnto quoq; redeũ ciuilis
te græci ioui olympio agonẽ celebrabãt. Addit is ãnus eudoxi octo e nr̃is cõtinẽs. Itẽ Chal- Trieteris
daicus q duodecim & Metonicus q Olympias
undeuigiti cõstare dr̃. ¶Nũc pri. ue. Annus
ele. ma. itis. Trãslatio est uelis ãt ma eudoxi
iorib⁹ dicit q̃ elegi nati ad q̃rimõia Annus
explicãdas ut eoꝝ nomẽ oñdit: nũc caldaicus
tractẽt sacra & seria nõ amores & lu Annus
drica. uidebat.n. hæc materia postu metonic⁹
lare carmẽ heroicũ qđ alibi oñdit: ut
sæpe dedi noste grã. ue. rati. ¶Lusit:
scripsit humilia Ludere q̃ uellẽ calamo pmisit agresti. ¶Hæc mea mi. ẽ
ge. q pos. ar. Bñ meremur de germa
nico carmie q eẽ nõ possumus. PAV.
Anus hẽt: Numa cum MAR.
ãno romuli duos addi
disset mẽses. Primũ Ia-
nuariũ nuncupauit: pri
múq; ãni mẽsem eẽ uo
luit. Secũdũ Februariũ uocauit februo deo dicatumq; lu
strationũ potẽs credit: ultimúq; ãni eẽ uolũt. Lustrari aũt
eo mẽse ciuitatẽ necesse erat. statuit ut iusta diis manibus
soluerent: sed postea a decẽ uiris Februari⁹ post ianuariũ
nũerat⁹ est. Diony. tñ asseret ur sacrificia hæc in februario
post brumã ab euãdro initiũ habuisse: q mos postea a ro
mãis suat⁹ est: Nec dissentit Var. februari⁹.n. inqt appella Februari⁹
tus a februo. Februare. purgare signĩt: eo mense purgabat uñ dicat.
antiq̃ ciuitas. i. palatiũ a nudis lupcis ab hoc de⁹ purgatio
nũ febru⁹ est noiat⁹: sed de hoc paulopost lati⁹ disseremus
Ianuariũ mẽsem primũ priore lib. diis aspicib⁹ absoluim⁹
nũc ad secũdũ his duob⁹ uersib⁹ trãsitionẽ poeta facit. ¶Ia
nus: hoc ẽ mẽsis Iano dicat⁹. ¶Hẽt finẽ: qa absolutus est.
¶Crescat & ãnus cũ car. Crescat ãnus p additionẽ mẽsiũ
& carmĩa ĩ qb⁹ aget. ¶Vt id alter mẽsis: secundus. s. ¶Sic
eat alter liber: quo secũdus ipse mẽsis describat qd mẽsis:
& uñ supi⁹ dixim⁹. Grauia grauiori stilo cõmẽdata erãt
s; cũ magis ĩgeniũ elegis accõmodatũ hret ẽt hæc q̃ grauia sũt: elegis decãtat: his.n. uersib⁹ mirabiles hoium ærũ-
næ & amoris q̃rimõiæ decãtant dicti ab ελεω qđ ẽ mi-
sereor. Inde ελεοσ materia: uertit ẽmonẽ ad ipos elegos Elegia
O elegi nũc primũ: q̃si nõ añ hac. sed nunc primũ ¶Istis uñ dicat.
ue. ma. sublimiore stilo & locupletiore materia p transla-
tionẽ a nauib⁹ & mari. ¶Memini eratis: nup opus exigua
materia: qa leuia leuiori stilo canebant. At nũc magna ca
nitis uerba sentẽtiis accõmodãdo. ¶Ipse elegias: de amo
rib⁹ multas scripserat: quaꝝ extãt ad corynna tres libelli.

¶P. Ouidii Nasonis Fastorum. Liber Secundus.

Anus hẽt finẽ
cũ carmie cre-
scat & annus
Alter ut hic
mensis sic li-
ber alter eat:
Nunc primũ
uelis elegi ma-
ioribus itis
Exiguum memini nuper eratis opus
Ipse ego uos habui faciles ĩ amor mini/
Cũ lusit nũeris pria iuẽta suis (stros
Inde sacra cano signataq; tẽpora fastis
Et quis ad hæc illinc crederet esse uiã
Hæc mea militia ẽ gerim⁹ q̃ possum⁹ ar
Dextraq; nõ oĩ mũere nr̃a uacat (ma
Si mihi nõ ualido torquent pila lacerto
Nec bellatoris terga præmunt equi
Nec galea tegimur nec acuto cingimur
(ense.

scripsit & artẽ & amoris remediũ. ¶Ipse ego ha. u. elegos. s. ¶Facile: benignos. ¶Mistros ĩ amore: & ut ex-
cusat⁹ hẽret subdidit. ¶Cũ pria iu. ipsa ætas iuuẽilis. ¶Lusit suis nu. q. d. cũ ea laudarẽ: q̃ iuuenes nõ dede-
cebãt. ¶Idẽ qđ de amore attigit: cũ hũilis eat materia: hũili ẽt sono exp̃ssit: hic uero cũ grauia dicat se totũ
ipso carmie attollit: uerbaq; reb⁹ accõmodat. Idẽ ego cano sacra: oĩa ad religionẽ faciẽtia. ¶Et tpa sig. de-
scripta. Fastis in fastoꝝ: oĩa hæc supi⁹ diffiniuim⁹. ¶Et qs cre. illinc: ex ipsa re amatoria. ¶Esse uiã ad hæc: sa
cra. s. & tpa describẽda. Hæc trahit sua quẽq; uoluptas: & cũ magno sit ornamẽto militaris idustria: cũ illi
se a pueris nõ dederit: hãc eẽ suã militiã inqt. nec oĩ ab officio uacare. Hæc ẽ mea militia poetice. s. sacra te- Hypbatõ
nere. ¶Ferim⁹ ar. q̃ pos. ac si diceret calami sũt mihi ꝓ hastis bellicis. ¶Dextra no. nõ ua. oĩ mu. oĩ officio. ĩ
mo aliqđ mun⁹ affert: nã si tela nõ torquet tractat calamo: qb⁹ ad scribẽdũ utit. ¶Si mihi: ut magis laborẽ
suũ grãmatico cõmẽdaret p lõgũ hypbathõ inq̃: Si a me nõ tractant arma non ꝑmit bellator equus non
f

**Illustration 3.** Lucrece's suicide in Marsus's edition of Ovid's *Fasti*.

Sackler Library, Oxford, Wind Collection, shelf mark #B3OVI folio: *P. Ovidii Nasonis fastorum libri diligenti emendatione typis impresse aptissimiqu[e] figuris ornata comentatoribus Antonio Constantio Fanensi: Paulo Marso Piscinate viris clarissimis additis quibusdam versibus qui deerunt in aliis codicibus* (Venice, 1508), fol. 41r. Reproduced by permission of the Bodleian Library.

The combination of Ovidian complaint and larger historical narrative in *Lucrece* may also suggest that the poem develops the strangely disarticulated relationship between Act 1 and the rest of *Titus Andronicus*. It is almost as though the young playwright looked at the historical frame given to the Ovidian tale of rape and barbarism by his elder collaborator, and then looked at Marsus's learned notes on the story in his edition of the *Fasti*, and sought in *Lucrece* to emulate their combination of political history and Ovidian violence. Shakespeare learnt from everything, including from himself and from his collaborators. The equivalent of Act 1 of the play is the prose Argument to the poem, which sets out the political and historical framework. This Argument (on very scant grounds) has sometimes been thought to be the work of a hand other than Shakespeare's own, since it presents a slightly different version of the story from that given in the poem. It may well represent Shakespeare attempting to mimic in prose the historical learning of George Peele, Master of Arts, in giving a larger political frame to the Ovidian passion and suffering of Lucretia. Certainly *Titus Andronicus* and *Lucrece* are very closely related, as are Lucretia and Philomela in Ovid's works. Philomela declares she will set shame aside and proclaim Tereus's actions to the people or to the very woods and rocks (6.544–8), and it is at this point that the tyrant is prompted to cut out her tongue. Philomela, that is, is a would-be Lucretia, who wants to make her suffering public. Ovid himself makes a connection between the two women at the very end of *Fasti* 2, when he says immediately after the end of the Lucretia story that spring is coming and Procne the swallow is returning, while her husband Tereus rejoices in the cold that she feels (2.855–6). Shakespeare's Lucrece compares her own lament to the wordless music of Philomela the nightingale, and the two violated women sing different words to the same old tune:

> Come, Philomel, that sing'st of ravishment,
> Make thy sad grove in my dishevelled hair.
> As the dank earth weeps at thy languishment,
> So I at each sad strain will strain a tear,
> And with deep groans the diapason bear;
>   For burden-wise I'll hum on Tarquin still,
>   While thou on Tereus descants better skill. (1128–34)

Unlike Philomela, however, Lucrece manages to utter the name of Tarquin just before her tongue becomes still for ever:

> Here with a sigh as if her heart would break
> She throws forth Tarquin's name. 'He, he,' she says—
> But more than 'he' her poor tongue could not speak,
> Till after many accents and delays,
> Untimely breathings, sick and short essays,
>   She utters this: 'He, he, fair lords, 'tis he
>   That guides this hand to give this wound to me.' (1716–22)

Her 'poor tongue' stammers; but it does get to the point that poor Philomela's tongue could not. Lucrece succeeds, unlike the muted Philomela, in publishing the crimes of Tarquin, and indirectly causes the exile of barbarous tyranny from Rome. Shakespeare's relationship to Ovid evolved partly by his habit of thinking back to his own earlier works, partly by his willingness to mull over the deep and recurrent preoccupations of his sources, partly as a result of the editions which he read, and partly too in response to the works of his rivals, contemporaries, and collaborators. But he also had an exceptional ear for the mute music of pain, which was perhaps Ovid's greatest and most lasting creation.

## Merrier Ovids

The previous chapter suggested that the way Shakespeare alluded to Virgil changed in the course of his career. That was partly because his contemporaries were changing how Virgil was understood, and partly because Shakespeare imitated Virgil in different ways in different genres. The deliberate way in which *Titus* draws attention to its Ovidian sources—even physically bringing them onstage—is similar to the direct and explicit ways Shakespeare alluded to Virgil in the earlier part of his career, by representing Virgilian speeches or Virgilian pictures. Marcus's attempt to use Ovidian allusions and Ovidian stories to understand what has happened to Lavinia and what she might be suffering is also in another respect analogous to the way in which Shakespeare presented allusions to Virgil's *Aeneid* in his early career: a present pain is set against a past example of analogous suffering, and the two (painfully) do not quite coincide.

In what way do Shakespeare's treatments of Ovid in the comedies differ from the tragic examples considered so far? In the last act of *A Midsummer Night's Dream* (1595/6) a company of amateur players, headed by Peter Quince the carpenter, put on a play to celebrate the wedding of Theseus and Hippolyta. Their play is based on the Ovidian story of the two lovers Pyramus and Thisbe (*Met.* 4.55–166). Ovid's tale has affinities with that of Romeo and Juliet in the tragedy Shakespeare wrote at almost the same time as *A Midsummer Night's Dream*: the two lovers Pyramus and Thisbe belong to different houses, converse through a chink in the wall, and try to elope to a wood to escape the opposition of their parents. Thisbe is surprised by a lioness and runs away, dropping her mantle, which the lioness then tears to pieces and smears in blood. Pyramus finds this rent fabric, and believes Thisbe is dead, and kills himself in despair. Thisbe finds him in his final moments, and also kills herself.

As so often in Ovid, the story of Pyramus and Thisbe has a fictional frame which interacts with the contents of the tale. It's related by one of the daughters of Minyas, who have refused to participate in the worship of Bacchus. They spend a day which should have been devoted to worship of this savage god (whose punishment of Pentheus for failing to worship him had been the subject of the last story of the previous book) spinning wool inside while they tell each other stories. Ovid weaves traces of the sisters' industrious spinning back into their literary creation, since the tragic tale of Pyramus and Thisbe which they relate turns on the rending apart of a delicate weave of fabric by the lioness. In the wider frame of the story, a tragic fate (and the fates also spin threads) clearly awaits these narrators who despise the punitive god Bacchus. The sisters do indeed eventually find their weaving transformed into tendrils of the vine; they flee as darkness falls, and the god turns them into squeaking insubstantial bats.

The story of Pyramus and Thisbe is woven into that of *A Midsummer Night's Dream* with similar artistry, although the first thing that strikes any audience of the play of Pyramus and Thisbe is that it is comically art*less*. Peter Quince's play is described as 'A tedious brief scene of young Pyramus | And his love Thisbe: very tragical mirth.' (5.1.56–7). It is a kind of botched tragicomedy, a deliberately clumsy version of a classical text, which is presented in a style so different from that of the surrounding drama that it seems to have quotation marks around it. Quince's play is composed in the relatively challenging form of decasyllabic quatrains, and its stylistic register is that of ballad-meets-popular-tragedy with heroical aspirations. The simplest of its many stylistic jokes is that any number of adjectives can be added in order to pad out a line or construct a rhyme:

> Anon comes Pyramus, sweet youth and tall,
> And finds his trusty Thisbe's mantle slain;
> Whereat with blade—with bloody, blameful blade—
> He bravely broached his boiling bloody breast;
> And Thisbe, tarrying in mulberry shade,
> His dagger drew and died . . . (5.1.143–8)

It has sometimes been thought that in this artless Ovidian play Shakespeare was satirizing Arthur Golding's translation of Ovid. Certainly the phrase 'boiling breast' is found in Golding, though not in the story of Pyramus and Thisbe (8.478). Direct satirical intent against a single target is hard to locate in such a slight verbal reminiscence, though, which here might just evoke a painstakingly literal translation of 'ferventi moriens e vulnere traxit' ('As he died he heaved the sword out of his boiling breast', *Met.*, 4.120) by a poet who is sitting with both Ovid and a dictionary to hand. Generally Quince's quatrains, like the course of true love in the play, do not run smooth. When passion strikes hard at the climax of the drama the form of the play changes from quatrains to what the enthusiastic Bottom calls 'eight and six', the alternating eight- and six-syllable rhyming lines favoured in ballads. This form may well suggest that Bottom is himself augmenting the role written for him by Peter Quince, as when he flies off in this high tragic aria:

> O dainty duck, O dear!
> Thy mantle good,
> What, stained with blood?
> Approach ye furies fell.
> O fates, come, come,
> Cut thread and thrum,
> Quail, crush, conclude, and quell. (5.1.275–81)

It's no accident that Bottom is a weaver, like the daughters of Minyas who relate the Ovidian tale of Pyramus and Thisbe. He seems to become at least part-author of the play here. A 'thrum' is very much a weaver's word: it means 'Each of the ends of the warp-threads left unwoven and remaining attached to the loom when the web is cut off' (*OED*). As with *Venus and Adonis*, Shakespeare's play doesn't just pluck a story from Ovid out of its context. It responds to the way that story is woven into the *Metamorphoses*. The larger comedy of the passage, though, lies in its interweaving of different vocabularies and poetic registers. The phrase 'furies fell' is often used in poetry from the second half of the sixteenth century to describe the fates. Usually it occurs at moments of high emotional drama. It was a stylistic intensifier that to a sophisticated audience in 1595 would have sounded hackneyed, but was certainly not the kind of phrase which they would expect to find alongside the artisanal vocabulary of 'thrums' and threads. This is a speech by a weaver who has, at some remove, read an Ovidian tale and who has some notion of the clichés of high tragic discourse.

There has been a lot of relatively fruitless argument about what the real object of Shakespeare's mockery might be in this play.[26] Is he taking a swipe at Golding's Ovid, or is the treatment of the mechanicals a professional playwright's way of mocking amateur artisan theatricals in mystery and miracle plays, or ballad writers? These questions will never be firmly settled for the simple reason that stylistic pastiche doesn't have to have a single specific object. Part of the fun of the play comes from the way its author(s) can't settle down to a single style, as different voices and styles weave into each other and chaotically collaborate. But there are some common features to all of the elements of pastiche in the style of the play. What makes it funny is the social and stylistic aspiration of the players. They are trying too hard to create a grand style that would suit a classically derived play and which would appeal to an audience of dukes and courtiers. They are, in a social sense, *translating* Ovid, and trying to move themselves out of one social sphere into another by using a classical text that they think will appeal to the audience (and, interestingly, when Bottom is literally metamorphosed into an ass he is said to be 'translated', 3.1.113). They get it wrong, and sound both socially and stylistically out of place. They also sound—within the elegant mix of vernacular and classical mythology dramatized in fluid blank verse and set-piece descriptive flights which is *A Midsummer*

*Night's Dream*—immensely old-fashioned. This brings to the play-within-the-play that flavour of self-mockery by the grammar-school educated glover's son Shakespeare which we have already found in the player's speech on Hecuba in *Hamlet*. One reason why the play-within-the-play is so edgily funny is that Shakespeare is here channelling traces of his own social and educational anxieties into comedy. Can someone with a relatively rudimentary grasp of Latin hope to dramatize an Ovidian play before a courtly audience, an audience used to the learned dramas of John Lyly and other university-trained dramatists, without falling flat on his face?

Shakespeare's way round or through that social and educational problem was to create comedy in which 'classical learning' is presented dramatically onstage with virtual quotation marks around it. The 'rude mechanicals'' play *sounds* old, because it is presented as a stylistic mingle-mangle, something that might derive from the rural youth of a sophisticated London dramatist rather than from his present-day self. That is entirely typical of Shakespeare's early theatrical uses of his classical learning. He wants to show his knowledge, but he is socially sensitive enough to realize that proudly displaying what might strike his audience as a rather rudimentary knowledge of Latin literature might actually show how little he knows rather than how much. By embedding his knowledge of Ovid in a play-within-a-play that sounds socially remote from the stylistic register and social class of the principal characters of *A Midsummer Night's Dream*, Shakespeare both shows what he knows and shows that he understands that those who show their knowledge too proudly can make themselves sound absurd.

That does not mean Shakespeare's deployment of Ovid in *A Midsummer Night's Dream* was *actually* clumsy or old-fashioned. Nor does it mean that all the jokes in the play are at the expense of the 'rude mechanicals'. Shakespeare uses the Ovidian play to radiate suggestions, and to hint at a darker possible plot which lurks within the comedy which is being enacted onstage, in 'tragical mirth'. The play-within-the-play seems to reveal a potential antique truth, learned from Ovid, that lovers meeting in the woods against the wishes of their parents are more likely to end in the kind of tragedy that meets Romeo and Juliet than in the fairy-led comic entanglements of *A Midsummer Night's Dream*. As Peter Holland has shown,

*A Midsummer Night's Dream* is haunted by dark myths which never quite appear in the play. Stories that present Theseus as a serial abandoner of women, which Shakespeare would know about from Plutarch's 'Life' of Theseus, as well as from Ovid's heroic epistle from Ariadne to Theseus, cluster around the evening celebration of Theseus's marriage to Hippolyta, hinting that comedy and tragedy are separated by the thinnest and most permeable of boundaries.[27] The audience members who are most scornful about the play-within-the-play are Hippolyta and Demetrius, who sit closest to the darkness. In many versions of the life of Theseus Hippolyta was carried off as a captured bride after the hero defeated the Amazons. Shakespeare's representation of Hippolyta as sulky and difficult hints that the wedding being celebrated is not a straightforwardly happy and consensual one. That other most scornful observer of the play, Demetrius, who at the end believes himself to be in love with Helena, is still under the influence of the magic juice squeezed into his eye by that native worker of tragicomic mischief, Robin Goodfellow.

The mechanicals' play therefore does not simply align 'ancient' Ovid with a socially aspirational but stylistically antiquated idiom. The Ovidian story glances over the shoulders of the onstage audience to the offstage audience. It hints that this comedy is a comedy which has a tragedy pressing at its edges. Behind the clumsy earnestness of the play is an artful playwright who is just as aware of the relationship between stories, narrators, and audiences as the Ovid who narrates the *Metamorphoses*.[28]

In this respect *A Midsummer Night's Dream* anticipates what was to become the dominant way that allusions to Ovid were to function in Shakespeare's drama in the later part of his career. In the works after around 1600, references to Ovidian stories very often function as narrative hints. They suggest different possible outcomes to the events and actions that we have seen. Usually those possible outcomes are darker than those that actually occur. This is particularly true of Ovid's role in the later romances. As we saw in the previous chapter, romances can allude to epic narratives, can include moments which appear to be tragic, and can also be amphibious with respect to the social status of their audience, appealing both to elite groups who want a richly allusive literary texture and to a popular audience (or to the spirit of the popular which is found hiding even in the most elite of elite audiences) who might enjoy marvels and sudden reversals of fortune. Shakespeare's romances often create moments which have the potential to be seen by different members of the onstage and offstage audience as either comic or tragic or both at once. Allusions to Ovid in the later plays tend to assist the creation of such moments. So in *Cymbeline* 2.2 Giacomo hides in a trunk which is carried into Innogen's bedchamber. He has made a bet with her husband Posthumus that he can persuade her to sleep with him. As he emerges from the trunk he describes the scene in this way:

> The crickets sing, and man's o'er-laboured sense
> Repairs itself by rest. Our Tarquin thus
> Did softly press the rushes ere he wakened
> The chastity he wounded. Cytherea,
> How bravely thou becom'st thy bed! Fresh lily,
> And whiter than the sheets!
> .....
> On her left breast
> A mole, cinque-spotted, like the crimson drops
> I'th' bottom of a cowslip. Here's a voucher
> Stronger than ever law could make. This secret
> Will force him think I have picked the lock and ta'en
> The treasure of her honour. No more. To what end?
> Why should I write this down that's riveted,
> Screwed to my memory? She hath been reading late
> The tale of Tereus. Here the leaf 's turned down
> Where Philomel gave up. I have enough.
> To th' trunk again, and shut the spring of it.
> Swift, swift, you dragons of the night, that dawning
> May bare the raven's eye! I lodge in fear.
> Though this' a heavenly angel, hell is here. (2.2.11–50)

Giacomo's speech is flanked by two allusions to classical rapes: it begins with Tarquin (and the allusion is partly to Shakespeare's own *Rape of Lucrece*, a new edition of which had appeared in 1607, and which is one source of the wager between the men about the chastity of Innogen at the start of the play) and ends with the rape of Philomela by Tereus in the copy of Ovid's *Metamorphoses* which Innogen has been reading. Giacomo has an instinctively male view of things: he sees this story as the 'tale of Tereus' rather than of

Philomela, despite the fact that Renaissance commentators such as Georgius Sabinus introduce it as a female tale, 'De Procne, Philomela, Tereo & Iti in aves'—the story of Procne, Philomela, Tereus and Itys turned to birds.[29] Those literary allusions are not static ornaments like the items in the inventory of Innogen's room which Giacomo greedily records in the part of this speech which is omitted from the quotation above. They add danger and possibility to the scene. Giacomo draws his notes on Innogen's chamber to a close once with 'No more', but then is compelled to pick up the book which she has been reading, as though driven by a compulsion to do more, to get closer to the sleeping woman. His note that 'the leaf 's turned down | Where Philomel gave up. I have enough' has an extraordinarily emphatic central pause after 'gave up'. That pause is loaded with threat (and also a measure of masculine obtuseness: Philomel never finally 'gave up', even pursuing her revenge when she is deprived of speech). In performance, that pause can and should carry huge charge: Giacomo is tempted for a moment to re-enact that Ovidian rape, before he tells himself 'I have enough.' This is the third time a copy of Ovid appears onstage in Shakespeare (we have already met the *Heroides* onstage in *Shrew* and the *Metamorphoses* onstage in *Titus*). The text of Ovid is again a carnal presence, which here raises the shadow of an onstage rape. The sight of a man onstage in a woman's chamber (and that word was often used in the period as a sexual pun) while she lies in bed, with her breast exposed, is itself a kind of sexual violation. And our presence observing the scene creates further unease and awkwardness: we spy on a spy, and are spying almost as much as Giacomo in the play or Actaeon in Ovid's *Metamorphoses*, pausing with him until we too 'have enough'. Observer and narrator are in a dangerous collusion, and the presence of Ovid onstage is a prompt to the audience to see this scene as a kind of violation. But it is simultaneously a kind of red herring, misleading the learned into thinking that a physical violation might be imminent. It creates an atmosphere and a set of expectations which are finally temptations and illusions rather than actions.

Giacomo's little piece of Ovid in the night fits in with the larger structures of the later romances, as well as with the ways in which they work on their audience and on characters within the plays. These are dramas in which characters onstage create and act on hypotheses, and where plot is not driven by a simple set of causally interconnected actions, but by imaginative possibilities which could either become violently real or remain as no more than threats or suggestions. So Posthumus mistakenly believes on the basis of Giacomo's detailed record of Innogen's chamber and body that he has slept with her, and sets out to kill his wife. *Cymbeline* repeatedly shows people making certainties out of tiny pieces of material evidence. The allusion to Ovid in Innogen's bedchamber extends that process of fictive extrapolation into the minds of the audience, turning allusions into illusions, and creating alternative moods and alternative grammatical modes for the action of the play. Innogen is not raped. Posthumus might believe she is, we might for a moment think she is about to be, but she is not.

The end of *The Winter's Tale* plays a rather different set of illusionistic tricks—although to call them 'tricks' rather than artistic miracles is to diminish them.[30] At the climax of the play Paulina reveals a statue of Hermione. Her husband Leontes and effectively the audience too have believed her to be dead. The statue is a kind of monument—both a moral admonition to Leontes and a reminder of Hermione's beauty. It has apparently no resemblance to the eroticized object of beauty which was Pygmalion's statue in Ovid, since it is untouchably beyond human contact, and beyond human power. As Paulina says:

> Either forbear,
> Quit presently the chapel, or resolve you
> For more amazement. If you can behold it,
> I'll make the statue move indeed, descend,
> And take you by the hand. But then you'll think—
> Which I protest against—I am assisted
> By wicked powers.
> . . . . .
> It is required
> You do awake your faith. Then, all stand still.
> Or those that think it is unlawful business
> I am about, let them depart. (5.3.85–97)

This moment is full of the deceptiveness and the self-consciousness of Ovid's story of Pygmalion. That word *reverentia*, which in Ovid prevents the statue from moving, and which leaks out into the relationship between the statue, its creator, and its observers, colours the whole scene, which is enacted in a chapel. In this reverent space Paulina warns her viewers not to fear that magic is about to occur. Orpheus, the singer of Ovid's tale of Pygmalion, is also a background presence in this tale about a man hoping to see his wife return to life through art, since Orpheus of course went to the underworld in a vain attempt to rescue his wife from death. As Paulina appeals to the characters onstage to 'awake your faith', the statue seems to breathe, to move, to become a piece of living art which marks a return from the dead. This isn't just a moment where Shakespeare winks at the more learned members of his audience and congratulates them on their ability to identify his source in Ovid's story of Pygmalion. The 'allusion' is all wrong and should come as a profound surprise, since the whole story is in a sense the wrong way around. A statue is made to come alive in Ovid as a result of the intercession of Venus in a morally queasy fable about the power of desire, mingled with that of art and a pagan goddess, to generate life. Here a living woman pretends to be a statue in order to pretend to come alive. The plot of the play goes into reverse as Hermione is shown not to have died. And Paulina is not the self-regarding artist described by Orpheus in Book X of the *Metamorphoses*: she is a kind of magical agent of regeneration cum morally admirable trickster.

The scene is in many ways outflanking all members of its audience, both onstage and offstage. Members of the offstage audience might initially assume that they are supposed to believe that the actor playing the statue is 'really' a statue. But Shakespeare holds the statue still onstage for so long—and as the focus of theatrical attention—that it is virtually inevitable that the unfortunate actor playing the part will move and show that it is 'in fact' alive.[31] The sceptical viewers who nudge each other as the statue shifts its balance or breathes eventually discover that their scepticism has revealed what they were in fact supposed to believe after all. It is trick. It is alive. To turn Ovid's writerly knowingness into such rootedly theatrical and illusionistic knowingness is indeed little short of a miracle. Allusions to Ovid, as we have seen, can in Shakespeare be in various ways 'framed' for their audience to notice: here there is a literal frame and curtain round the artwork, which marks it out for special attention.[32]

Allusions to Ovid can also be presented as in various ways 'antique': here Leontes remarks: 'But yet Paulina, | Hermione was not so much wrinkled, nothing | So agèd as this seems' (5.3.27–8). The desirable youthfulness of Pygmalion's statue was part of what made him want it to love: here the statue carries the marks of antiquity. Shakespeare's allusions to Ovid can also be interpreted in different ways by different characters: here in both the lengthy preceding scene of summary and anticipation by gentlemen and clowns, as well as in the varying attitudes of marvel and repentance of the observers of the scene itself, Ovid is once again the ancient poet most able to make Shakespeare explore the divergences between different points of view onstage. Allusions to Ovid can also hint at possible plots; but here a transformational imitation of Ovid—translating the Pygmalion episode from poem to stage, transforming the wish-fulfilling magic of Venus to the almost punitive illusionism of Paulina—creates a plot and a scene that seem to take us beyond the possible. Magic and miracle are possible, but here do not quite become reality.

Rather different, on the face of it, is the great Ovidian set piece towards the end of *The Tempest*. Prospero awaits the entry of his prisoners, and as he does so invokes Ovid in one of the closest allusions to the text of the *Metamorphoses* in the entire Shakespearian canon:

> Ye elves of hills, brooks, standing lakes and groves,
> And ye that on the sands with printless foot
> Do chase the ebbing Neptune, and do fly him
> When he comes back; you demi-puppets that
> By moonshine do the green sour ringlets make
> Whereof the ewe not bites; and you whose pastime
> Is to make midnight mushrooms, that rejoice
> To hear the solemn curfew; by whose aid,
> Weak masters though ye be, I have bedimmed
> The noontide sun, called forth the mutinous winds,
> And 'twixt the green sea and the azured vault
> Set roaring war—to the dread rattling thunder
> Have I given fire, and rifted Jove's stout oak
> With his own bolt; the strong-based promontory
> Have I made shake, and by the spurs plucked up
> The pine and cedar; graves at my command

> Have waked their sleepers, oped, and let 'em forth
> By my so potent art. But this rough magic
> I here abjure. (*The Tempest*, 5.1.33–51)

In Ovid's *Metamorphoses* (as translated by Golding) the sorceress Medea invokes her art in this way as she prepares to extend the life of her husband Jason's father Aeson by slaughtering him:

> Ye airs and winds, ye elves of hills, of brooks, of woods alone,
> Of standing lakes, and of the night, approach ye every one.
> Through help of whom (the crookèd banks much wondering at the thing)
> I have compellèd streams to run clean backward to their spring.
> By charms I make the calm seas rough, and make the rough seas plain [flat],
> And cover all the sky with clouds and chase them thence again;
> By charms I raise and lay the winds, and burst the viper's jaw
> And from the bowels of the earth both stones and trees do draw.
> Whole woods and forests I remove; I make the mountains shake,
> And even the earth itself to groan and fearfully to quake;
> I call up dead men from their graves; and thee, O lightsome moon,
> I darken oft, though beaten brass abate thy peril soon.
> Our sorcery dims the morning fair and darks the sun at noon.
> The flaming breath of fiery bulls ye quenchèd for my sake
> And causèd their unwieldy necks the bended yoke to take.
> Among the earth-bred brothers you a mortal war did set
> And brought asleep the dragon fell [dangerous] whose eyes were never shut.
> By means whereof deceiving him that had the golden fleece
> In charge to keep, you sent it thence by Jason into Greece.
> Now have I need of herbs that can by virtue of their juice
> To flowering prime of lusty youth old withered age reduce [bring back].
> I am assured ye will it grant. For not in vain have shone
> These twinkling stars, ne yet in vain this chariot all alone
> By draught of dragons hither comes. (pp. 208–9; cf. *Met.*, 7.192–219)

Prospero's speech has been described by Charles and Michelle Martindale as 'imitative not allusive; educated members of the audience would recognize the presence of Ovid, but there is no question of any such complex interplay between the divergent meanings of the two texts as our more ingenious critics often suppose'.[33] The speech is delivered while Ariel goes offstage to fetch Prospero's prisoners, and there is a simple theatrical need to fill in stage time. Yet to see Prospero's speech as principally a piece of stylistic imitation to occupy this pause in the action is theatrically rather naïve. Yes, critics can be over-ingenious. But Shakespeare could be more than ingenious. The speech comes immediately after Prospero's declaration that 'The rarer action is | In virtue than in vengeance' (5.1.27–8). At this point a potential revenge plot is being painfully avoided, and the speech comes right at the pivot in this transformation of the narrative outcome of the play. It is in that respect akin to the use of Ovid to mark the dark shadows of alternative possible plots beneath an unfolding comedy in *A Midsummer Night's Dream*, or the presence of Ovid during Giacomo's not-quite rape. And this perhaps makes sense both of the affinity and the savage incongruity between Ovid's Medea—a sorceress who can boil people in pots in order to rejuvenate them, and who goes on to kill her own children—and the bookish Prospero. Medea is something he might have been or which he could yet still almost be, and yet which he is not.

This thought also helps to explain many of Shakespeare's less obvious grammatical and syntactical transformations of Ovid's original speech here. In the larger action of *The Tempest* vengeful instincts are partially and with difficulty being tamed. That fact about the surrounding plot is registered in the syntax of the imitation. Prospero shifts Medea's invocation of her art from the present to the past tense. It is a magic he is giving up rather than one which he is summoning into being. He also strips away from Ovid's Medea the more obtrusively mythical elements. There are no dragons in his speech, and no 'flaming breath of fiery bulls' either, and in it there are no rivers flowing in reverse. The archaic magic and the vengeful impulses are both being written out—and many in Shakespeare's audience, who would have set pieces from Ovid such as this speech by heart, would hear that happening. The strange claim that 'graves at my command' have waked their sleepers suggests a dark and necromantic element to Prospero's magic which has not otherwise appeared in the play; but this detail too needs to be thought about in relation to its theatrical context. Prospero has not been shown reanimating corpses, but he *has* brought about a series of metaphorical and imagined deaths, of Ferdinand so far as his father is concerned, and of Alonso so far as Ferdinand is concerned.[34] The ancient barbarism of Ovid's Medea is registered, and then deflected into metaphor and illusion.

This is apparent in the most significant but least obvious change to the speech. Ovid's Medea is making an invocation, which, as Shakespeare would have been trained to notice, is in the 'vocative' case in Latin, one which calls to its addressees. It ends with a series of verbs in the imperative, which issue orders. As William Lily's *Grammar* (which Shakespeare would have been made to learn by heart) said 'the vocative is known by calling or speaking to as *O magister*, O master'.[35] In Prospero's version the speech does not conclude with an imperative. The elves are invoked, but they are not ordered to do anything. Prospero emphasizes as Ovid does not the relative freedom of the elves, who, for the first eight lines of his speech are not presented as obeying his commands, but are described as wandering through a landscape which seems very English, with its curfews, its mushrooms, and its fairy rings. Medea, by contrast, orders them to 'approach' right at the start of her speech. In Shakespeare the elves are neither subordinate powers nor 'masters' like the bossy schoolmaster in Lily's grammar: they are 'weak masters', invoked in order to be described and renounced rather than deployed. This syntactic muting of the passage is, as so often with Shakespeare's classical allusions, brilliantly in keeping with the movement of the whole play, in which everything is assembled for revenge and then at the last moment Prospero draws away from it. It is also steeped in the syntactic and practical habits of Prospero, who from the second scene onwards has been prone to bursts of rage which diffuse themselves out into fictional description. Here the description of the 'weak masters' seems to invite a verb of command as its conclusion; but in fact we get a 'But' that shrinks from the direct imperative: 'But this rough magic | I here abjure.' In performance those lines have to be hard to say, like Giacomo's renunciation of Ovid in 'I have enough': they run counter to the power of the invocation, and they defuse the authority of the imperative form into a simple statement of intention, a performance of giving up magic. The whole passage is a pointed transformation of Ovid, in which magical mastery is renounced even at the level of syntax, but in which the threatening potential of Medea remains just a distant possibility.

# 4

# *Roman Comedy*

When in 1598 Francis Meres put together a series of comparisons between contemporary English writers and their classical counterparts it seemed natural for him to compare Shakespeare not only to Ovid, but to the Roman comedian Plautus and the tragedian Seneca too:

> As Plautus and Seneca are accounted the best for comedy and tragedy among the Latins, so Shakespeare among the English is the most excellent in both kinds for the stage; for comedy, witness his *Gentlemen of Verona*, his *Errors*, his *Love Labours Lost*, his *Love Labours Won*, his *Midsummer's Night Dream*, and his *Merchant of Venice*; for tragedy his *Richard the Second*, *Richard the Third*, *Henry the Fourth*, *King John*, *Titus Andronicus* and his *Romeo and Juliet*.[1]

Meres was not doing literary criticism. His main aim in *Palladis Tamia* was to give smart young men a set of clever-sounding similes and comparisons to drop into their writing and conversation. He certainly would not have imagined that his every word about Shakespeare would be weighed and anatomized centuries later. Nonetheless, his comparison of Shakespeare with Roman drama may well have shocked some of its early readers. The two greatest names in Roman theatre are paired not with a symmetrical two English names, but with one: Shakespeare, the best in both kinds.

I shall return at the end of this chapter to Shakespeare's experiments in combining comedy and tragedy and what they might tell us about his responses to Roman drama. But first one general point needs to be made. Latin drama was perhaps the deepest and most pervasive influence on Shakespeare, but it is also one of the least visible. It is easy to point to moments when Shakespearian characters quote from Ovid or allude to Virgil, but it is not so easy to pin down moments when their author learnt from Roman stagecraft or from the tricks and stratagems enacted in classical comedies. This chapter will argue that although the influence of classical comedy is much less obvious than the influence of Ovid, it nonetheless runs just as deep or even deeper. It affects the shape and structure of Shakespeare's plots, has a surprising but strong influence on his interest in powerful and articulate women, and it extends right down into the filaments of his characters' minds, shaping the way he represents the relationship between their beliefs and their actions.

## Plautus

First some facts. Shakespeare certainly knew at least some of the works of the two major Roman comedians whose work survived into the Renaissance. These were Plautus (Titus Maccius Plautus, *c.*254–184 BC) and Terence (Publius Terentius Afer, 195/185–159 BC). These two playwrights, despite belonging to different generations, had a lot in common. Both wrote plays which were known in the Renaissance to have derived from Greek 'New Comedy' by Menander and others. Plautus was the earlier of the two, and twenty of his plays survive. He lived and wrote roughly two centuries before Virgil. This makes him the most 'antique' of the Latin writers known to Shakespeare, although there is nothing austerely ancient about the texture of his writing, which is dominated by quick-fire colloquial dialogue. He principally wrote what is called *fabula palliata*, in which the main characters wore cloaks (*pallia*), as Greeks did. Plautus was consequently a sort of hybrid 'ancient', who used Greek models from a century or so before to comment on Roman 'contemporary' life. Erich Segal describes this aspect of *fabula palliata* very well: 'Its basic premise, "it all takes place in Athens, folks", licensed behavior that was ordinarily forbidden.'[2] A 'Greek' world could mask satire on Roman customs, as well as licensing the representation of fornicating young men or disconcertingly loyal prostitutes. Scholars do not know how close Plautus and Terence were to their Greek models, because only fragments of these sources survive. Sixteenth-century readers would have known through commentaries and the patient explanations of schoolmasters that Menander existed and that Plautus and Terence were Romans who consciously put on Greek dress. That made Latin drama a major model of what we might call anachronistic theatre (or perhaps 'anatopic' theatre: plays which are not quite set in the right place). This kind of drama exploits the slippage between a fiction set 'back then and over there' and an immediately present now. One of the most significant inspirations for Shakespeare's comedies, John Lyly, was fond of setting fictions about England notionally in Greece, and when he did so he was following the example of Plautus.

A set of theatrical formulae runs through many of Plautus's plays, as does a store of stock character types. The plots of 'New Comedy' tend to be about generational conflicts between young men and their fathers. Clever slaves or parasites construct plots around and (mostly) for these young men in more or less consciously metatheatrical ways. When a slave in Plautus says 'I have a plan' ('*consilium*'), he tends also to mean 'I have an idea how this play might end,' or 'I can see a possible story ahead.'[3] The plays therefore associate drama with conjecture and anxiety about the future, turning comedy into a kind of improvised attempt to control and direct the onstage action. Plautus also often drew on the topoi of romance—lost children found, sea voyages—to bring about more or less self-consciously implausible unravellings of the plot. Roman virtues and values are often put under pressure as a result of the Greek setting: Plautus's plays often ask what it might mean for a father or a young man to be '*liberalis*' (which means both 'well born' and 'generous spirited'), or how soldiers and gods fit into domestic life, or about the relationship between being a citizen and being virtuous. Women (and their roles were always played on the Roman stage by men) often play a significant part in exploring these questions. Wives and prostitutes can influence the action and appear on the stage in *fabula palliata*, though young unmarried women (*virgines*) are rarely directly represented onstage. Sometimes there is a well-born *virgo* offstage whose status and actions have a determining influence over the plot; at other times there is a canny and loyal prostitute onstage who seems a better Roman (or Greek) than anyone else. Often these women are initially believed to be outsiders or slaves, and then when the plot unravels they turn out to be Greek citizens or relatives of the actors onstage.

Roman comedy was performed during public holidays on stages which seem to have been relatively small and intimate. The playing space was dominated by doors which lead into one or more household interiors, which remain out of bounds so far as the action of the play was concerned. As a result, the stage space usually represents a meeting place in the street or in the country, into which characters sometimes enter while still talking over their shoulders to the 'inside' space. The effect is very unlike later sixteenth-century drama for the popular stage, in which of course women (played by boys) are active onstage presences, and in which there is generally an easy movement between interior and exterior spaces. This does not mean that off-stage areas in Plautus or the women who sometimes occupy those offstage areas are insignificant. Indeed, the reverse is often true. Attempts by characters within the play to penetrate the offstage zone are some of the most powerful moments in Plautine comedy, and can be marked by *coups de théâtre*. At the end of the *Amphitryon*, for instance, the hero is enraged about his wife's supposed infidelity and declares: 'I'm going into the house right now' ('pergam in aedis nunciam', 1052). Instantly there is a thunderbolt from Jupiter which knocks him unconscious. This is a theatrical joke. Amphitryon has attempted to break theatrical convention by entering the hidden offstage space in which, earlier in the play, Jupiter himself had been having sex with his wife. The zone behind the doors is full of peril: in Plautus's *Menaechmi* the travelling Menaechmus twin says that he is going to go into the house of his brother's whore. His slave says: 'you're dead if you cross that threshold' ('periisti, si intrassis intra limen', 416). This is again a kind of serious joke: going into an offstage interior space *is* a kind of death for a character in a form of drama which by convention does not represent those spaces.

This is not to say that life for those who occupy the onstage space in Roman comedy is easy. Since the stage is usually imagined as a street on which people come and go, Plautus can sometimes suggest that people who are on the stage are, as we say now, out on the streets. So in *Menaechmi* the Menaechmus twin who belongs at Epidamnus is shut out by both his wife and his whore, forced onto the stage by being ousted from his home. He declares: 'she's gone inside. She's shut the door. Now I'm totally shut out' ('abiit intro, occlusit aedis. nunc ego sum exclusissimus', 698). 'Exclusissimus' occurs only at this point in Latin literature, and may carry the force of 'now I am completely on my own, shut off from everything I own'. That coinage tells us something about Roman comedy. Often its heroes depend on their relationship to an offstage space which we can never see, and which contains more or less everything they own, and sometimes we only see them before us because they have lost something, or are unable to go back inside to a domestic interior which is a defining element of their lives.

The traditional view used to be that characters in Plautus and Terence are just pantomimic types (whores, parasites, old men, braggart soldiers) who enact knockabout farces in which clever slaves rip off their masters. This is seriously misleading. Plautine characters can be people who are visibly hungry for elsewhere, desperate to get inside, to see the offstage girl, to return home. They also can be highly reflective beings. Indeed, Plautus very often puts characters in positions where they are made to ask radical questions about themselves as a result of what they see and hear. In Plautus's *Amphitryon*, the only Roman play to call itself a 'tragicomedia', a tragicomedy, and a play which Shakespeare certainly knew (it directly influences *The Comedy of Errors*), Mercury disguises himself as the slave Sosia. The god says that he has become the slave's *imago*. That word is a complex one. An *imago* could be a physical resemblance, a double, a reflection, or a pictorial representation, even a ghost, but it could also carry interior, mental senses—a sense impression, an illusion. When Sosia meets his *imago* Mercury he has a momentary crisis: 'he's as like me as I am like myself', he cries ('tam consimilest atque ego', 443). The physical presence of Mercury disguised as Sosia presents material evidence to the poor slave that he himself might not be who he thinks he is, and that he might be mad or deluded. As Mercury reels off facts about his (Sosia's) life he also receives *argumenta*, verbal proofs, that support the physical evidence before him. So Sosia tries rather desperately to respond in kind by relying on material evidence. He asks Mercury what reward Amphitryon was given for his battles. His double can even tell him this supposedly private piece of information: a golden bowl, which is hidden in a box, sealed with a *signum* or seal. This word means both a personal seal, a signature and a 'sign', and a token of a distinctive identity. It's an important word in the play, since a little while before this Mercury has told the audience that he can be differentiated from the real Sosia by a *signum*, a sign in his cap. But can we believe our senses? Do *signa* really tell the truth or show us who is who? When the real Amphitryon and Sosia look in the sealed box a little later on they find that, despite the unbroken *signum* or seal, the bowl has vanished. The *signum*, the material sign of ownership, identity, and even of truth, does not in fact testify to the truth. The whole series of events is described as a *mirum*, a wonderful, amazing thing, or a miracle, in which the gods turn upside-down the normal criteria for judging argument and evidence.

Shakespeare knew this play. He knew that Plautine comedy could represent moments where signs and arguments do not contribute to an earthy material certainty, but generate wonders, where the normal rules of evidence and proof break down, and can carry a person's sense of identity down with them. The traditional view is that Shakespeare read a worldly materialistic Roman comedy and brought to it the sophisticated scepticism of a Renaissance reader. This is not quite right. Plautine comedy repeatedly suggests that a combination of material evidence and argument can create wonders, or illusions, or even crises in personal identity. Shakespeare did not simply impose these imaginary marvels on Roman comedy. He found them there, and developed them.

## Terence

Terence was, like Plautus, 'antique' by the standards of classical Latin, since he too lived more than a century before Virgil (c.195–159 BC). He left behind six plays, which, like those of Plautus, were based on Greek New Comedies. Terence was consciously more 'polite' than raucous Plautus, and his plays are less varied in setting, mood, and theme than the work of the earlier dramatist, although their plots are typically more complex. Where Plautus's clever slaves often seem to resemble onstage playwrights or directors, who create plots and untie social tangles, Terence's equivalent slaves often seem to be fighting against a whole set of multiple plots which they can't fully control.[4] It's generally said that Terence had less influence on Shakespeare than Plautus. That's certainly true if 'influence' is limited to precise echoes of phrasing and details of plot. But Terence's complex plots, in which subplots and main plots struggle against each other, had a far stronger influence on the way that Shakespeare structured plays than any of Plautus's dramas, and Terence's favoured form of dramatized prologues, in which one character quizzes another about the circumstances which led to the action of the play, also shapes Shakespeare's opening moves, particularly in the later part of his career: in *The Tempest* 1.2 Prospero prompts Miranda to inquire further about his brother's treachery so that he can provide a distinctly Terentine dialogic prologue.

Shakespeare's acquaintance with Terence went back a long way. His plays featured in grammar-school curricula up and down the country because they were regarded as models of pure, colloquial Latin. The seventeenth-century writer on education Charles Hoole declared that a student ought to 'read Terence over and over, and to observe all the difficulties of grammar that he meets in him, and after he is once master of his style he will be pretty well able for any Latin book, of which I allow him to take his choice'.[5] Terence was a particular favourite among humanists: Desiderius Erasmus was reputed to have learned all of Terence's six plays by heart, and declared in his *De Ratione Studii* (1512): 'Again, among Latin writers who is more valuable as a standard of language than Terence? He is pure, concise, and closest to everyday speech and then, by the very nature of his subject-matter, is also congenial to the young.'[6] Terence was not just pleasing but also useful to schoolboys. Nicholas Udall's florilegium *Flowers for Latin Speaking Gathered out of Terence* included memorable sayings from Terence printed with English translations. It was reprinted five times between 1533 and 1581, and was typical of a much wider European tendency to extract memorable or useful phrases from classical drama. Udall's aim was to enable his pupils to *speak* Latin, and for this purpose Roman comedy was without doubt the most useful of all classical sources, since it has a wider range of colloquial registers than any other body of classical texts. Old men tend to be lugubrious or abruptly irascible, while slaves are sharp and abusive. Young men meet each other in the street, curse themselves or others, and frenziedly negotiate to win their lovers. And of course characters in plays tend to use the first person, which means that a beginner in Latin can simply repeat their words without bothering to change the person or number of Terence's verbs. In one of the most popular school textbooks of the period, the dialogues of Corderius (Maturin Cordier), pupils are described as hankering after a gilded new edition of Terence on which they lavish 10d.[7] This may be an educationalist's fantasy, but Terence was valuable: his 'hey you's, 'I just died's, his 'omygod's provided excellent models for a genuinely useful day-to-day Latin speech. As Gabriel Harvey put it when he attacked Thomas Nashe's learning in 1593, 'What peasant cannot say to a glorious soldier *Pulchre mehercule dictum, & sapienter*?'[8] That is, according to the notorious pedant Harvey at least, everyone knew the little piece of ironical flattery 'finely and wisely put, by Jove' from Terence's *Eunuchus* (416). The Pelian groves, Hyrcanian tigers, and rhetorical ornaments of tragic drama and epic poetry might be useful for orators composing funerary laments or florid addresses to monarchs on public occasions. But for buying a drink or negotiating in the playground under your master's eye, Terence was your man. Udall's *Flowers* includes phrases like 'In good sooth I know not what you mean'—a good phrase to use on a master who insists on deploying difficult Latin vocabulary—as well as the borderline profanity of 'God and all the saints in heaven give that old churl a mischief,' which one could well imagine being muttered from the back rows of a Tudor classroom. Sometimes pieces of wickedness slip under the radar even of the compilers of phrasebooks (and John Higgins, who expanded the *Flowers* to include all six plays of Terence, seems to have been more tolerant of sexually explicit material than Udall): 'credo abductum in ganeum | aliquo' (*Adelphoe*, 359–60) comes out loud and clear as 'I believe he is carried somewhither away into the brothel house, or stews.'[9] Lines like 'leno ego sum' ('I am a pimp', *Adelphoe*, 161) are perhaps unsurprisingly omitted—despite, presumably, having their uses for a certain type of reader.

This meant that Terence was one of the most 'contemporary' of ancient writers for Shakespeare and his fellow dramatists. He was part of how you learnt to speak. He was also built deep into the critical foundations of early-modern drama. Terence's plays were often printed in editions which include prefatory discussions about the structure and moral value of comedy. Anyone in the sixteenth century who wanted to know about how comic plays on classical models should be constructed would have looked first at editions of Terence by Erasmus, Melanchthon, Iodochus Willichius, and others.

There they would find, as well as sophisticated discussions of Terence's metre, detailed discussion of how he constructed plots. The commentators explained how to tie up a 'knot' of comedy through successive phases, and how to untangle it in a final scene. Aelius Donatus's commentary from the fourth century AD usually provides the skeleton to which later commentators added further flesh. Often they analysed the plays rhetorically as processes of accumulating proofs in support of a particular outcome or point of view, and often they interspersed these analyses with moral observations:

> The prologue is, as it were, the preface to the fable ... The *protasis* is the first act and the beginning of the drama; the *epitasis* the increase and progression of the agitation, and, as one might say, of the whole knot of errors; the *catastrophe* is the reversing of affairs toward a happy ending, a recognition having laid open all the action.[10]

The commentaries on Terence were the early-modern equivalent of a writer's guide to plot construction.[11] As a result the influence of Terence on Renaissance dramatic theory can scarcely be overstated. He also had a major influence on how early-modern playwrights thought about their own work in other ways. Terence's plays are unique among ancient drama for including self-defensive prologues. These state that he practised what he calls *contaminatio*; that is, he combined the plots of several Greek plays together in order to make his own. His prologues also say that he was accused of plagiarism, or *furtum* (theft), by a rival playwright, who was identified by Donatus as Luscius Lanuvinus. Terence therefore provided early-modern readers with a model for how a playwright might relate to his sources (eclectically) and to his contemporaries (aggressively). He also established a rough-and-ready template for relationships between an aspiring learned playwright and his audience, since he frequently complains that he has to compete for his spectators' attention against the attractions of jugglers, tightrope walkers, and other lowbrow forms of entertainment. He presents the playwright not as an isolated artist, but as a figure within a wider social and theatrical landscape, with rivals and debts, who does battle with a variety of noises off, ranging from musicians to critics.

This side of Terence had an incalculable influence on Ben Jonson—who emulated Terence's literary-critical prologues as well as adapting his concerns with plagiarism and theatrical rivalry when he constructed his own self-representations as 'the author' of his plays. But we should not exclude Shakespeare from the 'Terentine' style of theatrical authorship which Jonson was developing so energetically from the late 1590s onwards. Shakespeare's theatrical practice was often indirectly inspired by rivalry with and emulation of his contemporaries.[12] And he, accused in one of the earliest printed references to him of being 'an upstart crow beautified with our feathers',[13] knew all too well that a playwright could be accused of plagiarism. He would have read Terence, that is, not just for words and scenes, but for tips on how to be a playwright: how to make plots, work with sources, crush rivals.

I have emphasized the structural and foundational role of Terence within early-modern educational and theatrical practice for a reason. As we have seen, allusions to Ovid and Virgil in the first half (roughly) of Shakespeare's career are often in a variety of ways 'framed' in order to make it clear that they are allusions. The influence of classical comedy is quite different. Roman comedy provides Shakespeare with a set of conventions, structures, conversational rhythms, scenic ideas, methods, and themes for variation. It shapes almost everything, but rarely appears above the surface. It may even have provided a stimulus to the development of a fully vernacular style. Terence's drama looks on the page very like Shakespearian drama: its metre is mostly unshowy iambic trimeters, lines of which look on the page roughly similar to blank verse. Its linguistic texture feels Shakespearian: characters of different sexes and from different social groups are given quite distinct tricks of style and favour distinct grammatical forms. This feature of the plays was noted by Donatus, whose notes were widely reprinted in Renaissance editions, and was reiterated by the playwright Francis Beaumont in his preface to the 1598 edition of Geoffrey Chaucer's *Works*, where he defends Chaucer by comparing him to Plautus and Terence, who, he said, aimed through their demotic language 'to show the wantonness of some young women: the looseness of many young men: the crafty school-points of old bawds: the fawning flatteries of clawing parasites'.[14] Plautus and Terence were of course not the only places from which Shakespeare and his contemporaries could have got the idea that theatrical dialogue can be relaxed, that slaves and senior citizens can converse in their own distinctive registers and seek to get the better of each other conversationally, or that high tragic misery could meet with a lowbrow and tonally disjunct response. But Terence in particular was probably the *first* place in which Shakespeare would have encountered these possibilities. Terence could be said, paradoxically, to have been the greatest classical precedent for writing fully vernacular drama.

## *The Comedy of Errors*

If these distant parallels, influences, and filaments of learning and inspiration do not convince, let us turn instead to consider some strong and instantly visible parallels between a Roman comedy and the early Shakespearian play *The Comedy of Errors*. This play was performed at Gray's Inn during the Christmas revels of 1594, and may have been written for this occasion. It is based on the *Menaechmi* ('The Menaechmus Twins') of Plautus, though it takes some elements from the *Amphitryon* too. According to the traditional view of Shakespeare's play, its elite performance venue more or less inevitably went along with a stiffly classical manner: Shakespeare and most of his highly educated audience of lawyers at Gray's Inn would have read Plautus's play at school (and curiously the play includes a walk-on part for someone described in the stage directions as a 'schoolmaster' called Pinch, who is asked to diagnose the supposed madness of Antipholus of Ephesus: it is as though there was something inescapably schooly for Shakespeare about Plautine comedy). Its position within Shakespeare's career and its place of performance explain why it is so instantly recognizable as a 'classical' play: young Shakespeare, perhaps fresh from the success of the Latinate *Lucrece* and with a second edition of the Ovidian *Venus and Adonis* just out, was showing off to an audience of smartly Latinate young men. It has often been noted that Shakespeare doubles up the single set of twins in Plautus's *Menaechmi* to provide twin servants too, that he hybridizes the play with scenes and themes from another of Plautus's disguise and doubling plays, the *Amphitryon*, and that he multiplies the number of 'errors' in his sources.[15] It is also often and truly said that Shakespeare adds to the play's Plautine elements a large dash of Greek prose romance (voguish in the early 1590s) by supplying shipwrecks and seascapes just offstage. There are other ways in which the play learnedly contaminates the *Menaechmi* with other classical works. Egeon's long initial speech, which tells how one of his sons called Antipholus was lost at sea, adds a number of Virgilian echoes to a speech which is recognizably a narrative prologue of the kind frequently found in the plays of Plautus in particular, which is hybridized with the more dialogic 'prologues' of Terence. These transformations of Plautus, oddly enough, show how much *technique* Shakespeare had learned from Terence: the doubled plot, in which not one set of twins (as in Plautus's play) but two sets of twins are mistaken for each other is not just invented for the fun of it, but to make Plautus seem more like Terence, whose plays regularly have two sets of lovers. *The Comedy of Errors* is a consciously Terentine *contaminatio*, which mingles the plot of the *Menaechmi* with scenes and themes from Plautus's *Amphitryon*.[16] Shakespeare was trained at school to think not just about the words he read, but about the processes by which classical authors composed texts. He learnt to imitate those processes as much as their outcomes, and as a result could think of a classical author not as a static body of texts but as a set of practices and potentialities. In *The Comedy of Errors* it is almost as if Shakespeare had asked 'what would Terence have done with this play by Plautus?'

*The Comedy of Errors* is sometimes regarded as an early and therefore inflexibly classical play. This is not fair on the play, although its 'classicism' has become something of a self-perpetuating myth. Editions of the play tend to feed back the belief that *Errors* is a deeply classical comedy into the way in which they present the text. So the first Folio of 1623 (which prints the only extant version of the play) quite consistently refers to the place visited by the father of the Antipholus twins as 'Epidamium'. This (non-existent) place-name is emended in the single-volume Oxford edition to 'Epidamnus', which is the setting of Plautus's *Menaechmi*. (The editors of the Oxford *Complete Works* favour Alexander Pope's equally classicizing form 'Epidamnum'.) These emendations may correct a compositor's mistake (although it is a completely consistent mistake, if that's what it is), but they are also a sign that editors are determined to shift this play out of a not-quite Plautine world into one which is fully classical. Editors also routinely classicize the stagecraft of *The Comedy of Errors* in order to bring out its Latin genealogy. It's likely that in 1594 the play was put on in the hall at Gray's Inn, which has a line of screen doors at one end. Editors have often suggested that it adapts the conventions of classical comedy to this setting, and that, as in a classical comedy, characters come and go through these different doors into different houses, the interiors of which remain offstage throughout.[17] Both the Oxford *Collected Works* and the freestanding Oxford single-volume edition are again particularly keen to Latinize in this way: they often augment the simple exits and entrances given in the Folio text by adding 'to the Phoenix' or 'from the Centaur', which associates each of the supposed 'doors' off with particular locations. This implies an excessively rigid conception of both Shakespearian stagecraft and of how 'classical' stagecraft was understood in the sixteenth century. Editions of the Roman comedians did indeed sometimes include illustrations which had the doors used on the classical stage as background scenery, but Shakespeare could have known other rather more flexible models of classical scene setting (see Illustration 4). Thomas Goodwin in 1614 described the Roman theatre as having a 'house, whence the players came', but he also says 'that they might change their scene according to their pleasure, they made it either *versatilem*, so that with engines it might upon the sudden be turned round, and so bring the pictures of the other side into outward appearance: or otherwise *ductilem*, so that by the drawing aside of some wainscot shuttles (which before did hide the inward painting) a new partition might seem to be put up'.[18]

A less mechanized version of that scenic fluidity is apparent in *The Comedy of Errors*. It contains a much higher proportion of street scenes than most later Shakespearian plays, but (as with all Shakespearian drama) 'setting' is largely constructed by action and speech, and can shift even within a single period of onstage action in response to changing content and mood. The scenic conventions of 'antiquity' even in this play are less like a rigid language which determines the practice of stagecraft than a slightly foreign accent which comes and goes as social circumstances allow. That is, the presence of a Roman comedy underneath the Elizabethan comedy does not mean that always and in all circumstances characters enter through doors to particular houses. Instead Roman theatrical conventions operate when the particular nature of a scene allows. So when men are

**Illustration 4.** Sosia and Mercury appear in the *Amphitryon* against a classicizing background which suggests the doors used for entries and exits.

Codrington Library, All Souls College Oxford, shelf mark f.infra.1.10: *Marci Actii <sic> Plauti Linguae Latinae Principis: Comoediae*, ed. Lucas Olchinensis (Venice, 1518), sig. a7r. Reproduced by kind permission of the Warden and Fellows of All Souls College, Oxford.

onstage conversing together, the stagecraft has the feel of classical drama, as each character goes on or off to a house or to the 'mart' (market). Scenes involving intimate exchanges between women, however, tend to bring with them scene-setting cues which are far less clear, far less 'Roman', and far less unambiguously outdoor. So Adriana and Luciana have a conversation in 2.1 which the Oxford Shakespeare introduces in good classical fashion as a street scene: they are said to 'Enter from the Phoenix' at the start of the scene and 'Exeunt into the Phoenix' at the end. In the Folio text they are said simply to 'enter' and 'exit'. Since Antipholus's wife Adriana is waiting for her husband to return home, it would indeed be possible to play the scene as one in which the two women come out of the door of their house in order to look impatiently up and down the street. But the repeated references in 2.1 to Antipholus coming 'home' suggests that Shakespeare is, as it were, un-Romanly opening the doors to reveal a domestic interior. Throughout the scene the opposition between men and women is presented as a contrast between women who stay at home and men who go out: 'Why should their liberty than ours be more?' asks Adriana; and Luciana replies: 'Because their business still lies out o' door' (2.1.10–11). And as Adriana regretfully says, 'His company must do his minions grace, | Whilst I at home starve for a merry look' (2.1.86–7). These remarks could make sense in an 'outside' space, as the women, tired of waiting within, break out of the boundaries of the house. But this ignores the unclassical power of the scene, which implicitly constructs an 'inside' zone in which women patiently wait. We should not simply assume that stagecraft in *Errors* is 'Roman' because it is principally based on a Latin play. Shakespeare becomes more or less Roman in his stagecraft according to the gender of the speakers and according to the subject of conversation.

In the sixteenth century it was quite natural to associate women with interior spaces, since in that period married women often ran complex domestic economies based in the family home.[19] That feature of sixteenth-century English domestic life interacted powerfully with Roman comedy in *Errors*. In Plautus and Terence, as we have seen, offstage interior spaces, and offstage female characters, can have a great influence over the course of the play. In *The Comedy of Errors* that association between powerful women and offstage spaces can be developed almost to the point of parody. In 3.1, Shakespeare constructs a scene not from the *Menaechmi* but from Plautus's *Amphitryon*, in which the hero Amphitryon is shut out from his house by Jove and Mercury, who have assumed his identity and that of his slave in order to seduce his wife. In *Errors*, Antipholus and Dromio of Ephesus attempt to get into their own house, where Antipholus of Syracuse is having dinner with Adriana. As the men lay siege to the house, the Roman association between offstage interiors and femininity spawns a whole legion of women who otherwise do not appear at all in Shakespeare's play. The men outside shout for 'Maud, Bridget, Marian, Cicely, Gillian, Ginn!' (3.1.31), while another woman called (in the Folio) 'Luce' shouts from within. Later in the play 'Luce' (or perhaps another servingwoman who lives in the offstage interior) is renamed Nell. Later still Luce/Nell, or possibly yet another woman, is called Dowsabel. There is nothing specifically Roman about any of these aggressively English-sounding women. Their social class is from a classical perspective just plain wrong: women who remain offstage in Roman comedy tend to be *virgines*, unmarried women, or pregnant *matronae*, rather than slave girls. The extraordinary multiplicity of these offstage servants may simply be a sign that Shakespeare never finally decided on a name for his (one) offstage servant girl, or it could indicate that Shakespeare couldn't afford to waste his small number of boy players on bit-part servants, and so made a joke of this limitation by multiplying female offstage presences. Yet these offstage women 'within' are likely to be far more than just a slip of the pen or the product of theatrical convenience: they have their origin in Roman comedy and its association of women with interior and offstage spaces.

Stagecraft, then, is sometimes 'antique' and sometimes 'modern', and is usually a hybrid of the two in *The Comedy of Errors*. But even when it's at its most 'modern' and English, the play seems to be borrowing and multiplying energy from its Roman original. *Errors* shows the dialectical vigour that resulted from Shakespeare's attempt to present an 'ancient' play in modern dress. Roman comedy sought to represent 'Greek' behaviour on the Roman stage in ways that confused Roman and Greek behaviour. In *The Comedy of Errors*, 'antique' and modern social relationships sometimes converge and sometimes pull against each other in a similar way. This runs through the language of the play as well as its stagecraft, where again the relative strength of 'Roman' customs and contemporary English practices is dependent on occasion and circumstance. The Dromio twins are the bondmen and servants of the twin Antipholuses, but they are sometimes described as 'slaves'. This Roman-sounding word is exclusively used in conversational contexts where it could function as a term of abuse rather than as a formal description of social status. Calling someone 'slave' in the sense 'worthless scumbag' was not uncommon in early-modern English: Prince Harry in the English setting of *1 Henry IV* calls Falstaff (who is of course a knight) a 'slave' for hacking his sword and lying about who has assailed him. The Dromios become 'slaves' when characters are angry enough with them to call them that. Antipholus of Syracuse says: 'I'll to the Centaur to go seek this slave' (1.2.104) when he fears that Dromio has run off with his money. Adriana says to Dromio: 'Go back again, thou slave, and fetch him home' (2.1.74) when she believes Dromio has failed to seek out her husband. This is typical of Shakespeare's partially estranging not-quite-anachronisms: in an Anglo-Graeco-Roman drama, 'slave' is used when it makes sense in English usage, but with a faint underpresence, for those who want to hear it, of an ancient social relationship beneath.

*The Comedy of Errors* is about what happens when one person is substituted for another identical one. It is also a play with a deeper kind of substitutive logic, which determines how the actions and preoccupations of the *Menaechmi* are transformed to suit new times and a new playing environment. Plautus's play is grounded in a number of social practices which were very different from their early-modern English equivalents. At its centre is Menaechmus of Epidamnus's wife, who is a married woman with a dowry ('*uxor dotata*'). This was a stock type of powerful woman on the Roman stage, and their power derived from the fact that Roman women generally brought to their marriage a dowry given by their fathers, which could revert to the woman and to her family if the marriage were dissolved.[20] That gave them a degree of control over their husbands. There was no obvious sixteenth-century English equivalent for this economic and social relationship, since for Shakespeare and his contemporaries the property of women became that of their husband at marriage. Part of the process of transforming *Menaechmi* into *The Comedy of Errors* required the invention of a substitute for the straightforwardly economic power of the dowried woman in Roman comedy. This required not verbal imitation but cultural substitution. At this relatively early point in his career Shakespeare had to develop imaginative and analogical habits that could enable the successful cultural and theatrical adaptation of a classical play. He needed to make the actions and emotions of a classical drama plausible for an English audience, even if social customs were not quite the same. Simply removing the economic power of Menaechmus's wife would create a void or a zone of inexplicability in the plot: why is the husband quite so alienated? What kind of strength does his wife have to draw him back home? It's possible that Plautus himself wrestled with a similar kind of cultural translation when he wrote his own play. His lost source may have been founded on Greek conventions about marriage which were slightly different from their Roman equivalents. Greek women could not inherit a household, so if a Greek householder had a daughter he might adopt a young man as his son, and marry that adopted son to his daughter so that he would avoid the dissolution of his household after his death.[21] Fathers therefore might effectively bribe young men to marry their daughters, who might then feel bound, and inferior, to their wives. Since the source play of *Menaechmi* does not survive, we can't be sure that it represented the Greek equivalent of an arranged marriage; but it's likely that Plautus could not quite 'translate' a Greek marital practice into a Roman equivalent, and that at least some of the blank brutality of his married Menaechmus derives from this origin. Plautus, that is, probably preserved the behaviour that was the consequence of a Greek marital custom, without explicitly preserving the custom that gave rise to it.

Shakespeare would not have known about Plautus's difficulty, if, indeed, that is what it was; but he does seem to have felt that something was wanting, or that something needed changing, in the relationship between husband and wife in his original. A simple dramatist would have settled for making the wife of Antipholus of Ephesus a straightforward shrew or scold, and would have used that to explain why her husband treats her so high-handedly. Shakespeare did not do that. One of the main differences between *The Comedy of Errors* and the *Menaechmi* is the extreme articulacy and strength of Adriana, Antipholus's wife. Strong women are not unusual in Shakespeare, of course: his Venus is an ultra-articulate classical goddess, and Kate in *The Taming of the Shrew* certainly has a tongue, even if she finally uses it to declare her submission. We saw in the first chapter that articulate women figured strongly in Shakespeare's early education in the classics. But Adriana is something different. She may be adapted from the loyal Alcmena in the *Amphitryon*.[22] But she is also a Shakespearian invention, designed to make up for the absent convention of the *uxor dotata*. When Adriana sees what she believes is her husband (just after the 'interior' scene between her and her sister which is so 'unclassical' in its setting), she rebukes him with a power that comes not from her economic influence over him but from her highly elevated conception of marriage as a kind of incorporation:

> How comes it now, my husband, O how comes it
> That thou art then estrangèd from thyself?—

Thy 'self' I call it, being strange to me
That, undividable, incorporate,
Am better than thy dear self 's better part.
Ah, do not tear away thyself from me;
For know, my love, as easy mayst thou fall
A drop of water in the breaking gulf,
And take unmingled thence that drop again
Without addition or diminishing,
As take from me thyself, and not me too. (2.2.122–32)

This is great writing: 'fall' (128) works as a transitive verb ('let fall') as well as an intransitive verb, in which Antipholus becomes himself a water drop, lost in the undividing waves. But at a higher level it is astonishingly transformative writing. Plautus's wife has no equivalent speech. Plautus does briefly compare the two twins to identical drops of milk (*Menaechmi*, 1089–90; cf. *Amphitryon*, 601), but here the drops blend into the corporate union of marriage. A drop cannot be separated from the flood any more than Adriana can be separated from her husband. Adriana is not the Romano-Greek wife who wields domestic power because of her dowry: she articulates a notion of companionate marriage so powerful that it makes husband and wife the same self. This is an example not so much of Shakespeare learning from the classics, as of what could be called transformative substitution: Shakespeare was able to construct such a powerful alternative to his source because he recognized in it an alien social convention for which he had to make an alternative strong enough to fill the void it would leave when he removed it. The strong married women of Shakespeare's later plays—Desdemona, Innogen, perhaps even Cleopatra (although she is not technically married to Antony)—take part of their origin from this extraordinary act of transformative substitution early in Shakespeare's career.

## Tragicomedy

Shakespeare is often said to have been particularly 'unclassical' in his treatment of theatrical genres. He wrote tragicomedies, and he also wrote tragedies which contain comedy and comedies which blur over towards tragedy. As we have seen, only one play from the classical world describes itself as a 'tragicomoedia', and that is *Amphitryon* (59,

63), the play which Shakespeare hybridized with *Menaechmi* in *The Comedy of Errors*. The vernacular roots of formal tragicomedy lie in Giovanni Battista Guarini's *Il Pastor Fido* ('The Faithful Shepherd', 1590), and Shakespeare's adaptation of this form in the later romances is a subject in its own right.[23] Certainly the self-conscious illusionism of the classical comedians fed into both *Il Pastor Fido* and Shakespeare's romances. But in this section I would like to explore something slightly different. How was it that, well before he wrote *The Tempest* or *The Winter's Tale*, Shakespeare could take comic scenarios and conventions, and make them turn dark and near-tragic? How in particular could he write a play like *Othello*, that begins in Venice with a set of nocturnal confusions, an angry father, and an eloping couple, and which seems initially to be close in mood and setting to a classical comedy, but which ends with murder, rage, and darkness?

Obviously this is a huge question, to which Shakespeare's classical reading can only provide a partial answer. But we have seen that the classical comedians repeatedly raise questions about what people know and how they know it, and about the relationship between personal identity and belief. They also show people making inferences on the basis of partial or incorrect knowledge, which can lead them to act in a particular way. I shall suggest in this section that Shakespeare responded to these aspects of classical comedy in a way which enabled him to move from comedy to tragedy—and to occupy spaces between tragedy and comedy—far more readily than any surviving author from the classical period, and perhaps also far more convincingly than any other English dramatist. Again his debts are not a matter of verbal reminiscence. They go deep into the intellectual foundations of his art.

The best place to begin this large task is by saying a little more about the role of inference and belief in classical comedy, and probably the best way to do that is to discuss Terence's early play called the *Andria* (The Woman from Andros). It is not certain that Shakespeare read this play (though it usually appeared first in editions of Terence), but it does show very clearly some of the recurrent features of New Comedy on which he drew. The basic story is a fairly representative plot for a *fabula palliata*. A young man called Pamphilus has a mistress called Glycerium whom he wants to marry, against the wishes of his father. The father tries to arrange an alternative marriage for his son, but the proposed father-in-law will have none of it, since Pamphilus is a known philanderer. The father nonetheless pretends to continue with the preparations for the wedding in order to force his son to disobey him openly or to persuade him to change his mind. Towards the start of the play, Davus, the irrepressible slave, relates that the two lovers are attempting to make up a story to deceive Pamphilus's father Simo about the social origins of his mistress Glycerium. Davus does not think much of this fictional cover story, and he describes it in this way:

'fuit olim quidam senex
mercator. navem is fregit apud Andrum insulam.
is obiit mortem.' ibi tum hanc eiectam Chrysidis
patrem recepisse orbam parvam. fabulae!
miquidem hercle non fit veri simile. (221–5)

'Once upon a time there was some old merchant guy. He wrecked his ship on the isle of Andros. He snuffs it.' There Chrysis's father adopted the orphaned baby girl. Stories—fables I call them. Lord, they just don't have the idea of verisimilitude.

This is in all sorts of ways a joke. Davus the slave has a sophisticated conception of what fiction is and of what is lifelike, or 'verisimilar', as he says. This is itself deliberately un-verisimilar, because Davus the slave is incongruously using a literary term of art. The story he relates is a clichéd version of a romance plot of the kind which was the staple of Greek New Comedy, and indeed of Greek romances. Naturally enough, at the end of the play this fictional story, which even a slave can see is not remotely verisimilar, turns out in fact to be the plot of the play itself. We discover that Glycerium *was* in fact shipwrecked, and is the daughter of a wealthy Athenian nobleman. All ends like an old tale, or like a bad lie. The disillusioned perspective of the slave and the illusion-making structures of the play work together to create a story which is highly self-conscious about its own fictionality. The implausible becomes plausible because we see it being enacted before our eyes. This has a whiff of *Twelfth Night* to it, but also of the self-conscious illusion-making through illusion-breaking voiced by the second Gentleman at the end of *The Winter's Tale*:

The oracle is fulfilled. The King's daughter is found. Such a deal of wonder is broken out within this hour, that ballad-makers cannot be able to express it . . . This news which is called true is so like an old tale that the verity of it is in strong suspicion. Has the King found his heir? (5.2.22–9)

That self-consciousness about theatricality and illusion is deeply engrained in Terence's dramaturgy. And it is part of his much wider concern with the relationship between illusion and belief. Terence often makes his characters question the truth of what they are seeing. So, again in *Andria*, the father Simo finds himself outside the house in which his son's mistress Glycerium is (genuinely within the fiction of the play) giving birth to his illegitimate grandson. The slave Davus is with Simo and assumes that he will discover the truth, and the game will be up. Simo, however, believes that the timing of the offstage birth, just on the eve of his son's supposed wedding, is too good to be true. He assumes that it's an act put on by Davus to trick him into cancelling the marriage. He 'errs'—he assumes the birth is just a piece of theatre (which of course in one sense it is, although the audience is supposed to believe that the baby is real). And of course his doubt here depends upon the nature of the Roman stage, in which, as we've seen, any event which occurs inside the doors has to be 'performed' to those onstage through more or less clumsy and conventional stage effects—and in which the offstage scream of a woman giving birth was a tried and tested convention.

Shakespeare in various senses takes Roman comedy inside. As we have already seen, he takes us into domestic interiors even in the highly classical *Comedy of Errors*. But he also goes inside metaphorically. He works his way inside the illusion-building of Terence's characters. They live in a world of inference and belief rather than certainty. The *senex* Simo, overhearing the supposed (actual) birth of his son's bastard is not sure whose story he should believe. He has a lot of what look like facts in front of him (screams offstage as of a birth), and a lot of what seem like acts and stories which don't quite seem to fit the facts. He knows that Davus is a slave, and so likely to be a liar. Davus rapidly works out that it's better if Simo continues to believe that the baby is not real, so attempts to persuade him to see it all as a fiction. He says that Simo has to make inferences from a variety of different pieces of information: 'many things converge at the same time which now form this conjecture', he says ('multa concurrunt simul | qui coniecturam hanc nunc facio', 512–13). Davus, that is, encourages Simo to act not on the basis of what he knows, but on the basis of probabilities and conjectures—which turn out to be false.

The notion that people live and act on the basis of conjecture rather than certainty was crucial to Shakespeare, to Shakespearian comedy, to Shakespearian tragedy, and in particular to Shakespeare's ability to move through a realm between tragedy and comedy. It did not simply come to him from Roman comedy, but through a filter of legal, rhetorical, logical, and theatrical traditions that would take us well beyond the scope of this study to explore, although fortunately they have been the subject of a range of impressive studies.[24] But Roman comedy—in which characters make conjectures and act on the basis of those suppositions, and are perhaps fooled while doing so—was at the very root of it. And in the uncategorizable 'dark' comedies of Shakespeare's mid career the notion that people live and act on the basis of probabilities and conjectures began to play a role in the structure and texture of Shakespeare's dramaturgy and psychology. *Troilus and Cressida* is perhaps the clearest example. In Chapter 1 (pp. 25–7) it was suggested that in writing this elaborate *contaminatio* of a wide range of sources Shakespeare may have thought and read again about ideas of literary imitation. *Troilus* is also famously hard to pin down to a single genre. Probably as a result of a bibliographical accident it was slipped in late to the first Folio, and so sits in an anomalous position just after the Histories and just at the start of the Tragedies. It is not quite a comedy and not quite a tragedy and not quite a history either. It is also a play full of doubt and belief, supposition and inference, suspicion and disillusion, which occupies exactly the hinterland between the comic thinking of Plautus and Terence and a world of tragedy.

*Troilus* derives from many sources, but Plautus and Terence play a much larger part in the genesis of the play than has generally been appreciated. In Plautus's *Miles Gloriosus* ('The Braggart Soldier') a slave sees the mistress of the braggart Pyrgopolynices kissing her former lover. He is tricked into believing that the woman he saw was in fact the mistress's twin sister. The mistress (called Philocomasium) is later presented to him in different dress and pretends to be her own sister. She relates a dream that she was falsely accused of a crime, and that her sister was really to blame: 'I seemed pleased to have my sister come, but because of her I seemed to be subjected to a dreadful suspicion' ('ego laeta uisa, quia soror uenisset, propter eandem | suspicionem maxumam sum uisa sustinere', 387–8). The poor slave Sceledrus, who has witnessed his master's mistress kissing another man, doesn't know what he has seen: 'I didn't see her and yet I did see her,' he declares ('non uidi eam, etsi uidi', 407), and then a little later, as the girl manages to switch roles and scuttle from one house to another with impossible speed, he says 'etsi ea est, non est ea' (532), 'this is and is not her'. In Plautus the mistress performs a physical act of deception, which involves disguises and characters moving through holes in the wall between two houses, but it has psychological consequences. Who did the slave see? What are the grounds for believing your senses, when you hear a story that conflicts with what they show you?

Shorn of these material tricks, this episode was foundational to one of the great moments of Shakespearian jealous suspicion. In *Troilus and Cressida*, Cressida is handed over to the Greeks, and her lover the Trojan hero Troilus witnesses her kissing the Greek Diomed. He is a witness who can't believe what he sees. There are no twins here to save the appearances. She is the same woman that a few hours before had sworn to love him.

> If there be rule in unity itself,
> This is not she. O madness of discourse,
> That cause sets up with and against thyself!
> Bifold authority, where reason can revolt
> Without perdition, and loss assume all reason
> Without revolt! This is and is not Cressid. (5.2.144–9)

This is and is not Plautus, too. There is no simple 'source' for these lines in *Miles Gloriosus*: the poor slave makes no long, grand speeches. He simply complains briefly that what he has seen doesn't appear to be what he thought he saw. He is not the idealistic and deceivable Troilus, and he has no direct emotional connection with the infidelity which he thought he witnessed. But Shakespeare turned the physical trickery in Plautus into a psychological crisis in which what Troilus sees and what he wants to believe are completely at odds with each other. Plautus's 'etsi ea est, non est ea', this is and is not her, becomes a perceptual crisis in which Troilus experiences several realities at once: one is grounded in the visible fact of Cressida's infidelity, and the other depends on his belief in her truth.

It is very probable that Plautus, or a transformed memory of Plautus, lies behind this moment—though the world of literary genetics, like that of comedy, is one driven by probabilities rather than certainties. The probability is increased by the fact that *Miles Gloriosus* was one of the most widely read and imitated classical dramas. It is also increased by the fact that *Troilus and Cressida* is repeatedly concerned with mock-heroical braggadocchio. The main character of *Miles Gloriosus*, Pyrgopolynices (whose name means something like 'Conqueror of many fortresses', but might also suggest 'Many burning conflicts'), is a braggart soldier surrounded by flatterers. He regards himself as a new Achilles, and the memory of Homer's hero struts repeatedly through the play as a means of deflating Pyrgopolynices. At one point he is persuaded that his neighbour's wife wants to sleep with him, and is urged on by her maid with 'Go on, my Achilles, grant my prayer; graciously rescue that graceful girl, express your benevolent nature, you capturer of towns, you killer of kings' ('age, mi Achilles, fuat quod te oro, serua illam pulchram pulchre, | exprome benignum ex te ingenium, urbicape, occisor regum', 1054–5). The braggart is flattered into thinking of himself as a hero. In *Troilus and Cressida* 2.3 Ajax (who is rather dim and very vain) is persuaded by his fellow Greeks that he is superior to Achilles: 'You are as strong, as valiant, as wise, no less noble, much more gentle, and altogether more tractable' (2.3.147–9), says Agamemnon. Meanwhile Achilles himself is overwhelmed by his own imagination of his excellence:

> Imagined worth
> Holds in his blood such swoll'n and hot discourse
> That 'twixt his mental and his active parts
> Kingdomed Achilles in commotion rages
> And batters 'gainst himself. (2.3.170–4)

It is not just that even the real Greek heroes become braggarts in this play. It's more that everyone has beliefs about themselves which don't quite fit what anyone, including the audience, actually sees: worth becomes almost inseparable from 'imagined worth'. Shakespeare massively extends the pride of Plautus's braggart soldier, transforming physical deception and simple flattery into a more or less universal condition of mental deception and self-persuasion, a state of mind which also shapes the desires and the behaviour of the lovers in the play.

The uneasy alternation between belief and experience, and between acts of persuasion and truth, was an absolutely central feature not just of Shakespeare's response to Roman drama, but of Shakespeare full stop. And his interest in how people could be persuaded to believe things that contradict the physical realities before them had a profound consequence. It was one of the major reasons why, throughout his career, Shakespeare could put such creative pressure on the generic division between tragedy and comedy. If mental illusion, suspicion, and conjecture are substituted for the physical acts of deception which prevail in Roman comedy, and if people create their own realities out of beliefs and desires which may not be true, then comic confusions become something potentially threatening to the whole way in which a person perceives the world. Cressida kissing Diomed is not Cressida's twin or Cressida pretending to be Cressida's twin. She is Cressida. The person who loves her has to try to adjust his beliefs and inferences and suppositions about her in order to accommodate both what he sees and what he wants to believe. Troilus ends up tortured in a double reality which goes far beyond anything in classical comedy. He participates indeed in a kind of tragedy of misperception which has its roots in Plautus and Terence, but which seems to be pushing far beyond any kind of comic resolution.

How does this lead Shakespeare to blur the classical division between comedy and tragedy? The reason is straightforward. Shakespeare was encouraged by his reading in classical comedy to think of human agents as forming beliefs and performing actions on the basis of conjecture and probability rather than certain knowledge. He was also encouraged by those same comic plays to think that human characters occupied a world that was partially invented through illusion—either as a result of what they themselves want to believe or as a result of what others want them to believe. This enabled him to see the potential for tragedy within a comic plot. Imagine a scenario in which a bluff soldier (he doesn't have to be a braggart for the story to work, but he could be) believes that his wife loves him. He holds this belief on reasonable but not certain grounds. Then an insinuating 'slave' or lower-class character, who perhaps is not loyal to him, draws attention to the fragile foundations of his belief, and tells him stories, drops little pieces of evidence before him. Imagine this soldier being led from one kind of probable belief (that his wife loves him) to another (that his wife is sleeping with someone else). This kind of inferential chain, in which belief becomes doubt, and doubt leads on to a kind of proof which falls tragically short of certainty, but which can nonetheless serve as a sufficient foundation for action, underlies the plot of *Othello*. That play moves from a first act (substantially invented by Shakespeare) which is set unmistakably in the realm of Roman comedy, in which deluded fathers bumble around at night trying to find out what their daughters are up to, and which is studded with references to probability and belief (''Tis probable, and palpable to thinking', 1.2.77, declares the *senex* Brabanzio), to a final climax of shattering violence. *Othello* builds magnificently on Shakespeare's introduction of domestic interiors to Roman comedy in *The Comedy of Errors*: it takes us inside houses and even inside bedchambers. It also takes the habitual concern of Roman comedy with inference and uncertainty right inside the mind of its hero. For Othello is a person who cannot live with suspicion:

> Think'st thou I'd make a life of jealousy,
> To follow still the changes of the moon
> With fresh suspicions? No, to be once in doubt
> Is once to be resolved.
> . . . . .
> No, Iago,
> I'll see before I doubt; when I doubt, prove;
> And on the proof, there is no more but this:
> Away at once with love or jealousy. (3.3.181–96)

This is almost a confession that Othello cannot live in a Shakespearian play, or that one way or another he will refuse to live in a classical comedy, with its blurred distinctions between physical evidence, belief, persuasion, and illusion. That does not mean that Othello is simply a braggart soldier or that he is too noble for the world he inhabits, as traditional arguments about the play would have it. The roots of this tragedy lie in Roman comedy and in its thinking about belief and inference. Othello wants a degree of certainty which is incompatible with comedy as written by Plautus and Terence and as explored by Shakespeare in the years leading up to the composition of this play in around 1604. Iago is consequently not in any simply moralized way a devilish trickster. His role is chiefly to pull Othello into the realm of inference and uncertainty and to await the consequences. In his reply to Othello's declaration that he'll see before he doubts, Iago says 'I speak not yet of proof' (3.3.200):

> I am to pray you not to strain my speech
> To grosser issues, nor to larger reach
> Than to suspicion. (3.3.222–4)

That is a killing suggestion: it implies that a desire for evidence and proof is 'gross'—and that particular word is repeatedly associated in the play both with certain knowledge and with sexual defilement. Through its first usage, when Roderigo talks of Desdemona in the 'gross clasps of a lascivious Moor' (1.1.128), making a 'gross revolt' (1.1.136), it also carries a taint of racial slur. When Othello insists on 'the ocular proof' (3.3.365), Iago drives home his suggestion that being able to live with suspicion is far more sophisticated, far more Venetian, and that a desire for knowledge is by comparison 'gross' and carnal: 'Would you, the supervisor, grossly gape on, | Behold her topped?' (3.3.400–1). He insists that it is 'imputation, and strong circumstances' rather than gross knowledge 'Which lead directly to the door of truth' (3.3.411–12). Like the slave in Terence's *Andria*, he persuades Othello that 'many things converge at the same time which now form this conjecture' ('multa concurrunt simul | qui coniecturam hanc nunc facio', 512–13). By the end of the scene, Iago's attempt to turn 'imputation and strong circumstance' into the foundation of knowledge and action has worked on Othello; and he, a man who cannot live with less than certainty, declares himself a violent force of nature:

> Never, Iago. Like to the Pontic Sea,
> Whose icy current and compulsive course
> Ne'er knows retiring ebb, but keeps due on

> To the Propontic and the Hellespont,
> Even so my bloody thoughts with violent pace
> Shall ne'er look back, ne'er ebb to humble love,
> Till that a capable and wide revenge
> Swallow them up. (3.3.456–63)

There are no doubts here, no contingencies. Othello's rhetoric just rushes forward: the Pontic swells in sound into the Pro*ponti*c, and into the Helles*pont*, just as his thoughts flow onwards towards vengeful certainty. The language of this speech surges beyond anything in classical comedy, just as the whole play turns the fragile trickster plots of Roman comedy hinted at by its opening into psychological horror. With a violence which is generic as much as personal, *Othello* drags its audience from its classically 'comic' opening street scenes, and takes them inside—not just into the house, that domestic space pushed to the wings in Roman comedy, but into the very bedroom of Desdemona—and on into the realm of tragedy.

Francis Meres blandly described Shakespeare as 'the most excellent in both kinds for the stage' in 1598. He wrote those words half a dozen or so years before *Othello* was composed. He could not have anticipated the violence and originality of this play, which propels its audience inside the house and inside the mind, away from the material confusions of classical comedy and towards the rhetoric and violent actions of Senecan tragedy. But Shakespeare's interest in the plausible and probable in classical comedy enabled him to make that great generic leap, from one world into another. He would, however, not have been able to represent the agony or the violence of Othello if he had not read Seneca as well as Plautus and Terence. And it is to that other great classical influence on Shakespearian drama that we turn next.

# 5

# *Seneca*

When the travelling players arrive at Elsinore, Polonius praises their versatility by saying that for them 'Seneca cannot be too heavy, nor Plautus too light' (*Hamlet*, 2.2.400–1). Could Shakespeare have shared the ponderous Polonius's admiration for 'heavy' Seneca as well as for 'light' Plautus? Several scholars in the past thought not. T. W. Baldwin claimed that Seneca's tragedies rarely figured in the curricula of early-modern grammar schools, and concluded that if Shakespeare was aware of them at all it was via intermediaries.[1] Baldwin, though, had a tendency to suppose that the reading life began and ended in school, and so was likely to believe that if Shakespeare hadn't read Seneca by the time he was fourteen, then Seneca could not have mattered much to him. Repeatedly scholars have sought out precise verbal parallels between Seneca and Shakespeare, and repeatedly other scholars have found these thin and unconvincing.[2] Others have found deep and pervasive influences.[3] Where does the truth lie?

There is an overwhelmingly strong *prima facie* case that Shakespeare read and was influenced by Seneca. He was the only surviving classical tragedian whom Shakespeare could have read comfortably in the original language, and Shakespeare would have been mad not to have done so. Seneca was *the* high-status model for drama in the formative years of the English professional stage, and playwrights who influenced Shakespeare at the start of his career—Kyd, Marlowe, Peele—not only read but showed their audiences that they had read Senecan tragedy. Shakespeare was in touch with fashion, and he wanted to win and retain a place among the leading dramatists of his age, most of whom had university degrees as he did not. Not to have read Seneca at this point in his career would have been like (to use a gory Senecan metaphor) chopping off one of his own hands.

Nonetheless, Baldwin's scepticism lives on. The most recent editors of Seneca's *Phaedra* declare that 'Seneca was for the most part a remote influence on Shakespeare,'[4] while editors of Shakespeare's plays—pushed by fashion into attaching more weight to the performance history of Shakespearian drama than to its origins—have been astonishingly reluctant to discuss Seneca in their introductions, or to record even evident and well-established parallels in their notes. This obscures from view not only a vital element of the origins of Shakespearian drama, but also, often, a crucial component of theatrical meaning, since, as we shall see, allusions to Seneca—even 'remote' ones—can often contribute to the overall force of a line or a scene, or even of a whole play.

The clichéd view of Senecan drama used to be that it is declamatory, overblown, rhetorical, and relentless, and is stuffed with stuffy *sententiae*, or generalized moral maxims. Combine that view with an equally wrong view of Shakespeare, deeply entrenched in the critical tradition since at least the later eighteenth century, that he was a poet of native fluency, whose receptiveness to life was matched only by his endlessly creative desire to warble his native woodnotes wild, then it is not surprising that so many people have believed Shakespeare did not owe much to Seneca, the jumped-up son of a late-imperial rhetorician, who, moreover, acted as tutor and advisor to the tyrannical emperor Nero. Somewhere not very deep in the anti-Seneca prejudice lies a genteelly poisonous and deeply Whiggish national complacency: for many anti-Senecans, 'native' traditions (mystery plays, moralities), and the native freedoms of the imagination, mattered to Shakespeare more than the bastard offspring of Augustan Rome. Even T. S. Eliot in his largely sympathetic account of Senecan tragedy—which was indeed one of the turning points in the appreciation of Seneca's plays—represented it as sharing the general vices of later Roman imperial writing, which were of course quite un-English and embedded in an alien 'race'.[5]

A widespread reappraisal of later Latin writing has raised Seneca's stock today. But how was he regarded in sixteenth-century England? Seneca was widely read and admired by young and old alike in this period. Jasper Heywood described his translation of Seneca's *Hercules Furens* as done 'for the profit of young scholars so faithfully translated into English metre, that ye may see verse for verse turned as far as the phrase of the English permitteth'.[6] That is, the translation provided a crib for students, whether at university (Heywood was a Fellow of All Souls College, Oxford, where, rumour has it, they have no need of cribs) or at school. Despite the existence of these accessible translations, it's possible that many English readers in the sixteenth century did not read Seneca's plays as wholes, but rather came upon his *disiecta membra*, his plays in pieces. Charles Hoole, writing of grammar-school education in the later seventeenth century, seems to have had in mind a very selective survey of Seneca's tragedies for his pupils: 'As for Lucan, Seneca's tragedies, Martial, and the rest of the finest Latin poets, you may do well to give them a taste of each, and show them how and wherein they may imitate them, or borrow something out of them.'[7] The choruses of Seneca's tragedies seem to have provided such a 'taste' for those who wanted to 'borrow something out of them'. In the extremely popular miscellany of poems (called *Songs and Sonnets*) from the early sixteenth century published by Richard Tottel in 1557, there are two translations or paraphrases of choruses from Seneca, one by Thomas Wyatt, and another by an unknown author.[8] Seneca's choruses are among the finest meditative and lyric poetry from the later Roman empire, and often include general reflections which are detachable from their dramatic setting. This made them favourite translation exercises for classicizing poets in the sixteenth century, as well as, quite probably, for schoolchildren. English translators certainly were at their freest when they worked on the choruses: Jasper Heywood, who added an entire soliloquy to the *Thyestes*, also added a chorus to the *Troas*, while John Studley made big alterations to the first chorus in *Medea* when he translated it. If, as some scholars believe, Senecan tragedy was originally designed to be performed in excerpts, there is additional reason for seeing these plays as intrinsically fragmentable, and as therefore prone to have had a fragmentary influence on those who read them.[9] Nonetheless, Seneca was available as a whole to English readers in the later sixteenth century. Jasper Heywood's translations were gathered together by Thomas Newton in 1581, along with the versions by John Studley and others, in a collected edition.

So Seneca was out there, valued, and available. What was his influence on Shakespeare? That influence was extensive but (as with Plautus and Terence) elusive. This is partly because Seneca was himself strongly influenced in theme and style by Ovid, who composed a lost drama about Medea which may well have influenced Seneca's own play of that name. Seneca also influenced Shakespeare's contemporaries, who in turn influenced Shakespeare. As a result it is often impossible, and probably undesirable, to try to unpick a Senecan thread from a radial web of other influences. *Titus Andronicus* is the best illustration of this. The climax of the play, in which Titus Andronicus serves up the children of Tamora in a pie, is close kin to the end of Seneca's *Thyestes*, in which Atreus dishes up the children of Thyestes to their father. Shakespeare's scene, however, takes rather more than hints and savours for its stew from Ovid's story of Tereus and Philomela, a story which in turn had influenced Seneca.[10] Seneca himself declared in his 84th Epistle that those who imitated works from the past should seek to resemble bees, flitting around and reading a number of sources, before finally digesting the savours of that reading into something all of their own ('concoquamus illa', we should 'digest' or 'cook up' our reading).[11] At the end of *Titus Andronicus* Shakespeare seems to have taken this advice literally: Ovid and Seneca are all part of an intertextual concoction. Earlier sections of the play also hit exactly the points of crossover between Seneca and Ovid. The rape of Lavinia occurs in a wood, around a hunt. That is just the landscape evoked at the opening of Seneca's *Hippolytus* (the play is generally called *Phaedra* today; sixteenth-century editions tended to call it by the name of its chaste huntsman hero rather than by that of his libidinous stepmother), when Hippolytus describes a morning hunt in a rural landscape. At the start of 2.2 Titus makes a much shorter speech to mark the start of a hunting scene ('The hunt is up, the morn is bright and grey, | The fields are fragrant and the woods are green', 2.2.1–2). Violence in a pastoral or a woodland landscape is, however, also a recurrent scenario in Ovid's *Metamorphoses*, inescapably sinister, almost always hinting at tragic outcomes.[12] The moods and moments when Seneca and Ovid were more or less indistinguishable were the ones which tended to catch Shakespeare's eye in both writers—when, as it were, they seem to be amplifying and reinforcing each other's preoccupations, and co-writing a classical scene. And the fact that Shakespeare first ventured into this area in a play which was itself probably a collaboration with George Peele makes it very difficult to be sure about agency or authorship here.[13] On the other hand there is no reason at all (apart from an anti-Senecan prejudice) to claim that all of these moments spring only from Ovid, or that Seneca meant little or nothing to Shakespeare. Shakespeare professionally melted sources together. It is impossible and undesirable to distil his fusion into single elements.

## Seneca the Philosopher

There are other reasons why listing parallels between passages of Shakespeare and bits of Seneca will not get to the heart of this rich relationship. Seneca was a philosopher as well as a playwright. In the Renaissance these two parts of his output were always printed separately, and sometimes were believed to be the work of different people. Seneca's philosophical works, often printed as his *Opera* ('Works'), were diffused into early-modern culture at a deep level. This was particularly true of the treatises *De Beneficiis* ('Concerning Benefits') and *De Clementia* ('Concerning Clemency'), both of which have a deep but indirect influence on Shakespeare as well as on most of his educated contemporaries. *De Beneficiis* is a treatise about gift-giving and gratitude, and argues that the attitude of mind displayed by the recipient of a gift matters more than any material return. Seneca's treatise addressed questions over which more or less every person in early-modern Europe would have puzzled on practically every day of their lives: how do we repay a patron, acknowledge a debt, or give due weight to a friendship, when we have no adequate material means to reciprocate those favours? For the client of a wealthy patron this was not just a recurrent practical problem, but more or less a state of being. How should children show gratitude to their parents? How should a servant express gratitude to a master? How can we measure a monetary return against an immaterial gift? And how should we respond to the infinite generosity of nature, and to the gift of our own being? These questions were vital for early-modern England (in which 'credit' connoted both 'high social status' and 'being the dispenser of favours', as well as our notion of 'creditworthiness'), and are of course central to a number of Shakespeare's plays—and particularly, as we shall see at the end of this chapter, to *King Lear* (*c*.1605).

Seneca was, however, principally known in the later sixteenth century as the most notable Roman expositor of Stoic thought. Stoicism was a complete philosophy, encompassing what are now called physics, geography, and cosmology, as well as ethics. The ethical components of Stoic thought were what most people in the Renaissance (as today) would have thought of as 'Stoicism'. Stoic ethics had as their goal life according to nature, which Stoic thinkers aligned with life according to reason. The passions should be mastered so that man (Stoic thought is quite emphatic that '*vir*tue' is about being a '*vir*', a man) can avoid unnecessarily subjecting himself to fortune. A '*vir virtutis*' (a man of virtue) stands constant, is firm and secure in himself, and controls passions within him so that he can avoid subjection to the world around him. Anger with those more powerful than yourself is pointless. It perturbs the reason, and it might also potentially destroy the self and the body too if the object of one's anger retaliates against it. If the man of virtue, or the ideal figure of the 'sage', was finally overwhelmed by Fortune and rendered unable to control his passions, he would rationally choose to kill himself in order to avoid subjecting himself to external events, achieving sovereignty over his own being even when he had lost control of his body and his fate.

Seneca's form of Stoicism was adapted to life in the later Roman Empire, and was related to his own experience as tutor and subsequently advisor to the Emperor Nero, whose reputation as a whimsical tyrant (though it has been questioned recently) was not undeserved.[14] Seneca himself committed suicide when he was implicated in a plot against the Emperor. His ethics have been described by Gordon Braden as advocating a form of self-government particularly well-suited to periods of absolutism: the sage seeks autarchy (self-rule) as a compensation for his lack of control over the political world.[15] His rage at unjust treatment or tyranny is partly checked out of prudence, though he may boil within against his oppressors.

This strand of Senecan philosophy probably reached Shakespeare in second-hand or even shorthand form: he is well aware of the traditional criticism of Stoics, that they are 'stocks' or lumps of wood, insensible to all passions, and echoes that traditional pun when Tranio in *The Taming of the Shrew* says 'Let's be no Stoics nor no stocks' (1.1.31). By the early seventeenth century he had also absorbed Montaigne's *Essays*, in which Stoic strands of thought are richly entangled with threads of epicureanism and scepticism, and weave in and out of Montaigne's 'frisks, skips and jumps' through his reading.[16] Shakespearian drama tends to focus on characters who are perplexed or overwhelmed by what they see or experience rather than on people who are in control of themselves and their passions. That does not mean that Shakespeare has no room for Stoic sages; it is rather that they tend to be for him foils to set off multifaceted heroes. Hamlet rather wistfully describes the broadly Stoic simplicity of his friend Horatio's ethical life:

> For thou hast been
> As one in suff'ring all that suffers nothing,
> A man that Fortune's buffets and rewards
> Hast ta'en with equal thanks; and blest are those
> Whose blood and judgment are so well commingled
> That they are not a pipe for Fortune's finger
> To sound what stop she please. Give me that man
> That is not passion's slave, and I will wear him
> In my heart's core, ay, in my heart of heart,
> As I do thee. Something too much of this. (3.2.63–72)

In *Antony and Cleopatra*, Pompey is presented as a similar conqueror of Fortune:

> Well, I know not
> What counts harsh fortune casts upon my face,
> But in my bosom shall she never come
> To make my heart her vassal. (2.6.53–6)

Pompey is shuffled to the margins of the play, outmanoeuvred by the political canniness of Octavius, upstaged by the fascinatingly mutable and infinitely desirable Cleopatra, while at the play's centre Antony makes his heart vassal to the Egyptian queen. Antony notably fails to be a Stoic Roman in his death, botching his attempt at suicide. Philosophical arguments seem generally to have meant most to Shakespeare when they infused situations with a number of conceptually incommensurable ways of thinking about them; but identifiable philosophical positions could also provide shorthand ways of characterizing a distinct point of view. 'Stoicism' provided Shakespeare with (to hazard a dreadful pun) a stock type of character, whose Roman virtue would express itself through his desire to order his passions or to control his fortune. The chief theatrical value of these 'philosophical' characters was to provide a clear background against which he could develop complex foreground characters who seem incapable of such moral simplicity.

## Tragic Seneca

Seneca's plays contain hardly any such 'Stoic' heroes, and stand in a complex relationship to Stoic philosophy. This is partly what makes them interesting today, and is also part of what made them interesting for Shakespeare. Ten plays comprise the traditional canon of Seneca the tragedian, and these are on subjects ranging from the mythological (*Medea*, *The Madness of Hercules*) to the topical. Even in the sixteenth century there were doubts about the canon of Seneca's plays and their authorship. Erasmus was sure that they were not all written by one man,[17] and in 1588 Justus Lipsius argued that they might have as many as four authors. For Lipsius (who was the greatest scholar of Stoicism in sixteenth-century Europe), only the *Medea* was the work of Lucius Annaeus Seneca the philosopher, while the historical play *Octavia* (in which Seneca himself appears) was written by an uncertain author.[18] The phrase 'Seneca's Tragedies' therefore covered a wide range of ground in this period: the plays were regarded as a diverse group, possibly by several authors. The inclusion of the *Octavia* within the canon meant that Seneca gave a clear classical precedent for writing historical dramas. This was the underlying reason why Shakespeare could people historical plays such as *Richard III* with characters who frequently sound like Seneca's heroes, although he was by no means the first playwright to treat English historical topics in a Senecan style.

Seneca's plays were in various respects 'ancient' so far as Shakespeare was concerned. Many of them (*Medea*, *Troades*, *Agamemnon*, *Hippolytus*) treated subjects which had already been dramatized by Greek tragedians from the fifth century. The actions of these plays were set in the very distant past, and often dramatized mythological acts of violence—Medea slaying her children in order to avenge herself on Jason, or Hercules being driven mad by the gods and slaughtering his children. This gave them the kind of 'mythological' antiquity which Shakespeare also found in Ovid: they relate, perhaps even release, a primary substrate of human savagery in historical settings which were ancient even for the Romans. Despite their mythological subject matter, though, Seneca's plays are often consciously 'late' in the style of their Latin. They frequently echo Ovid and (to a lesser extent) Virgil. Anyone who had read those authors would encounter so many echoes of their writing in Seneca's dramas that they might well feel that Seneca was a kind of epic poet of the stage, as well as a latecomer to the feast of ancient literature. Seneca's play the *Trojan Women* (*Troades*) takes this further. It is a deliberately and insistently post-heroic work, in which a younger generation of heroic characters are denied a chance to re-enact the heroic actions of their elders: Astyanax, the son of Hector, is cut off by death from emulating the deeds of his father, as though the play self-consciously presents a literary generation which can only remember rather than re-enact the deeds of their heroic ancestors. In the (pseudo-Senecan) *Octavia* the playwright himself appears as a character who is literally old. He is called from philosophical retirement to pummel philosophy into the wilful heart of the tyrannically inclined emperor Nero. Seneca the character describes the Rome of his present as having fallen away from its earlier republican virtue, and broadens his picture to represent the whole cosmos as senile, on the verge of an apocalyptic destruction from which a new world might be reborn:

> Qui si senescit, tantus in caecum chaos
> casurus iterum, nunc adest mundo dies
> supremus ille, qui premat genus impium
> caeli ruina, rursus ut stirpem novam
> generet renascens melior, ut quondam tulit
> iuvenis, tenente regna Saturno poli. (*Octavia*, 391–6)

If the heavens are getting old, and so great a thing is fated to fall again into blind chaos, now is the last day of the universe, which will crush this impious race under the falling sky. The result will be that a better world reborn will generate new offspring, as it once bore in its youth, when Saturn occupied the throne of heaven.

The doctrine here is broadly in harmony with Stoic cosmology, according to which the universe would periodically destroy itself—by fire, or in some versions of the theory by water—and be reborn to re-enact an identical cycle of history all over again. For a Renaissance author those lines would give great authority to Seneca as a sage who predicted the apocalypse, and the 'new heaven and a new earth' (*Revelations* 21.1) which would follow (and letters supposed to be from Seneca to St Paul were frequently printed among Seneca's works in the period). They would also have a particular charge for Seneca's Renaissance readers: the old man Seneca admits to his vision of terminal decline a renaissance, 'renascens melior', something better coming into being.[19] For Seneca's poetic successors those would be words of hope. Like Ovid, Seneca was a writer who seemed to talk to the future, who seemed to be inviting the resurrection and renewal of his own world. Even in the plays which are more securely part of the canon, Seneca is very self-conscious about his position within a literary tradition. At the end of the *Hippolytus* Theseus is left literally with the *disiecta membra* (1256), the torn limbs, of his son Hippolytus which he tries to piece together. The phrase is a conscious echo of Horace in his *Satires*, who had talked about the *disiecti membra poetae* (1.4.62), the limbs of a scattered poet: piecing together a classical tradition after its apparent death and destruction is a central part of Seneca's project, though he often pessimistically leaves his readers with ruins and torn limbs rather than with a full rebirth.[20]

The plays of Seneca the younger were 'old' for Shakespeare in other respects too. Most of the high-profile translations and all of the early adaptations of Seneca's plays in Elizabethan England were made by men associated with the Inns of Court in the 1560s, 1570s, and 1580s, and these provided the core of the collected volume of *Seneca's Ten Tragedies* put together by Thomas Newton in 1581. Unlike Cicero, or Homer, or Plutarch, or Ovid, or indeed Seneca's philosophical works (a complete translation of which by Thomas Lodge appeared in 1614), Seneca's dramas were not translated afresh at the very end of the sixteenth century or at the beginning of the seventeenth. Seneca in English was as a consequence, from the viewpoint of the late sixteenth-century vernacular reader, stylistically old-fashioned. Indeed, the earliest translators of Seneca seem to have used a style that would have sounded slightly 'antiqued' even at the time of their composition. Jasper Heywood added some stanzas to the second chorus of *Troades* which explicitly compare the play to Chaucer's 'double sorrow' of *Troilus* ('The double cares of Hector's wife to wail, | Good ladies, have your tears in readiness'),[21] and throughout his translation he echoes the neo-medieval idiom of *The Mirror for Magistrates*. And yet Heywood clearly also thought of his revival of Seneca as a modish and modern affair. In his prologue to the translation of *Thyestes* (1560) he explains to Seneca himself (who appears to the translator in a vision) that 'In Lincoln's Inn and Temples twain, Gray's Inn and other mo, | Thou shalt them find whose painful pen thy verse shall flourish so, | That Melpomen thou wouldst well ween had taught them for to write.'[22] He declares that Thomas Norton, Thomas Sackville, and Christopher Yelverton's works will bring about Seneca's rebirth 'as Pallas was, of mighty Jove his brain'. Heywood's Seneca is therefore a curious being: he is set for modish rebirth, but he is also presented as a literary antiquity. The translator goes on to describe a volume containing the true text of Seneca's plays as an illuminated manuscript, written on vellum, which has escaped the ravages of time and of printers' errors which he complains have beset his own works: 'These leaves that fine as velvet feel, and parchment-like in sight, | Of feat [elegant] fine fawns they are the skins, such as no mortal wight | May come unto' (sig. X4r). In Heywood's fantasy, Seneca becomes a medieval manuscript the contents of which could be reborn by the activities of a small clique of writers in the Inns of Court. He was old, but ripe for renewal.

By 1590 the idiom used by these early translators of Seneca would have certainly sounded as though it came from a different world. Their thickly alliterative style, with long fourteeners and awkward rhymes would have marked the English Seneca as belonging to the landscape of the 1560s and 1570s rather than that of the 1590s. It is no surprise that Thomas Nashe should have insisted on the hackneyed character of English Seneca in 1589:

> English Seneca read by candlelight yields many good sentences, as 'blood is a beggar', and so forth; and if you entreat him fair in a frosty morning, he will afford you whole *Hamlets*, I should say handfuls, of tragical speeches. But O grief! *Tempus edax rerum* [Time the consumer of things], what's that will last always? The sea exhaled by drops will in continuance be dry, and Seneca,

let blood line by line and page by page, at length must needs die to our stage; which makes his famished followers imitate the Kid in *Aesop*, who, enamoured with the Fox's newfangledness, forsook all hopes of life to leap into a new occupation . . .[23]

Nashe made his living by being slightly ahead of literary fashion, and where he was not ahead of fashion he had a habit of making it look as though he was. This he usually did by exaggerating his own modernity and by overstating the outmodedness of everyone else. As a result, writers in the 1590s under thirty tended to listen to Nashe as they listened to no one else, since he sounded like the voice of the future. Seneca, English or otherwise, was in actual fact not out of fashion by this date, since he remained a continuing influence on Thomas Kyd (on whose name Nashe knowingly plays) and Christopher Marlowe. But Nashe makes something negative out of what was to Heywood something positive: English Seneca was *old*. In that respect he was entirely in tune with Shakespeare's desire to renovate Senecan drama in a more thoroughgoing way than any of his predecessors or contemporaries had attempted.

## Old *Hamlet*

Nashe's old-fashioned Senecan ghosts stalk the stage of Shakespeare's *Hamlet*, which was written in about 1599. Shakespeare's play was probably based in some way on the drama to which Nashe had taken exception around a decade before. The existence of an earlier 'Senecan' treatment of the Hamlet story, even though it does not survive, is a significant clue to understanding Shakespeare's play. Shakespeare's *Hamlet* is a densely historical work, not in the sense that it is embedded in *fin de siècle* England and its politics, or because it is about history, but in its deeply layered allusions to different kinds of past. There are of course fictional pasts to which the play looks back—to the time when Hamlet's father was alive, to the time young Hamlet sported with Yorick, to the more questionable and recent past of his father's death. But the play also registers literary pasts. And that is partly because it was probably a kind of remake. One aspect of its literary past is the English Senecan tragedy which the play probably 'modernizes'. In Shakespeare's *Hamlet* an 'ancient' bloodiness is a little out of date, theatrically speaking: it belongs to the generation of drama just before Shakespeare, and it is enacted by resolute and relatively simple characters on the edges of the play, like Fortinbras or Laertes. But that ancient kind of heroism is also attractive to the hero as something real because it is archaic. A simple 'Senecan' style of bloody revenge in *Hamlet* is at once a temptation and a kind of delusion. 'If only I could be like Medea or Atreus' is part of Hamlet's ambition; and part of Hamlet's problem is that in his particular circumstances, surrounded by courtly elegances, with a head stuffed full of fashionable ideas (you feel he would certainly have read Nashe), he can't simply re-enact a Senecan past. Repeatedly he uses Senecan pastiche to stand in for murder, or as a method of self-persuasion. He has good ancient precedent for this. At the start of *Thyestes* Atreus berates himself for failing to kill his brother:

> Ignave, iners, enervis et (quod maximum
> probrum tyranno rebus in summis reor)
> inulte, post tot scelera, post fratris dolos
> fasque omne ruptum questibus vanis agis
> iratus Atreus? fremere iam totus tuis
> debebat armis orbis, et geminum mare
> utrimque classes agere; iam flammis agros
> lucere et urbes decuit, ac strictum undique
> micare ferrum. (*Thyestes*, 176–84)

Lazy, useless, gutless, and (what I think is the worst failing in a tyrant who is dealing with the most important matters of all) unavenged! Angry Atreus, after so many crimes, after your brother's trickery and the violation of all good principles, are you just whining on with vain complaints? Now the whole world should thunder with your weapons, and fleets should be setting sail from both shores of the twin sea; now the fields ought to be alight with flames and the cities too, and the drawn sword should flash on all sides.

Shakespeare offers a quizzical and sceptical variation on this theme, in which he transforms the first speech of the most violent avenger in the entire Senecan canon into—a speech...

> O, what a rogue and peasant slave am I!
> .....
> Why, what an ass am I? Ay, sure, this is most brave,
> That I, the son of the dear murderèd,

> Prompted to my revenge by heaven and hell,
> Must, like a whore, unpack my heart with words
> And fall a-cursing like a very drab,
> A scullion! Fie upon't, foh! (2.2.551–89)

This soliloquy, of course, occurs at one of the most self-consciously classical moments (as well as one of the most self-consciously theatrical moments) in the entire play, just after the First Player has recited his speech on the death of Priam and the grief of Hecuba (see pp. 62–71 above), and a few stage moments after old Polonius has said that Seneca could not be too 'heavy' for the actors. The allusion to Atreus would to many in Shakespeare's audience have been absolutely unmissable. Many of the 'wiser sort', whom Gabriel Harvey said *Hamlet* pleased, would have underlined Atreus's speech at school, and probably a few of them had it by heart.[24] The 'modern' transformation of the Senecan speech would also have seemed insinuatingly audacious. Hamlet and Shakespeare are both in their different ways critical readers of Seneca. They recognize that a Senecan revenge plot begins not with actions, but with a string of modal verbs: in Atreus's speech ships *ought* to sail, fires *ought* to crackle through fields and cities. And yet they don't. Shakespeare's play has a seam of satire in it (and satire deriving from classical origins was one of the most exciting and innovative genres in the late 1590s), some of which is probably directed against earlier Elizabethan Senecan heroes who talk big and act bloody; but it is also animated by an extremely acute reading of Seneca himself, whose high rhetoric so often is subjunctive, imperative, or optative, and as a result often seems to usurp actuality and indeed action. In *Hamlet* Shakespeare took up these rhetorical features of Seneca's plays and ran with them—or perhaps it's better to say that he crawled with them, since he used Seneca's habitually subjunctive rhetoric to create a hero who infamously and repeatedly stalls on his journey to revenge, unpacking his heart with words which seem to suggest that he thinks *alluding* to Atreus is a sufficient substitute for actual revenge.

Learned Hamlet is haunted not just by the ghost under the stage, but by a whole range of classical actions and modes of speech which threaten to absorb him, and which keep on coming out of his mouth sounding like allusions to earlier works or parodies of them:

> 'Tis now the very witching time of night,
> When churchyards yawn, and hell itself breathes out
> Contagion to this world. Now could I drink hot blood,
> And do such bitter business as the day
> Would quake to look on. Soft, now to my mother.
> O heart, lose not thy nature! Let not ever
> The soul of Nero enter this firm bosom. (3.2.377–83)

This is a rhetorical exercise known as 'chronographia' or a formal description of a time of day. It is done in a *grand guignol* manner by Hamlet, who has his moments of being a little ham. At the motivational level, however, the speech is a piece of self-persuasion to act: the implied logic of this moment runs 'I will describe the night in this way; that will make an atmosphere which is sympathetic to dark and murderous deeds; I will then be able to do those dark deeds.' Having rehearsed this Senecan performance, replete with modal verbs which make it quite clear that the actions he proposes are only hypothetical ('could . . . would'), what does Hamlet do?

Nothing. Or rather he proceeds to give his mother a really tough talking to. The Senecan moment is marked by the reference to Nero and by that cosily neo-Stoic phrase 'this firm bosom': marble-constant like his Stoic friend Horatio, Hamlet will emulate Seneca the philosopher and be a model of tranquillity, rather than raging with the heroes of Seneca's tragedies. Killing is so difficult for Hamlet because to perform his murder he will have to become a Senecan tyrant like Atreus rather than a reflective would-be neo-Stoic heir to the throne who is not quite an heir to the throne. In this stagey piece of Senecanism the cosmic atmosphere for killing is created rhetorically rather than being generated by the action of the hero, and the result is a rhetoric of dark deeds which is detached from actually performing them. Doing, setting out to kill Claudius, becomes not just 'acting' in the sense of performing a deed; it becomes a Senecan performance, a matter of acting the villain, drawing on the energies of Senecan heroes and their rhetorical mannerisms, and perhaps finally being absorbed and overwhelmed by them. Hamlet is not just trying to be like 'old Hamlet', to live up to his father: he is trying to be and to sound old, theatrically. His 'antic disposition' is madness, but the words 'antic' and 'antique' are not fully separated from each other in Shakespeare's English. A process of stylistic recreation of an 'antique' style becomes in turn its own end, distracting the hero from performing the act for which he adopted this stylistic mask in the first place. The modernity of Hamlet the hero—who makes the comparatively simple desire for vengeance of Laertes or young Fortinbras seem to belong to a different century—is dependent on his awareness of 'antiquity', of earlier styles of English drama and of the idiom of a wide palate of Senecan drama, and on his brilliance as a stylistic mimic. His inaction is partly the consequence of his troubled and hybrid inheritance from classical and native Senecanism.

## The Play's the Thing: Seneca's *Hippolytus*

One reason why Seneca the dramatist was such a valuable resource for playwrights was that his writing could be mined for purple patches and fine phrases. He is famous for his *sententiae*, phrases which conveyed a moral truth or falsehood in a sharply epigrammatic style. Nashe's example in the Preface to *Menaphon*, 'Blood is a beggar', illustrates the style of these maxims. Often alliterative, and often shaped by rhetorical figures which emphasize the symmetry of the thought, Senecan *sententiae* are a gift to people who want to sound learned, and to the compilers of printed phrasebooks which could stock the minds of fashionable young men with clever-sounding things to say. A reader could cut Seneca up, indeed make him bleed to death, Nashe suggests, by slicing whole handfuls or whole *Hamlets* of these phrases out of his texts for reuse in their own.

Senecan drama certainly was presented in Renaissance editions in digestible chunks, divided up into five acts, with separate choruses, and with *sententiae* sometimes marked in the margins for easy recall. But there is another aspect of Senecan tragedy which was equally important for Shakespeare and his contemporaries. Seneca provided the clearest example of poetic drama, in which action and metaphor, and perhaps a substrate of philosophical and metaphysical thinking, cooperate to create plays which not only hang together, but which knit together mental experiences, material catastrophes, rhetorical mood, and metaphorical structures. They are as a result simultaneously plays which can be shattered into fragments by an eclectic imitator and works which could be read as unified dramas of the mind from which readers could learn how to write plays which have the texture and overall coherence of single poems.

Seneca's *Hippolytus* is the best play in relation to which to explore this aspect of his work, and from which to gain a sense of Shakespeare's response to it. *Hippolytus* displays the almost suffocating unity of imagery and theme, and indeed of past and present, in much Senecan drama. It also had a deeper and more sustained influence on Shakespeare than any other play by Seneca, and perhaps than any other play by any author. The *Hippolytus* is haunted by a beastly mythic past. Phaedra's mother Pasiphae had, long before the play begins, loved a bull in a union which produced the minotaur. Theseus defeated the minotaur, escaped from the labyrinth, abandoned Ariadne, and married Minos's daughter Phaedra. Before the play begins, Theseus has gone to rescue Persephone from the underworld. In the meantime his wife Phaedra is overwhelmed by a frenzied desire (called *furor*) for her son-in-law Hippolytus. He is an obsessive hunter, whose devotion to Diana, the chaste goddess of the hunt, leads him to despise women. Phaedra persuades her nurse to proposition Hippolytus, which she does in general terms, reminding him that the world will die in one generation unless people breed. Phaedra herself then attempts a more direct approach. Hippolytus rejects his mother-in-law's advances in horror. Theseus then returns from the underworld, and Phaedra, out of a desire for vengeance and self-protection, suggests that Hippolytus has raped her. Theseus appeals to his father Neptune, god of the sea, to punish his son. A beast, bull-like and raging, emerges from the waters to destroy Hippolytus, who is torn limb from limb as his horses flee in panic (see Illustration 5).

This sounds extremely unlike any play by Shakespeare. Bulls from the sea do not rip people apart in Shakespearian tragedy. But the superficial differences conceal deeper affinities. At every stage of Seneca's *Hippolytus* there are allusions to the sea, and to water. Repeatedly the language of the drama dwells on the bestiality of passion, as though the house of Minos is haunted by an earlier generation of bullish lust. The climactic destruction of Hippolytus by a sea-beast-bull (a moment of destruction which, like many climaxes in Senecan drama, is related by a messenger) reads like the final pulling together of the past and of the deep undercurrents of the play's imagery: the sea, the bull, the raging elements all converge at

**Illustration 5.** *Metamorphoses*, Book XV: The bull rises from the sea and Hippolytus crashes in the background.

Codrington Library, All Souls College, Oxford, shelf mark b. infra.1.22: *Ovid's Metamorphosis Englished, Mythologized, and Represented in Figures*, trans. George Sandys (London, 1632), facing p. 491. Reproduced by kind permission of the Warden and Fellows of All Souls College, Oxford.

the moment of destruction, in which the hero's physical body is shattered into pieces:

> haec dum stupentes quaerimus, totum en mare
> immugit, omnes undique scopuli astrepunt,
> tumidumque monstro pelagus in terras ruit.
> summum cacumen rorat expulso sale,
> spumat vomitque vicibus alternis aquas,
> qualis per alta vehitur Oceani freta
> fluctum refundens ore physeter capax.
> inhorruit concussus undarum globus
> solvitque sese et litori invexit malum
> maius timore; pontus in terras ruit
> suumque monstrum sequitur. (*Hippolytus*, 1025–34)

While we were agape asking these questions, behold the whole sea moos like a bull, and all the rocks and waves roared too; swelling with a monster the sea rushes towards the land. The topmost peak bursts with breaking foam, boiling and spewing out alternately, as a powerful sperm-whale carried through the high seas of the ocean blows out of its mouth the wave it has swallowed. The sphere of waves bristled as it was struck, burst and bore to the shore an evil beyond fear. The sea rushes onto the land, chasing its own monster.

This is phantasmagorically vivid: the bellowing moo ('immugit' is a word that could be used of cattle as well as of the booming of waves) of the ocean builds into a simile which compares the action of the sea with that of a genuine sea-monster, a huge sperm whale. The waves finally burst into a fully formed sea-bull, a monster which embodies both the terror of the elements and awful memories of the house of Minos. Sea and myth are united in a single poetic fable and texture.

Critics sometimes ascribe the connectedness of elements in Senecan drama—passions reverberate with the world, the 'literal' reality seems to refract the mental reality of the characters—to Stoic cosmology.[25] There is one particular element of that cosmology which does seem to have influenced the way Seneca constructed his plays, and that is the doctrine termed *sumpatheia*. According to Stoic physics all aspects of the universe, from man to beast through waves and stars, are animated by a single *pneuma* or spirit, which made the cosmos a unity akin to that of an animate being.[26] The origins of this doctrine probably lay in the work of Chrysippus (although the fragmentary nature of the surviving early Stoic texts makes this uncertain), and the doctrine itself underwent significant transformation in the eclectic, and on the whole not philosophically rigorous, work of Roman Stoics. The unity of the Stoic cosmos meant that for many Stoics when one element in the universe stretches or deforms, the rest of the world connectedly deforms. As a result, a personal passion might cause a reverberation in the cosmos. The interconnectedness of objects and beings in Stoic thought extends through time as well as space, through a complex system of causes. That means a past event can connectedly cause a predetermined subsequent event.[27]

This vision of the cosmos is a powerful heuristic tool for the analysis of Seneca's plays, and has played a strong part in the critical re-evaluation of his work. It gives a cosmic resonance to human emotion: as man or woman rages, so the world might vibrate in sympathy. It also gives a philosophical underpinning to the metaphorical relationships between human passions and the elements, or between human self-destruction and the destruction of the cosmos, which are such a frequent element in the climaxes of Senecan drama. With a little metaphorical stretching it might also explain the powerful impression created by Seneca's plays of unity between imagery and action and of a close relationship between the past and present: the mythical stories of Pasiphae's love for a bull tug at the present action in *Hippolytus*, as it were, shaping the figure of the climactic destructive bull-wave out of the watery element of the sea.[28] The concept of *sumpatheia* and Stoic cosmology more generally can also help to explain how Seneca *Philosophus*, the author of Stoic works advocating a life in which human beings attempt to follow reason and thereby free themselves from fortune, could also be Seneca *Tragicus*, the author of tragic dramas in which the universe seems to bend and buckle as heroes and heroines boil with fury or desire. Life in harmony with nature is the Stoic end of living; but Senecan drama shows how that ideal when put under pressure pulls at the self and the world at once.

This bold attempt to unify the Senecan canon and Senecan drama by invoking the concept of *sumpatheia* can, however, be a little too tidy. It does not take full account of the rhetoric of the plays, or, more precisely, of the ways that Seneca's rhetorical methods and preferences cut against his presumed Stoic cosmology. Again and again in

Seneca's drama the universe is not simply represented as reverberating to the strains of human passion, nor do cosmic or natural forces simply act as natural means of amplifying human passions. Generally heroes and heroines have to force *sumpatheia* on the world. They urge, beg, curse, order that the cosmos will in fact reflect their emotions, as Atreus did in the speech to which Hamlet alludes. After Phaedra discovers that Hippolytus has been killed, she cries out:

> Me me, profundi saeve dominator freti,
> invade, et in me monstra caerulei maris
> emitte, quidquid intimo Tethys sinu
> extrema gestat, quidquid Oceanus vagis
> complexus undis ultimo fluctu tegit. (*Hippolytus*, 1159–63)

Assault me, me not him, you savage overlord of the deep waters, and send out the monsters of the sky-blue sea against me, whatever terrible things Tethys hides in her inmost recess, and whatever the Ocean embraces with its wandering ways and hides in its most distant currents.

The language of this speech is blended almost obsessively into the texture of the play and its climax, with sea-monsters, deep undercurrents, and hideous punishments. It is in perfect 'sympathy', we might say, with the action of the play. But what Phaedra asks for does not happen. The hyperbolic, hyper-intense language is tragically separated from any causal connection with the universal forces which she calls down upon herself: as Thomas Rosenmeyer puts it, 'The vast bulk of imperatives in Seneca are not practicable orders or requests urged upon plausible executors, but "rhetorical" imperatives, that is, imaginary, inoperable, and channelled toward levels of authority unresponsive to the speaker's wishes.'[29] Senecan heroes and heroines can indeed sometimes appear merely to 'unpack their hearts with words' rather than to control the universe or even successfully shape a plot which follows their own wishes.

It is worth staying with the single example of *Hippolytus* to see whether and how these aspects of Senecan drama influenced Shakespeare, because this play stayed with him throughout his career. The persistence of its influence makes the old claim that Shakespeare took his Seneca from second-hand sources and *florilegia* look extremely improbable. Traditional source-study, of the kind that lists direct allusions, tended to group parallels between Seneca and Shakespeare according to Shakespeare's plays rather than Seneca's—so we are given lists by Cunliffe of incidental connections and relationships between, say, *Macbeth* and a range of sections from Seneca's plays. This approach feeds the view that Seneca's influence on Shakespeare was shallow and sporadic, rather than deep and continuous, because it makes it look as though he simply flitted from play to play as he wrote, culling a thought here and a phrase there from different Senecan plays. The example of *Hippolytus* suggests something different. There are two quotations from Seneca in Latin in *Titus Andronicus*. Both of these are from *Hippolytus*, although both occur in sections of the play which have been ascribed to George Peele. Titus says: '*Magni dominator poli,* | *Tam lentus audis scelera, tam lentus vides?*'—'O ruler of the great heaven, how can you be so slow to hear crimes, so slow to see them?' (4.1.81–2). The language of this fuses together *Hippolytus* 671–2 with a passage from Seneca's *Epistulae Morales* 107.11 in a way that may well reflect an attempt to remember or reproduce a Senecan commonplace that was learnt at school or found in a handbook. There is another quotation in Latin from the same play, when the wicked Demetrius exits with '*Per Styga, per manes vehor*' ('I am dragged through Stygian regions, through hell', 2.1.236). This transforms Phaedra's own cry, 'per Styga, per amnes igneos amens sequar' (1180), 'I will madly follow you through the Styx and through fiery rivers.' This is often described as a 'mangled' reminiscence (critics seem to have a deep-seated wish to associate Seneca with dismemberment). It is certainly curious the way 'amens' (madly) is transformed anagrammatically into 'manes' (underworld): there is a poetical memory at work there, a mind punning in memory, recombining letters to remake something new, just as the source text puns on 'amens' (madly) and 'amnes' (rivers).[30] It is not a simple example of Shakespeare—or Peele—trundling out a mangled Senecan hyperbolic *sententia*. The quotation comes from passion, from a desire characteristic of early Shakespearian tragic characters in general and of characters in *Titus* in particular to set themselves alongside the massive passions of the past and only partially lay claim to them. 'I am Phaedra, wishing death on myself, on the world,' the quotation says, while its performance perhaps ironizes that aspiration slightly by asking 'Are you really? Aren't you just (mis)quoting? And might you not be falling tragically short of that archetype of self-destructive passion?'

*Hippolytus*, a play haunted by a mythic past which its characters seem compelled by *furor* to re-enact, flickers through other works from the early 1590s. Even if it was Peele rather than Shakespeare who was responsible for the allusions to this play in *Titus*, Shakespeare rapidly responded to his cue. As Peter Holland has shown, *A Midsummer Night's Dream* is haunted by myths that are not quite there—by the fact that Theseus left Ariadne, by the fact that he will leave the Amazon Hippolyta, who is in some versions of the Theseus story the mother of Hippolytus.[31] Running through the *Dream* is a dark underpresence, along with more obvious Ovidian shades, of Senecan tragedy, of beasts in the wood, of hunts, of lovers desperate as Phaedra to get their man, and madly to pursue him through all dangers.[32] That kind of Ovidian–Senecan hybrid, in which *Hippolytus* is a recurrent element, is a signature note of Shakespeare's work around 1593–4. We have already met it at the start of *Titus Andronicus* in the hunting scene which is found exactly on the dividing line between what are thought to be Shakespeare's and Peele's portions of that play. Even the sunny *Venus and Adonis* has a shadow of Senecan tragedy beneath its Ovidian humour. When Venus attempts to persuade the petulant huntsman Adonis to stay with her and sleep with her, she does so in a very different way from her chief source in Ovid, who, as we have seen (pp. 103–5 below), tells the story of Atalanta and Hippomanes to her ephebic lover in order to keep him with her. Instead Shakespeare's goddess urges him to breed. There is much in Ovid's story of Venus and Adonis that might prompt recollections of *Hippolytus*—the hunt, the chaste boy, perhaps even the name of Hippomanes, which might recall that of Hippolytus, that other misogynistic horse-mad huntsmen. These associations between the two stories may well have triggered a reminiscence of the moment when the Nurse in *Hippolytus* tries to lure the young huntsman into his stepmother's bed by reminding him that nature would die in a single generation if he did not breed. The Nurse's extended *suasoria*, or formal speech of persuasion, to love sounds exactly like a versified 'theme', or a schoolroom essay on the benefits of marriage.[33] Her speech to Hippolytus consequently bridged the gap between schoolroom and stage, and that was the most likely reason why Shakespeare made his Venus focus her 'idle theme' (422) on arguments from procreation as Ovid's did not: he hybridizes Ovid's Venus (as well as the voice of the *preceptor amoris* in the *Ars Amatoria*) with Seneca's nurse.

There are also tantalizing signs in the earlier plays that Shakespeare responded to *Hippolytus* scenically—that is, he read it with an eye for action and gesture—and that he was particularly drawn to the closing and climactic stages of the play. This is again a speculative claim, but life without speculation would be unutterably tedious, and this particular speculation opens up a range of fascinating possibilities. Critics have recently suggested that Shakespeare's plays were sometimes printed in versions that might have been designed to be read rather than to be performed. They can elicit what Harry Berger has called 'imaginary audition', in which readers imaginatively create the scenes which they were reading.[34] The evidence that Shakespeare remembered scenic structures and episodes from plays he saw himself was brilliantly explored by Emrys Jones, and has an intrinsic appeal.[35] It is quite likely that he could also respond to plays which he read as though he had seen them, having read them with the eye of the mind, and with specifically a *playwright's* mental eye. In Act I Scene 2 of *Richard III* the future King Richard courts Queen Anne, despite having killed both her husband and her father. This scene takes as its starting point a Senecan situation, a structure of relationships rather than a set of Senecan words. Its main origin lies in *Hercules Furens* when the tyrant Lycus courts the wife of Hercules while her husband is believed to be dead. Hercules is not in fact dead, and Megara does not consent to the tyrant's wishes. That allusion in itself suggests the imaginative depth of Shakespeare's engagement with Seneca: Hercules is dead offstage, in the background of *Hercules Furens*; in *Richard III* Shakespeare brings the body of Anne's husband physically onto the stage. His eloquent tyrant has a greater persuasive facility than his main Senecan prototype, indeed enough persuasiveness to invert the outcome of the Senecan scene which he is reenacting, since he wins Anne over. And Richard is also hybridized with the eloquent Phaedra, who also woos an unsuitable partner while a greater hero is apparently dead offstage. At the climax of Shakespeare's scene Richard goes down on his knees and invites Anne to impale him with his own sword. This is very likely to have been inspired by the moment when Hippolytus pulls back Phaedra's hair to kill her with his sword as she is kneeling to him. This is the main physical gesture in Seneca's play, a gesture which centres on the hero's sword, which is the chief prop in the drama. It is just about possible that Shakespeare could have seen a performance of that scene. Seneca's plays were sometimes staged in elite London schools such as Westminster and at the universities, but these environments were slightly out of Shakespeare's sphere. It is more likely that he 'saw' the bodily relationships behind the words as he read them, and remembered the 'action' of the play text as much as its words.

## British Seneca: *King Lear* and *Macbeth*

There is more to say about the role of Seneca in general and the *Hippolytus* in particular in Shakespeare's later tragedies. But first it might be a good idea to draw back and take a wider view of some ways in which the cultural significance of Seneca changed through Shakespeare's career. The greatest of these changes—or at any rate the easiest to pin down—occurred around the very end of the sixteenth century and ran on through the reign of James I. Neo-Stoic thought had become fashionable through the later sixteenth century, largely through continental intermediaries such as Justus Lipsius and Michel de Montaigne. It went along with a rising interest in the philosophy and historiography of the late-imperial period in Rome, and frequently brought together reflections on the passions with arguments about how citizens should respond to tyrannical rule. These philosophical systems were particularly significant for well-educated and powerful magnates within political environments which concentrated political authority on the monarch. As European kingdoms increasingly came to deploy imagery associated with imperial absolutism, so Tacitus and Seneca, those wily critics of late-imperial decadence, became valuable examples for aristocratic readers who felt their own authority to be diminished by the imperial ambitions of their rulers, as well as for scholars who wished to articulate a philosophical system which would preserve their intellectual autonomy.

In England several writers in the circle of the Earl of Essex (who was executed in 1601), and before him among the family and admirers of Sir Philip Sidney (who died in 1586), were interested in adapting the work of Tacitus and other late-imperial historians to sustain new ways of thinking about political life, about passions, and about relationships between aristocratic elites and rulers.[36] William Cornwallis, who served under Essex in Ireland, published in 1601 his *Discourses upon Seneca the Tragedian*, which use tags from Seneca's plays as pretexts for meditations on ethics and politics. The extent to which Shakespeare was aware of or affected by these developments is open to debate. Certainly his contemporary dramatists Ben Jonson and George Chapman were not only influenced by this new fashion but wanted to show that they were influenced by it. Shakespeare, as we have already seen, did not just live on planet Shakespeare, sublimely unaware of what was going on around him. He appears in the cast list of actors for Jonson's highly Senecan and Tacitean *Sejanus*, which was performed in 1603. It would be strange to suppose that he simply recited his lines and then went home to bed afterwards, rather than reflecting on what made this play different from his own. He tended to register intellectual innovations in indirect and oblique ways, rather than (as Chapman or indeed Jonson might) by declaring his immersion in fashionable new learning through ostentatious displays of his knowledge in footnotes, or by direct translation from a modish source. The accession of King James in 1603, and the subsequent transformation of the Lord Chamberlain's Men into the King's Men, did, however, put an instant pressure on Shakespeare to rethink how he wrote in general and how he registered the presence of Seneca in his works in particular. James's tutor during his childhood in Scotland, George Buchanan, had composed Latin neo-Senecan dramas which raised questions about the relationship between kings and tyrants. At the turn of the century too there was an increasing interest in British antiquity, and in particular in the relics of ancient Rome found in these islands, with Ben Jonson's teacher and friend William Camden at the heart of that movement. Britishness, and indeed Romano-Britishness, was a hot topic in the early seventeenth century.

The result of all this, briefly put, was a phase in Shakespeare's career in which he experimented with what might be called British Senecanism. The tragedies of *Macbeth* (set in the near-mythical past of the Scottish monarchy, and dealing in questions of succession and tyranny) and *King Lear* were the main results. These plays were not

'Senecan' in the sense that Chapman's *Revenge of Bussy Dambois* (1613) was. Chapman's hero quotes passages of Epictetus and tries to live the neo-Stoic life; Shakespeare's heroes do neither of these things. But in these two tragedies Shakespeare adapted his response to classical antiquity in order to suit his environment and his audience. He sought to create tragedies in which entire worlds seemed to vibrate with the passions and desires of heroes from early British history, whose actions and whose words seem often to have shadowy prototypes in Seneca. Both *Lear* and *Macbeth* are in their different ways meditations on the Scottish King James VI's proposed union between England and Scotland. They also explore relationships between Britishness and classical antiquity.

Both these tragedies have attracted the eyes of traditional source-hunters. *Macbeth* in particular has given rich pickings to the gleaners after Senecan *sententiae*. Cunliffe suggested that Macbeth's 'Things bad begun make strong themselves by ill' (3.2.56) is a version of the Senecan *sententia* 'the only safe path from bad deeds is through bad deeds' ('per scelera semper sceleribus tutum est iter', *Agamemnon*, 115). That is quite likely. Versions of this particular Seneca tag were commonplace on the early-modern stage, and were meant to be noticed. In John Marston's *The Malcontent* (*c.*1603) Mendoza says: 'Black deed only through black deed safely flies' (5.3.13), which instantly prompts Malevole to quote Seneca's Latin original back at him. This in turn prompts the incredulous response, 'What, art a scholar?'[37] Although it is only a tiny example, Shakespeare's treatment of this particular 'Senecan' *sententia* shows how capable he was of making Seneca sound completely Shakespearian. Seneca repeats, unambiguously, the word 'crimes' (*scelera*). Marston, keen to bring his source to the minds of 'scholars' in the audience, follows Seneca by hammering out 'black deed' twice. Shakespeare, however, makes the sharp edges of the *sententia* melt: 'Things bad begun make strong themselves by ill' uses 'bad' as both an adjective and as an adverb, and by that simple expedient manages to suggest that the *sententia* is not a universal truth but an act of self-persuasion. If the project of evil is badly or ineffectively begun, Macbeth attempts to persuade himself, then doing 'ill' (bad deeds) ensures that it can be properly carried through. The Senecan thought is filtered through Macbeth's curiously vulnerable psychology of action, according to which if you have started to do something and you know it to be wrong, then the only way to make it work out is to carry it through to the end:

> I am in blood
> Stepped in so far that, should I wade no more,
> Returning were as tedious as go o'er. (3.4.135–7)

This is not the only moment in *Macbeth* where a Senecan phrase is adapted so completely to the concerns of the hero that it seems to be entirely 'engrafted' into the play. So Hercules gives up everything, even his *furor* in *Hercules Furens*: 'now I have lost all good things: my mind, my weapons, my reputation, my wife, my children, my band of friends [or "hands"—*manus* could mean either] even my madness' ('cuncta iam amisi bona, | mentem arma famam coniugem gnatos manus, | etiam furorem', 1259–61). This is ancestor to Macbeth's:

> I have lived long enough. My way of life
> Is fall'n into the sear, the yellow leaf,
> And that which should accompany old age,
> As honour, love, obedience, troops of friends,
> I must not look to have . . . (5.3.24–8)[38]

The dazzling flash of those yellow leaves ('or none, or few', as Sonnet 73.2 has it) puts a Shakespearian stamp on the passage, but Macbeth's lines are also steeped in his own distinctive preoccupations and experiences. 'I must not look to have' means simply 'I cannot hope to have', but 'looking' in this play has come to carry a disturbing charge. After the murder, Macbeth said: 'I am afraid to think what I have done, | Look on't again I dare not' (2.2.48–9), and at his second visit to the witches the sight of Banquo's future heirs 'does sear mine eyeballs . . . I'll see no more . . . Horrible sight! Now I see 'tis true' (4.1.129–38). It is as though Shakespeare or Macbeth has *un*remembered the words in the original (*coniugem*, *gnatos*—wife and children) which best suit the plight of Hercules, and which it best suits Macbeth to forget, or from which he must look away. The stately abstract nouns, 'honour, love, obedience' which replace Hercules's wife and children seem incongruous, since 'honour' and 'troops of friends' are not high on the list of things that Macbeth has seemed to possess or to expect up to this point. But their incongruity creates an effect of erasure: children—well, as Macduff says, Macbeth 'has no children' (4.3.217). His wife is by this stage still alive but madly lost to him. Macbeth's weary lament for his life is a piece of Seneca with the wife, the children, killed dead out of it. And that's a major part of its point.

These phrases point to one way in which Seneca functions within *Macbeth*. Senecan *sententiae* are so completely incorporated into the body of the play that they become hard to identify as pieces of Seneca. But this is by no means the only aspect of Seneca's influence in this play, and indeed there is another strand to the Senecanism of *Macbeth* which pulls in a diametrically opposite direction. Senecan drama is old, violent, and strange. And several of the play's allusions to Seneca seem to jut out from the surrounding action as though they are designed to be noticed as something that doesn't quite fit with their surroundings, like the *disiecta membra*, the scattered limbs, of an earlier poet from an earlier age. Once again *Hippolytus* runs beneath this play like a dark current. After Phaedra has propositioned him, Hippolytus cries out to be cleansed by the waters of the sea:

> quis eluet me Tanais aut quae barbaris
> Maeotis undis Pontico incumbens mari?
> non ipse toto magnus Oceano pater
> tantum expiarit sceleris. (*Hippolytus*, 715–18)

What water in the Tanais sea will cleanse me, or the Maeotis pouring its barbarous waters into the Pontic sea? Not the great father himself could expiate such a crime with the entire ocean.[39]

This is often proposed as a verbal source for Macbeth's guilty meditation:

> Will all great Neptune's ocean wash this blood
> Clean from my hand? No, this my hand will rather
> The multitudinous seas incarnadine,
> Making the green one red. (2.2.58–61)

*Macbeth* is, apart from this passage, a relatively sea-free zone (it may be significant that all other references to the sea are associated with the witches, who are 'Posters of the sea and land' (1.3.31) and who use 'gulf | Of the ravined sea-salt shark' (4.1.23–4) in their brew). And Neptune here is the only allusion to the classical pantheon in the entire play, which is otherwise unusually rich in mild Christian imprecations ('God bless us', 'God help thee', and the like). This passage as a result sticks out. It also stands out from the surrounding play because of its shockingly unfamiliar vocabulary: the words 'incarnadine' and 'multitudinous' are not found in English before this passage. Their far-fetched and dense Latinity seems almost to stand in for the allusions to distant places—the barbarous waters of the Maeotis—in the Senecan original. Macbeth seems to be reaching out to a pagan world of pollution and ritual cleansing which cannot quite be translated into English.

That little detail points to a much wider fact about the play and about the role of Seneca within it. *Macbeth* is in a near-literal sense a *strange* play. It is set long ago and in Scotland. Its audience is encouraged to think about the contrast between the world it represents and a more familiar, English, world by the long scene set in England which contrasts the tyrannies of Macbeth to Edward the Confessor's benign touching of his subjects for the King's evil (4.3). And throughout, although the play keeps us intimate with the intentions and desires of Macbeth, those desires take us to strange places. The word 'strange' is indeed a particular favourite of Macbeth's: 'I have a strange infirmity which is nothing' (3.4.85); 'You make me strange | Even to the disposition that I owe' (3.4.111–12); 'Strange things I have in head that will to hand' (3.4.138); 'My strange and self-abuse | Is the initiate fear that wants hard use' (3.4.141–2). He seems to travel in the course of the play to a strange and foreign country, through strange words ('assassination' is another word first recorded in the *OED* from this play—though in fact it had been used in English a little before—along with 'incarnadine') and stranger deeds.

His wife helps him on that journey, of course. But so does Seneca. As we have seen, Hamlet is partly driven by a desire to become a Senecan avenger, a desire which he finds it very difficult to realize. Macbeth and his wife are throughout the early acts also attempting to create a Seneca drama around themselves, so that they can perform the acts of regicide and infanticide that will give them the status that they desire. This means that they tend to force the mood of the play in deliberately unnatural directions. Lady Macbeth plays a particularly strong role in this. Repeatedly she seems to be attempting to transform herself into an ancient Scottish equivalent to Seneca's child-killing mother and witch Medea.[40] The effort of translating herself into this ancient character seems sometimes to lead her to rewrite her own past. She says in one of the strangest moments of the play:

> I have given suck, and know
> How tender 'tis to love the babe that milks me.
> I would, while it was smiling in my face,
> Have plucked my nipple from his boneless gums
> And dashed the brains out, had I so sworn
> As you have done to this. (1.7.54–9)

'How many children had Lady Macbeth?' is a famously inappropriate question to ask. As L. C. Knights showed long ago, it implies a simple literal-mindedness about the real lives of characters in fiction. But it is quite legitimate to ask some kind of question about this very strange moment. The play comes to be dominated by the fact that Macbeth 'has no children' and therefore no heirs. If Lady Macbeth did have children, if we are to think about them literally, they must have died before the play begins. But at a less literal level they are literary ghosts, brought into the play by a memory of Seneca. Lady Macbeth invokes her children to create a possible alternative world in which she becomes Medea, Seneca's most violent and self-destructive heroine, who kills her own children to avenge herself on her husband Jason. In Seneca's play Medea is presented as something archaic, who seeks within herself what she calls the 'ancient vigour' ('si quid antiqui tibi | remanet vigoris', 41–2) to kill her children. She also refers to her infanticidal revenge as a 'birth' (25). Her deliberate and conscious attempt to make herself kill is the clearest classical precedent for the terrifyingly deliberate murder performed by Macbeth, which he undertakes without experiencing any blinding rush of rage, or Senecan *furor*. Lady Macbeth's call to the 'murdering ministers' to 'unsex me here' is one moment when she echoes the prayers and invocations of Seneca's Medea. But her hypothetical children probably come from another passage in which Seneca's Medea is invoking the gods in order to prepare herself for infanticide. The language of Lady Macbeth's speech has more in common with the English translation of *Medea* by John Studley than with the original, which is less direct about the murder which Medea intends:

With naked breast and dugs laid out I'll prick with sacred blade
Mine arm, that for the bubbling blood an issue may be made,
With trilling streams my purple blood let drop on th' altar stones.
My tender children's crushéd flesh, and broken bruiséd bones
Learn how to brook with hardened heart: in practice put the trade
To flourish fierce, and keep a coil, with naked glitt'ring blade.[41]

tibi nudato pectore maenas
sacro feriam bracchia cultro.
manet noster sanguis ad aras:
assuesce, manus, stringere ferrum
carosque pati posse cruores—
sacrum laticem percussa dedi. (*Medea*, 806–11)

For you [Diana, the moon] like a maenad with breast bared I shall strike my arms with the sacred knife. Let my blood flow onto the altar. Practise, my hand, drawing the sword and enduring the shedding of your own dear blood. With a blow I have given the flowing sacrament.

'My tender children's crushéd flesh': that addition to the Latin in the English translation seems to have struck Shakespeare's eye. Lady Macbeth is trying to turn herself into a British Medea, but she is not quite succeeding. Rather than contemplating murder herself, she attempts to goad her husband into following through his promise to kill his king. And that detail is important. Seneca's Medea in the passage just quoted speaks as she acts, and describes the act of cutting herself to make a sacrifice to Diana as she does it: she moves from the future tense ('I shall strike my arms'), to the present, to the perfect tense, having by the end of the speech shed her own blood. Lady Macbeth, however, speaks in the past conditional: 'I *would*, while it was smiling in my face, | Have plucked my nipple from his boneless gums | And dashed the brains out'. This is very much her grammatical mood: she says while her husband is killing Duncan: 'Had he not resembled | My father as he slept, I had done't' (2.2.12–13)—letting 'I dare not' wait upon 'I would' like the poor cat i'th'adage. Seneca's heroes and heroine often imagine universal destruction or self-destruction in the future or in a conditional mood. Lady Macbeth is in this respect an heir to Seneca. The act of violence against her child which she imagines seems in the context of the play to be not just hypothetical but more or less imaginary, since it is performed on a child who, the rest of the play suggests, may never even have been born.

Macbeth is more of a woman than his wife, and takes on the mantle of Medea. He plans and more or less instantly performs child murders when he discovers that Macduff is fled to England:

> Time, thou anticipat'st my dread exploits.
> The flighty purpose never is o'ertook
> Unless the deed go with it. From this moment
> The very firstlings of my heart shall be
> The firstlings of my hand. And even now,
> To crown my thoughts with acts, be it thought and done:
> The castle of Macduff I will surprise,
> Seize upon Fife, give to th'edge o'th' sword
> His wife, his babes, and all unfortunate souls
> That trace him in his line. (4.1.160–9)

There is nothing hypothetical here: he accelerates towards present and instant violence. He begins with a *sententia* which is effectively a euphemism: 'The flighty purpose never is o'ertook | Unless the deed go with it'. The 'flighty purpose' is his intention to kill Macduff; 'the deed' means murder. But that states his aim: to do things almost before they are thought of, to 'overtake', not simply to attain or reach, his purpose. Then child murder starts seeping into his language: 'firstlings' suggests newborn children (a lamb can be described as 'the firstling of the flock'), which are here imagined as thoughts, which must now turn instantly to murder. And by the end of the speech he has stated an intention literally to perform murder, a murder which is seen onstage, instantly, in the very next scene. We see the future in the instant: action, bloody, bold, and Senecan.

Is what emerges from *Macbeth* a triumphant fusion of British and Roman drama, in which, as Camden says, Briton and Roman 'by a blessed and joyful mutual engrafting, as it were, have grown in one stock and nation'?[42] *Macbeth* is the most completely unified and focused of Shakespeare's tragedies. Its theatrical movement has none of the studious leisure of *Hamlet*. It proceeds with a sharp dramatic thrust from Macbeth's desire for the throne to its achievement, and can be performed without an interval as though in a single heated burst of movement after the battle which immediately precedes the play. Its language is oppressively unified in metaphor and theme. Seneca seems sometimes to be welded into that structure, and to have been domesticated into its language. But at other times Senecan tragedy seems to bring out the archaism, the violence, and the strangeness of ancient Scotland, propelling the hero towards murder and more murder. The play as a result suggests a cultural unease which parallels the uncertainty and discomfort experienced by many English people early in the reign of their new Scottish king: is there something strange and unsettling about a union between different nations, different languages, and different moral universes? Can 'Britons', English and Scots, comfortably speak the same language as the Romans? Those questions were pursued and developed in *King Lear*.

## *King Lear*: Senecan Amnesia

*King Lear* is in many respects the Senecan climax to Shakespeare's career, despite the fact that its editors have been extraordinarily reluctant to acknowledge any Senecan presence in it at all. Even the eager Cunliffe found it 'further removed than *Macbeth* from the spirit of Senecan tragedy', while one of the play's most recent editors dismissively lists Seneca as one of 'many other works and events' which 'contributed something to the play'.[43] The plot of *King Lear*, in which a kingdom is divided into three by an ageing monarch, clearly reflects both anxious memories of the uncertainty surrounding the succession of the English crown in the later years of Elizabeth and the planned union of England and Scotland which dominated political discussion during the first years of James VI and I's reign. Set deep in the British history related by Geoffrey of Monmouth and adapted in Holinshed's *Chronicles*, the story of King Lear invited Shakespeare to think about the identity and integrity of Britain. The social and geographical capaciousness of the play, ranging around the south of England through heaths and hovels, shivering with madmen, and slumming it with corrupt courtiers, makes it a picture of a whole nation, tied together by reciprocal bonds of service and reward which seem to be losing their grip over the geographical realm covered by the play.

The play and its king both brood on ingratitude, on the kinds of return which children owe their parents, and on the limits to that debt. These are central themes in Seneca's philosophical works, and of the *De Beneficiis* in particular. It is very likely that Shakespeare read or reread this work early in the seventeenth century (there had been two English translations by this date, but there is no reason to suppose that Shakespeare did not read the Latin). *Timon of Athens* has been linked to Seneca's thought on benefits,[44] and *King Lear* is closely related to *Timon* in both theme and time of composition. But Seneca is again less a source than an under-presence, a text which is obliquely evoked in ways that seem almost casual or accidental. There is one particularly oblique example. When Lear and his Fool are waiting for his horses to be made ready, just after Goneril has asked her father to reduce the number of his followers, the Fool says:

> FOOL: The reason why the seven stars are no more than seven is a pretty reason.
> LEAR: Because they are not eight.
> FOOL: Yes, indeed, thou wouldst make a good fool.
> LEAR: To take't again perforce—monster ingratitude! (1.5.35–9)

This is an offbeat moment between scenes. The characters talk to fill in time while the horses are made ready for their departure, and each pursues his own track, with the Fool attempting to distract his master. But it has a little shadow of Seneca behind it. In a passage on the abundance of the universe, and the gratitude which is consequently owed to nature, Seneca says: 'For there is no reason why you should think only seven stars move, and the rest are fixed; there are a few whose motions we understand, but there are countless deities beyond our ken which come and go, and many of these which our eyes can perceive go with an invisible motion and hide their movements' (4.23.4). Seneca goes on to provide extensive discussion of the benefits given and received between parents and children ('few reach the age when they can reap some true reward from their children', 5.5.2), and by Book 6 we are told: 'We owe filial duty to our parents, and yet many at the time of their union had no thought of begetting us' (6.23.5)—what would the bastard Edmund say to that? Nature, Seneca argues, has given mankind a whole universe, which is a debt so great that it can never possibly be repaid. The allusion to the *De Beneficiis* is so oblique that it is almost beyond the boundaries of an allusion, but Seneca's association of the seven stars with gratitude feeds in to the apparent non-sequitur of the exchange between Lear and his Fool.

As this example indicates, Senecan thought does not come through *Lear* as anything which remotely resembles a naked slab of doctrine, nor does it quite have the character of a 'source' as it is traditionally conceived, though it can sometimes come closer to that than critics have tended to recognize. Seneca at one point in the *De Beneficiis* (7.9.5) constructs a fictional diatribe by the Cynic Demetrius, who declaims against luxury: 'I see your silk garments, if garments they can be called, in which there is nothing that could protect either the body or our sense of modesty, and while you're wearing them you could barely say that you weren't naked' ('Video sericas vestes, si vestes vocandae sunt, in quibus nihil est, quo defendi aut corpus aut denique pudor possit, quibus sumptis parum liquido nudam non esse iurabit'). That diatribe, attacking luxury, expressing wonder about the accidental generosity of the world and the meanness of men, runs like a distant chorus through Lear's madness. Lear's attack on his daughter Regan fuses together that cynical diatribe with a passage of *echt* Senecan tragic rhetoric:

> O, reason not the need! Our basest beggars
> Are in the poorest thing superfluous.
> Allow not nature more than nature needs,
> Man's life is cheap as beast's. Thou art a lady.
> If only to go warm were gorgeous,
> Why, nature needs not what thou, gorgeous, wear'st,
> Which scarcely keeps thee warm. But for true need—
> You heavens give me that patience, patience I need.
> (2.2.438–45)

The theatrical point here is not that a 'source' is slapped down before us, or that Lear suddenly sounds like a Cynic. Rather the fragmentariness of the allusion to Seneca, the effect of a diatribe which is half-forgotten and which loses its own impetus, is what makes this such a powerful evocation of an old man's attempt to articulate what his daughter owes to him and to the abundance of nature. Patience, that quintessential Stoic virtue, enters as Lear shifts from using the word 'need' in the material sense of 'lack of goods' to a moral sense: his need is becoming philosophic, a need for some kind of ethical system which will keep his diatribe within the bounds of social decorum and the ties which bind a family together. But the speech then suddenly shifts gear from the realm of Seneca *Philosophicus* to Seneca *Tragicus*, as though Lear's mind has skipped on to a different volume in his mental library:

> No, you unnatural hags,
> I will have such revenges on you both
> That all the world shall—I will do such things—
> What they are, yet I know not; but they shall be
> The terrors of the earth. (2.2.452–6)

Lear's outburst here without doubt does not just derive from Seneca but is meant to sound 'Senecan'. Its violence comes directly from *Thyestes*, when Atreus is asked what he is planning to do:

> Nescioquid animo maius et solito amplius
> supraque fines moris humani tumet
> instatque pigris manibus. haud quid sit scio,
> sed grande quiddam est! ita sic. Hoc, anime, occupa. (*Thyestes*, 267–70)

Something, I don't know what, larger than usual, and beyond the bounds of human limits, swells and drives on my sluggish hands. What it will be I know not, but it is something huge. This will be it. Seize on it, my soul.

Lear presents an old man's Seneca—even perhaps an 'antique' Seneca in the Shakespearian sense of 'antic', meaning both 'old' and 'mad'. He roughly jolts from one part of Seneca's works to another, shifting violently from a fractured memory of the *De Beneficiis* to the frenzy of Atreus. Lear seems just too old to be able quite to recall his Senecan texts; it all seems too distant, the thread too hard to follow. Editors are now extremely reluctant to acknowledge even the very clear echo of Atreus here, perhaps with some reason. It is easy to assume that when an editor notes a source it simply means 'Shakespeare got these words from this place.' That is not what is at stake in pointing out these fragmented allusions to Seneca, which are a profound part of the meaning of the scene and of the larger drama. Shakespeare's greatest play comes from deep and continued thinking about Seneca, and about the way that ingratitude in particular could bridge the gap between Senecan ethics, Stoic cosmology, and Senecan drama. The wider concern of the *De Beneficiis* with problems of gratitude (does one owe gratitude to parents who conceived one even if they did so unwittingly and accidentally?) rings and finally roars through *King Lear*, which seems partly to be made from a Senecan thought experiment. What would happen if the flow and exchange of benefits which unite servant to master, which sustain the love of parents and children for each other, and which hold together families and realms in early-modern Britain, were radically disrupted? What if the gratitude of child to parent were turned into a bare expression of reciprocal return, as when Cordelia says in the play's opening scene, 'You have begot me, bred me, loved me. | I return those duties back as are right fit' (1.1.96–7)? What would that disruption of the complex reciprocal relationships of familial love and debt then do to a society, to the passions and rhetoric of an individual man, and then to the cosmos? Could it lead to and provide an explanation for a climax of Senecan *furor* which makes the very heavens shake?

Lear on the heath is the most powerful example in Shakespeare of Senecan rhetorical mannerisms in action, where impossible commands ('Blow, winds, and crack your cheeks! Rage, blow, | You cataracts and hurricanoes', 3.2.1–2), and apocalyptic threats rage around a central warping anger at filial ingratitude. It is not remotely 'Senecan' in the traditional staid, mannered, speechifying way. But running through this play is a desire to create a British equivalent to Seneca. That Senecan vision of society is founded on a complex system of exchanges between emotions and material goods. When that system broke down it could unleash the uncontrolled rage of a would-be tyrant who can control nothing, not even his own self:

Let the great gods,
That keep this dreadful pother o'er our heads,
Find out their enemies now. Tremble, thou wretch
That hast within thee undivulgèd crimes
Unwhipped of justice; hide thee, thou bloody hand,
Thou perjured and thou simular of virtue
That art incestuous; caitiff, to pieces shake,
That under covert and convenient seeming
Has practised on man's life; close pent up guilts,

Rive your concealing continents and cry
These dreadful summoners grace. I am a man
More sinned against than sinning. (3.2.49–59)

Critics and audiences have often experienced this scene as a breakdown of everything. In performance it can be shattering. It has a mass of origins, but somewhere behind it lies yet another distant, broken memory of Shakespeare's oldest favourite Senecan play, the *Hippolytus*:

Magne regnator deum,
tam lentus audis scelera? tam lentus vides?
et quando saeva fulmen emittes manu,
si nunc serenum est? omnis impulsus ruat
aether et atris nubibus condat diem,
ac versa retro sidera obliquos agant
retorta cursus. tuque, sidereum caput,
radiate Titan, tu nefas stirpis tuae
speculare? lucem merge et in tenebras fuge.
cur dextra, divum rector atque hominum, vacat
tua, nec trisulca mundus ardescit face?
in me tona, me fige, me velox cremet
transactus ignis: sum nocens, merui mori. (671–83)

Great king of the gods, are you so slow to hear about crimes? Are you so slow to see them? And when will you send the lightning bolt from your vengeful hand, since now the heavens are clear? Let the whole sky collapse inwards and hide the day in black clouds, let the stars turn backwards and swerving run their course askew. And you, head of stars, radiant Titan, do you look down at this crime by your offspring? Drown the light, and flee into darkness. Why is your hand empty, ruler of gods and men, why do you not singe the world with your three-pronged brand? Strike me with lightning, transfix me, let the swift fire cremate me: I am guilty. I deserve to die.

Again a mighty act of erasure and amnesia transforms this passage of Seneca into a passage of Shakespeare. What stayed with Shakespeare above all from this speech by Hippolytus—and that play remains the anchor point of his response to the Roman tragedian, its climax a recurring point in the climaxes of his dramas—was the mood of the speech. I do not use 'mood' in the fuzzy sense of 'atmosphere', but in the more precise sense of its grammatical mood. All of this *should* happen, might happen, but is not quite happening as Hippolytus wants it to happen. 'Let the great gods...': there is a shade of the faintly ironical treatment of Seneca that had run through *Hamlet* even here in this later and infinitely unplayful play. A man 'more sinned against than sinning' emerges out of Hippolytus, who declares his own guilt when he is in fact innocent; metaphorical thunderclaps and lightning become actual bolts of thought-executing fire which crash around the hero. The grateful circulation of benefits between father and child has broken down, leaving a man roaring to the elements, begging that they will display *sumpatheia* with his passion. Lear turns Senecan drama outside-in and raises it to a higher power: Stoic conceptions of the sympathetic relationship between the 'little world of man' (Quarto text, 8.9) and the cosmos are pushed to their outer limit, while the raging ineffectiveness of human rhetoric is dramatized with a completeness close to cruelty. Lear orders the elements to rage with him, and for criminals to cower. Do the wretches tremble with fear rather than just with cold? And do the elements rage because he orders them to do so or because they would be raging anyway? Is the only kind of *sumpatheia* on offer in this scene the human emotions which Lear elicits from his onstage audience of fools and madmen, and from his offstage audience of powerless spectators? The whole world, of which Britain is a tiny, fractured, northern part, is broken apart by the collapse of grateful exchanges between parent and child. The result is a Senecan apocalypse.

# 6

# *Plutarch*

With Plutarch, Shakespeare left memories of school far behind. The preface to the version of Plutarch's *Lives* which Shakespeare used, Sir Thomas North's translation from the French version by Jacques Amyot, states grandly: 'there is no profane [i.e. secular] study better than Plutarch. All other learning is private, fitter for Universities than cities, fuller of contemplation than experience, more commendable in the students themselves, than profitable unto others.'[1] This, North suggested, was a worldly book. It was also a book to which Shakespeare came just at the point he was making his mark in the world. North's translation first appeared in 1579, but Shakespeare probably first encountered it in around 1595, when a new edition was printed by Richard Field, the stationer from Stratford-upon-Avon who had printed *Lucrece* in 1594, and who issued a reprint of *Venus and Adonis* in 1595. This fits with the first unequivocal sign that Shakespeare had read the *Lives*, which comes from around 1595, when he took details from the 'Life' of Theseus for *A Midsummer Night's Dream*.[2] That play with no clear sources, so lightly woven together from hints out of Ovid, Chaucer, and John Lyly, was also the place where Shakespeare first registered his interest in what was probably one of the most expensive books he ever owned, and what was certainly the book from which he took most. The *Lives* provide the main sources for *Julius Caesar* in 1599, and remained with Shakespeare for almost a decade, through *Antony and Cleopatra* (1606–7), and *Coriolanus* (1608). Shakespeare may also have learnt tricks from Plutarchan biographies when he fashioned plays out of Holinshed's *Chronicles* on the lives of Henry IV and Henry V, and, as we'll see, he did far more with Plutarch than simply extract good moments for the stage from the 'Lives' from which he wanted to create plays.[3]

What are Plutarch's *Parallel Lives* like? In the form in which Shakespeare read them they were called *The Lives of the Most Noble Grecians and Romans, Compared Together by that Grave Learned Philosopher and Historiographer Plutarch of Chaeronea.* The full title of the work is a bit of a mouthful but it is a significant mouthful. Plutarch's *Lives* were not just biographical records of ancient heroes. They were explicitly framed to encourage comparisons between historical and mythological figures from Greece and Rome. Plutarch himself was a Greek, born in around 45 AD, who wrote his *Lives* under Roman rule at some point around the early second century AD. He spent most of his life in Chaeronea, which is relatively close to the centre of mainland Greece and to Delphi, where he became a priest. He wrote for educated Greeks, and believed, like most of his early audience, in the superiority of Greek culture and education over their Roman counterparts, although he was not about to risk an overt assertion of superiority over his rulers.[4] This resulted in perhaps the most obvious fact about the *Lives*, but one which had immense consequences for Shakespeare. Plutarch's *Lives* tend to assume that their readers would know more about the history and political institutions of Greek states than they would about Rome. This means that he tends to explain Rome's customs and institutions as though they belonged to a slightly foreign country—which they did, so far as he was concerned. In the 'Life' of Romulus, Plutarch describes the festival of Lupercalia, as 'a feast of great antiquity', in which:

> two young boys, noble men's sons, whose foreheads they touch with the knife be-bloodied with the blood of the goats that are sacrificed. By and by they dry their foreheads with wool dipped in milk... That done they cut the goats' skins, and make thongs of them, which they take in their hands, and run with them all about the city stark naked (saving they have a cloth before their secrets) and so they strike with these thongs all they meet in their way. (i, 98)

Christopher Pelling notes 'a *detachment* in the way Plutarch approaches Rome', and that detachment can resemble the position of an ethnographer who is describing an alien culture.[5] Plutarch's Rome would consequently have seemed to a sixteenth-century reader more like 'antiquity' than his Greece because it was more thickly described as a place with its own distinct and distant customs—and this was probably one of the major reasons why Shakespeare was drawn more to the Roman 'Lives' than to the Greek. They seem to describe not just a life, but a world.

Although Plutarch at one point describes himself as travelling 'far into antiquity' (i, 29), as though history is a journey across both space and time, his *Lives* are by no means simply exercises in historical anthropology. Most of his pairings of Greek and Roman parallel lives end with a formal *synkrisis*, or comparison of the two heroes and their respective virtues and vices. These generally include both positive and negative judgements on Greek and Roman alike. Shakespeare poked gentle fun at historical *synkrisis* in Fluellen's parodic comparison of Henry V with Alexander, which was probably composed immediately before *Julius Caesar*:

> I tell you, captain, if you look in the maps of the world I warrant you sall find, in the comparisons between Macedon and Monmouth, that the situations, look you, is both alike. There is a river in Macedon, and there is also moreover a river at Monmouth. It is called Wye at Monmouth, but it is out of my prains what is the name of the other river—but 'tis all one, 'tis alike as my fingers is to my fingers, and there is salmons in both. (*Henry V*, 4.7.22–30)

The joke here is not just on Fluellen and his Welsh 'prains', and poor memory for classical river names: cross-cultural comparison was a deep part of both history and literary history in the sixteenth century. As we have seen, Francis Meres undertook his own *synkrisis* of English and classical writers when he compared Shakespeare to Plautus and Seneca. Shakespeare never explicitly made comparisons between Greek and Roman lives, but the habit of *synkrisis* may leave its mark on his choice of subjects later in his career: *Antony and Cleopatra* and *Coriolanus* may have been conceived as a pair of Roman parallel lives, which represent heroes driven respectively by passion and anger.[6] The study of Greek misanthropy in *Timon of Athens* (which derives partly from a digression in Plutarch's 'Life of Antony', and which Shakespeare seems not to have finished) also may have been designed originally as a parallel for the life of the vehemently antisocial Roman Coriolanus, and is one of the few points where Shakespeare's Plutarchan plays venture into Greece.

Nonetheless, Plutarch's cross-cultural comparisons between Greek and Roman heroes were significant for Shakespeare. This was because they added a transtemporal ethical perspective, which assumes that human actions can be judged according to the same criteria irrespective of time and place, to the ethnographical perspective of individual lives.[7] That meant Plutarch allowed Shakespeare to think (according to present-day perspectives, anyway) both historically and unhistorically at once: he could imagine Rome as a distinct and distant culture, with its own customs, and its own characteristic political, religious, and ethical priorities, but he could also see it as a stage on which to explore questions which were independent of ancient Roman or ancient Greek history. How good a man was Brutus and why did he act as he did? What can be learnt from the patrician severity of Coriolanus or the misanthropy of Timon? And can ancient politics reveal parallels to the present? This was not simply a matter of seeing 'salmons in both' the past and the present. The plays explicitly based on Plutarch, perhaps more than any other works by Shakespeare, tend to raise questions about here and now in England: *Coriolanus* reflects on corn riots in the Midlands in 1607–8, *Julius Caesar* has often been related to the dark anxieties about succession in the last years of Elizabeth I, while over *Antony and Cleopatra* there hang memories of the captivating dead queen Elizabeth.

Plutarch also mattered to Shakespeare because he was a remarkably *literary* historian. Most Greek historians quote from poets and dramatists. They also shape their representations of history according to a wide range of literary and rhetorical techniques. Plutarch went further. He regularly cites literary texts, from Homer, through Plato the comedian (who was distinct from Plato the philosopher) and Aristophanes, to the tragedians Euripides and Sophocles, as sources of factual evidence:[8] 'Aeschylus the poet, in a tragedy which he entitled the *Persians*, knowing certainly the truth, sayeth thus…' (i, 298). He believed poets could be historians. It is quite likely that this was one aspect of Plutarch that struck Shakespeare's eye. As the last chapter showed, the *Hippolytus* had a more sustained influence on Shakespeare than any other of Seneca's works. Plutarch's 'Life of Theseus', from which Shakespeare borrowed several details for *A Midsummer Night's Dream*, treats Euripides's *Hippolytus* (which is, perhaps at several removes, a source of Seneca's play) as a source of historical fact (i, 58). His favourite books must have seemed at that moment to be in conversation with each other.

Plutarch also had an eye for drama. At the end of the 'Life' of Crassus, he describes a performance of Euripides's *Bacchae* before the Parthians, just after Crassus had been defeated. In this play Agave (Pentheus's mother) enters triumphantly carrying her son's head (although North in his translation makes a mistake about her gender). In the history which Plutarch is relating the real head of a defeated Roman enemy is presented to the king of the Parthians. He weaves the play and the historical event into a single tableau of horror:

> The same night Crassus' head was brought, the tables being all taken up, Jason a common player of interludes (born in the city of Tralles) came before the kings, and recited a place of the tragedy of the *Bacchants* of Euripides, telling of the misfortune of Agave, who struck off his son's head. And as every man took great pleasure to hear him, Sillaces coming into the hall, after his humble duty first done to the king, delivered him Crassus' head before them all. The Parthians seeing that, fell a clapping of their hands, and made an outcry of joy. The gentlemen ushers by the king's commandment, did set Sillaces at the table. Jason casting off his apparel representing Pentheus' person, gave it to another player to put on him, and counterfeiting the Bacchants possessed with fury, began to rehearse these verses, with a gesture, tune, and voice of a man mad, and beside himself.
>
> Behold, we from the forest bring a stag now newly slain.
> A worthy booty and reward beseeming well our pain. (iii, 89)

There is no hard evidence that Shakespeare read this passage. The affinities between its spectacular violence and the climax of *Titus Andronicus* may be no more than accidents, since it's probable that Shakespeare wrote *Titus* slightly before he began to read Plutarch. But it's hard to believe that this extraordinary piece of writing about the political use of drama would have not caught the eye of a 'common player of interludes' as he scanned through North's Plutarch in search of matter for his own dramas in the mid 1590s. And it gives an extraordinarily multiple perspective on the cultural function of tragedy: a Greek author describes how a tribe he thought of as barbarous incorporated a victory over Rome and an actual decapitation of a powerful Roman general into a Greek play, which becomes in performance an occasion of savage cultural revenge. How far is the Greek Plutarch rejoicing with the Parthians here? And could that sacrificial blend of triumph and tragedy have fed Shakespeare's understanding of how tragedy can be used by and move its audiences?

These are unanswerable questions. But this passage illustrates why Plutarch was such a good theatrical source. He knew what theatre could do, and he could use literary sources and quotations artfully to create dramatic climaxes to his *Lives*. Although individual *Lives* tend to follow a single principal historical source—and scholars accept that in the age of the papyrus scroll it was difficult to do otherwise, since it is far harder to find a particular point in a roll than it is in a codex—nonetheless Plutarch is keen to stress that he worked from several different kinds of historical record. Often this allows into his writing several different historical perspectives. He frequently notes discrepancies between different pieces of evidence and offers a range of versions of several major events—including even the foundation of Rome. He says early in the *Lives* that 'We are not to marvel if the history of things so ancient be found so diversely written' (i, 57), and his awareness of diversity in representations of the truth often seems a constitutive part of his method. The 'Life of Marcus Antonius', the principal source for *Antony and Cleopatra*, is particularly self-conscious about the sources of its information and their potential inaccuracy and biases. Plutarch does not simply describe the beauty and allure of Cleopatra, but says: 'Now her beauty (as it is reported) was not so passing, as unmatchable of other women, nor yet such, as upon present view did enamour men with her: but so sweet was her company and conversation, that a man could not possibly but be taken' (vi, 26–7). That innocent and readily overlooked parenthesis '(as it is reported)' mattered to Shakespeare. Beauty is in the eye of the reporter rather than in the eye of the beholder in Plutarch, and so it is for Shakespeare's play based on Plutarch. Plutarch goes on to describe the mutual feasts of the lovers, which they termed *amimetobion*, a life which could not be imitated, 'exceeding all measure and reason', and he does so in ways that draw attention to the sources of the information and to their possible inaccuracies:

And for proof hereof, I have heard my grandfather Lampryas report, that one Philotas a physician, born in the city of Amphissa, told him that he was at that present time in Alexandria, and studied physic: and that having acquaintance with one of Antonius' cooks, he took him with him to Antonius' house, (being a young man desirous to see things) to show him the wonderful sumptuous charge and preparation of one only supper. When he was in the kitchen, and saw a world of diversities of meats, and amongst others eight wild boars roasted whole, he began to wonder at it, and said 'Sure you have a great number of guests to supper.' The cook fell a-laughing, and answered him 'No' (quoth he), 'Not many guests, nor above twelve in all'... Philotas the physician told my grandfather this tale. (vi, 27–8 )

This story is referred to in Shakespeare's play but does not directly generate a scene in it. Nonetheless, it is highly suggestive. It indicates how Plutarch's practice as a historian informs Shakespeare's theatrical realization of ancient Egypt and Rome: knowledge of the past is dependent on potentially unreliable chains of testimony, which could include both textual sources and oral testimony. The opening of the play, 'Nay, but this dotage of our General's | O'erflows the measure' (1.1.1–2), is partly inspired by the description of these feasts which 'exceed all measure and reason'. The wonder of the first-hand observer Philotas the physician, seeing 'a world of diversities', also becomes that of the observer of the play, who feels his or her way through a plethora of witnesses and descriptions towards an understanding of the inimitable singularity that those witnesses all represent in slightly different ways. Plutarch did not just provide the matter of *Antony and Cleopatra* but also inspired its main representational strategies. Reports and their reliability, the processes of learning about and recording historical events, messengers: these become part of the texture of the play. At one extreme Cleopatra hectors and beats a messenger into reporting to her the image of Octavia that she wants to hear (3.3). At the other is Enobarbus's set-piece description of Cleopatra's meeting with Antony ('The barge she sat in', 2.2.197–233). This is, famously, a very close versification of North's Plutarch, and takes many phrases directly from its source. But even here Enobarbus is doing more than simply reporting facts: he is another reporter who wants to make an impression on his Roman audience by showing that he has experience of exotic marvels. Much of the love of Antony and Cleopatra, and much of the heroic past of Antony himself, is presented in the play through reports and stories which are pitched on the boundary between credible historical record and deceptive fiction.

These features of the play are not simply Shakespearian inventions. They leak through from Plutarch's interest in the processes by which a historian comes to acquire knowledge. So Plutarch gives a vivid description of the death of Cleopatra which Shakespeare quite closely follows: 'they found Cleopatra stark dead, laid upon a bed of gold, attired and arrayed in her royal robes, and one of her two women, which was called Iras, dead at her feet: and her other woman called Charmion half dead and trembling, trimming the diadem which Cleopatra wore upon her head' (vi, 87). Plutarch then goes on to offer a number of alternative versions of her death:

> Some report that this aspic [asp] was brought unto her in the basket with figs, and that she had commanded them to hide it under the fig leaves, that when she should think to take out the figs, the aspic should bite her before she should see her: howbeit, that when she would have taken away the leaves for the figs, she perceived it, and said 'Art thou here then?' And so, her arm being naked, she put it to the aspic to be bitten. Other say again, she kept it in a box... Howbeit few can tell the truth. For they report also, that she had hidden poison in a hollow razor which she carried in the hair of her head... But it was reported only, that there were seen certain fresh steps or tracks where it had gone, on the tomb's side toward the sea, and specially by the door's side. Some say also, that they found two little pretty bitings in her arm, scant to be discerned: the which it seemeth Caesar himself gave credit unto, because in his triumph he carried Cleopatra's image with an aspic biting of her arm. And thus goeth the report of her death. (vi, 87)

The glimmering delight and perplexity of Shakespeare's play, in which audiences and producers are often required to hold together several incompatible perspectives on Cleopatra, and in which what we witness ourselves and what we hear from witnesses do not quite add up, grow from North's Plutarch, where the reiterations of the word 'report' give a faint cadence of doubt even to the apparently resolute declaration 'thus goeth the *report* of her death'. What we see here is a paradox to which Shakespeare responded actively: Cleopatra's death in Plutarch is a vividly realized and stageable 'scene' which nonetheless accommodates a variety of historical perspectives. Which 'report' do we believe? Amyot uses the neutral verb '*dire*' ('some say') at all of the points above where North talks of 'reports' (and this reflects Plutarch, who tends in these places to use forms of the verb *legō*, I say). *Antony and Cleopatra* takes up the word 'report' from North and runs with it: the play contains significantly more occurrences of the word than any other by Shakespeare (though *Cymbeline* runs it a close second). And where North, a lawyer, may invest 'reports' with something of the force of legal testimony or record, Shakespeare's usages tend to imply that a 'report' is a repetition at one remove from the truth. The 're-' prefix is particularly audible in the curious rhyme on the word in the lines uttered by one of Caesar's messengers: 'To the ports | The discontents repair, and men's reports | Give him much wronged' (1.4.38–40). The quality of information received by a particular character through 'report' is carefully calibrated in the play, and again follows cues and prompts in Plutarch. So Plutarch relates Antony's elevation of Cleopatra to a throne in direct speech as simple fact, and then says 'Octavius Caesar reporting all these things unto the Senate . . .' (vi, 57). Shakespeare caught the eerie correspondence implied here between Caesar's information and the historical truth, and uses it to characterize Octavius, who relates these events to Agrippa and Maecenus with entire confidence in his own sources of information: 'As 'tis reported, so' (3.6.19).

That way of characterizing Octavius simply through his use of spies and reporters to gain reliable information is also in its way Plutarchan. For Plutarch, in a much-quoted passage from the 'Life of Alexander', states that he aimed not to present an authoritative history, but to tell stories or relate anecdotes which revealed character:

> For the noblest deeds do not always show men's virtues and vices, but oftentimes a light occasion, a word, or some sport makes men's natural dispositions and manners appear more plain than the famous battles won, wherein are slain ten thousand men, or the great armies, or cities won by siege or assault. (ii, 298)

This is probably more of a comment on Plutarch's 'Life of Alexander' than a statement of his general method,[9] but it does again indicate why this Greek historian could mean so much to a dramatist for whom the typifying quirk mattered more than a grand and comprehensive narrative.

Although there is harmony, synergy, and sparks of affinity flying between the representational methods of Plutarch and those of Shakespeare (and how often has the world spawned a historian who can describe and even think in scenes?), the two writers were not simply in agreement about everything. Indeed, the areas where they differed were probably more creatively significant than those in which they thought in similar ways. In the realms of ethics and politics in particular, Plutarch would not have told Shakespeare exactly what he would have expected to hear about Rome. Educated early-modern Englishmen would generally have thought that Roman moral agents were concerned with the performance of particular offices within the commonwealth, and that they would have regarded themselves as agents bound by reciprocal responsibilities to state and family. As Nicholas Grimald's frequently reprinted translation of Cicero's *De Officiis* put it, 'we be born not for ourselves alone, but somedeal of our birth our country, somedeal our parents, somedeal our friends do claim'.[10] From his reading in Seneca, and indeed in Cicero, Shakespeare might have also identified 'Roman' with Stoic ethics, and have thought (as Hamlet does) that being an 'ancient Roman' entailed attempting to suppress passion and consequently avoid subjection to *fortuna*.[11] Plutarch wrote *Moralia*, or Moral Essays, as well as his *Lives*, and these were distinctively Greek rather than Roman in their emphasis. The *Moralia* had a wide influence on early-modern ethical writing even before the appearance of a complete translation by Philemon Holland in 1603. Before that date Shakespeare could have read the French translation by Jacques Amyot, and would also have come across elements from the *Moralia* embedded in his reading of Montaigne (who declares, modestly but falsely, 'I have not dealt or had commerce with any excellent book, except Plutarch or Seneca').[12] The *Lives* themselves are suffused with ethical thinking, and this too was not quite 'Roman' ethical thinking, since Plutarch, although he was well read in Stoicism, could be explicitly anti-Stoic. He could accept that Scaevola burning his hand was evidence of 'the Roman's noble mind and great courage' (i, 269), but he did not believe that the human good could be obtained only by those who effectively controlled their passions with reason. Rather his character studies tend to dwell on people like Mark Antony, who are subject to strong and almost uncontrollable passions which they have learnt to direct towards noble ends, but which finally they prove unable fully to control. The 'Life' of Coriolanus is conceived partly as a study in how anger can become uncontrollable in someone who has not had a proper—and 'proper' for Plutarch would mean Greek—education. There is an aesthetic relish in his portrayals of these un-Stoic Romans, and perhaps too a faint suggestion of Greek *schadenfreude*, as he presents the conquerors conquered by their un-Roman passions: the butchered Roman general Crassus whose head becomes a prop in a Greek play put on by a barbarous tribe is in this respect not entirely alien to Plutarch's larger concern with putting Romans in their place.

Plutarch applies particular stress to one aspect of ancient masculinity: its competitiveness. Plutarch's Alexander the Great competes with his father to have more realms to conquer ('For he delighting neither in pleasure nor riches, but only in valiantness and honour, thought that the greater conquests and realms his father should leave him, the less he should have to do with for himself', iv, 302), Cicero was 'by nature ambitious of honour' (ii, 317) and had an 'extreme covetous desire of honour in his head' (ii, 337), while Julius Caesar competes even with himself:

> the prosperous good success he had of his former conquests bred no desire in him quietly to enjoy the fruits of his labours, but rather gave him hope of things to come, still kindling more and more in him thoughts of greater enterprises, and desire of new glory, as if that which he had present were stale and nothing worth. This humour of his was no other but an emulation with himself as with another man, and a certain contention to overcome the things he prepared to attempt. (v, 59)

Plutarch's emphasis on the aspiring, emulous, and contentious minds of his Romans created a set of conflicts within Shakespeare's conception of Romanness. Were Romans constant creatures, driven by a desire to fulfil their public offices and to control their passions, or were they beings driven by what Plutarch terms 'greedy desire of honour' (v, 17)? Or were they all of these things?

The Greek perspective on Rome provided by Plutarch was misaligned by several degrees from what Shakespeare would have regarded as 'Roman'. This was the greatest single source of the apparent three-dimensionality of Shakespeare's Plutarchan plays. His Romans are often internally self-contradictory or at odds with themselves, their peers, or their political environments. The scornful patrician Coriolanus fails to fit a Rome increasingly dominated by the Tribunes of the People. The reflective Brutus cannot succeed in a world dominated by intrigue and rhetoric, in which emulation and aspiration become the principal drive of the conspirators. The passionate Antony is set to lose the competition with Octavius Caesar, partly because of his susceptibility to Cleopatra, but also because he lacks the control over information which Caesar displays, and which Shakespeare presents as the crucial emerging virtue in the dawning of Augustan Rome. These characters stand out from their background because they do not quite fit in with it. And that was partly because what Plutarch told Shakespeare about these characters did not quite correspond to what he believed about Rome.

Plutarch's view of Roman politics was also slightly askew from what Shakespeare might have believed about Rome from other sources. Most grammar-school-educated Elizabethans read some Livy, some of Ovid's *Fasti*, and perhaps delved a little in other Roman and Italian historians. They would have thought of Rome as a dynamic polity, which repeatedly moved between republican aristocratic forms of government and various forms of monarchy or empire. Plutarch, however, tended to present the Roman state and Roman society as divided between a small group of the nobility and a much larger and more unstable group of common people. His political ideal was, broadly speaking, a kind of oligarchical republicanism, where a small group of highly educated (and ideally Greek-educated) patricians rule over a more or less benignly treated group of plebeians, whose interests are almost intrinsically at odds with those of the patricians. This leads Plutarch often to present political conflict at Rome—and indeed in Greece—in starkly polarized ways. At one point the nobility might seize too much wealth, with the result that the plebeians will rise against them. At another the avaricious plebeians might insist that the nobility yield more of the common good. North's translation very often adapts this rather simplified model of Roman politics to an Elizabethan political vocabulary, and makes it seem as though Rome was a kind of mixed or balanced constitution akin to England, which was always in danger of collapsing into tyranny: he says that Caesar 'brought the commonwealth of Rome into an absolute monarchy' (ii, 334). Early-modern English political language was very flexible: a 'commonwealth' could be equivalent to our 'republic' or refer more neutrally to a 'common doing of a multitude of free men collected together and united by common accord';[13] but most Elizabethans would have regarded an 'absolute monarchy' as something to fear.

The balanced ethical judgements of the *Lives*, their perplexing blend of anti-Stoicism and their apparent valorization of passion, their conjunction of political analysis and gossip, their constant and self-conscious attempts to reconcile a whole range of conflicting historical sources—all these were exciting in themselves. But they were particularly exciting for Shakespeare in 1598–9, when he began work on his first Plutarchan play. He had over the previous few years been writing plays about English history, which were based largely on chronicle sources. There was a huge gulf in historiographical theory and in practice between the *Chronicles* of Holinshed from which Shakespeare chiefly worked for his English history plays, and the philosophically informed, rhetorically shaped *Lives* of Plutarch. Those differences would not have been quite so obvious to Shakespeare as they appear today, however. Holinshed compiled together a number of different sources, and the treatments of different reigns covered by the *Chronicles* vary in their perspective as a result of the eclectic blend of different historical documents and different historiographical methods from which they derive.[14] Holinshed often seemed to present Britain as a commonwealth of potentially disparate elements—nobility, commons, kings—which periodically overreached themselves. The repeated references in North's Plutarch to mixed constitutions, to the balance between the needs of the rich and those of the poor, came from historical origins which were wildly different from the chaotic mixed constitutionalism that emerged from Shakespeare's reading of Holinshed. But the apparent similarities between the two was probably why Shakespeare turned to Rome after he had completed his series of plays on Henry V. The first of these was *Julius Caesar.*

## Antique Romans: *Julius Caesar*

*Julius Caesar*, written in or around 1599 in the anxious last years of Elizabeth I, is set in 44 BC. It is much preoccupied with time. Allusions to the hour of day lace the speeches of the conspirators: an anachronistic clock chimes three as they decide not to kill Antony along with Caesar, and Caesar rises in his nightshirt a little before it strikes eight (2.2.114). There were of course no clocks in Rome, let alone nightshirts. Does this mean that Shakespeare's view of Rome was completely lacking in any sense of the antiquity of the action presented onstage or of the customs of that alien place?

Very much not. The onstage clock is, oddly enough, an attempt at fidelity to his source: North states that this event happened 'past three of the clock in the afternoon' (iii, 231). Shakespeare simply took the most direct route to indicate this onstage, which was to make a clock sound. The anachronistic but timely chiming clock, though, tells us more than this. Rome in *Julius Caesar* is not about only one place or time. It is built up from several strata of pasts, and reflects the complexity both of Plutarch and of Shakespeare's reading of Plutarch. The brilliance of the play lies in the ways in which it moves almost invisibly from one of those levels of the past to the next. Markers of 'antiquity', which represent the action on the stage as belonging to a distant and culturally distinct past, tend to occur at specific kinds of moment. So when Shakespeare represents a religious ritual, he, like Plutarch before him, will tend to emphasize the alienness of Roman customs. The feast of the Lupercalia is a good example. Shakespeare learnt about this through Plutarch, whose Greek curiosity about Roman religious rites prompted him to describe it several times. Caesar offers almost a footnote on this ancient rite when he urges Antony, who in 1.2 is stripped and ready for the race in which matrons were struck with goatskin thongs, 'To touch Calpurnia, for our elders say | The barren, touchèd in this holy chase, | Shake off their sterile curse' (1.2.9–11).

There are other kinds of scene, however, when the division between the play's historical setting and the Elizabethan present breaks down. This is particularly true of crowd scenes. The cocky cobbler in 1.1, who 'lives by his awl', is not a Roman, nor is his friend the carpenter, and the crowd does not include olive-oil sellers, freedmen, or any kind of Roman local colour. The reason for this is straightforward, and does not have much to do with Plutarch. Whenever the scene represented onstage roughly approximates to the crowd gathered at the Globe theatre, then the Roman people and the Elizabethan theatre-going public seem to blend together. As a result, it is in crowd scenes that Rome is particularly prone to sound like Shakespeare's own 'commonwealth'. Part of the theatrical risk taken in this play is to make a crowd of angry and rebellious Roman plebeians blend into the audience at the Globe, and one of the reasons why Shakespeare could get away with doing this was because he combined these very English moments with historical details about specifically Roman practices drawn from Plutarch. These made the action of the play seem historically remote, and partly served to defuse any potentially disturbing resemblances between the near-monarchy of Julius Caesar and late Elizabethan England.

*Julius Caesar* is intent on representing a Rome which is not only ancient, but ancient in multiple different ways and along several different axes. This is a profound truth about the play, but it is not one that instantly leaps out either from performance or from the page. The language of *Julius Caesar* was described by E. K. Chambers as 'deliberately experimenting in a classical manner, with an extreme simplicity both of vocabulary and phrasing'.[15] The play's lack of obtrusive imagery, the relative absence from it of puns or lexical innovations, its tendency to rely heavily on monosyllables, its relish in extended forensic displays, all make it seem as though Shakespeare was trying to signal 'Roman' language by holding back on some of his own most obvious stylistic signatures and by creating characters who instinctively make speeches rather than conversing. If the play is set beside the exuberantly 'English' prose of Falstaff (written at most a couple of years before), it seems dry, focused, and programmatically disambiguated, as though Rome lives in a state of spare certainty. When Julius Caesar's wife Calpurnia warns him of the portentous 'horrid sights seen by the watch' (2.2.16), he insists that these will not keep him at home because 'Cowards die many times before their deaths; | The valiant never taste of death but once' (2.2.32–3). That sententious declaration is typical of this play's 'Roman' style: certain and declarative, Shakespeare's Romans utter truths with which it is impossible to argue, and Shakespeare seems to have made them do this almost to the point of comedy. Ben Jonson wickedly recorded that in an early version of the play Julius Caesar uttered the magnificent line (which is either an oxymoron or a tautology, or perhaps a miraculous fusion of the two) 'Caesar did never wrong, but with just cause.' The play as we have it does not include that phrase, although Caesar does say to Metellus 'Know Caesar doth not wrong, nor without cause | Will he be satisfied' (3.1.47–8: the one-volume Oxford edition emends 'nor without cause' to 'but with just cause' on the grounds that Jonson records the performed version; the text quoted here follows the Folio). It may be that here Shakespeare felt that his attempt to evoke absolute moral authority had gone too far, and revised the original line.

Despite this marmoreal clarity of style, *Julius Caesar* is often said to mark a turning point in Shakespeare's career, in which he was rehearsing for the kind of psychological inwardness which is often supposed to be represented in *Hamlet*. Brutus is sometimes said to be the first character on the English stage to have an inner life (something which could only be said if one ignores large sections of Marlowe and Kyd, and indeed many earlier moments in Shakespeare, but people do say some strange things about Shakespeare).[16] The psychological complexity of Shakespeare's Romans is probably not the result of a blinding moment at which Shakespeare suddenly realized that people have things going on inside their heads as well as around them. It is to a great extent a product of their temporal complexity. Hamlet, as we have seen, has an awareness of the past in various different respects: he has a sense of an 'ancient' style which is appropriate for 'epic' actions in the speech about Hecuba (discussed above, pp. 62–71), he has a past before the play, and he has perhaps also an 'archaic' notion of revenge with which the 'modern' hero feels uncomfortable. *Julius Caesar* shows a similarly layered and multiple awareness of antiquity. And part of that historical awareness derives, oddly enough, from the way the play makes Shakespeare's ancient Romans be afraid that they might be 'modern'—which in Shakespeare's vocabulary usually meant 'inferior to the past'. This is because Rome for Shakespeare's Romans is not just where they live. It is also a historical idea which they have to live up to. This is relentlessly played on, and perhaps even exploited, by the conspirators. When Cassius is leading Casca on into the conspiracy he declares that:

> Romans now
> Have thews and limbs like to their ancestors.
> But woe the while! Our fathers' minds are dead,
> And we are governed with our mothers' spirits. (1.3.79–82)

The earliest usages of the word 'thews' tend to mean 'customs'. It then comes (as here) to mean 'bodily proportions' (usually implying that they are ample: wimps and weaklings do not have either 'thews' or sinews). The word asserts physical continuity between the Roman past and its present and insists that there is nothing defective about modern Roman physiques, before Cassius goes on to suggest that it is modern behaviour ('thews' in the old sense) which has declined into effeminacy. The conspiracy against Julius Caesar is partly an attempt by Romans to recover the past—to reanimate a spirit of ancient Rome and ancient Roman virtue, which brings with it republicanism and tyrannicide. Within this project there lives an animating spark of parricidal emulation which is historically and politically regressive: the conspirators are prone to believe that if they kill Caesar they can become true 'ancient' Romans again, free from his control, like their own fathers. This desire on the part of the conspirators to bring back the ancient Roman past of the early republic is why they so often seem to be (in the play's own phrase) 'Roman actors', or people who are acting in accordance with an idea of Rome and Romanness which they do not seem quite to inhabit by instinct. Plutarch's portrayal of Brutus played a central role in this, since he is a man of many roles, both a public actor and a nocturnal soliloquist:

> When he was out of his house, he did so frame and fashion his countenance and looks that no man could discern he had anything to trouble his mind. But when night came that he was in his own house, then he was clean changed. For, either care did wake him against his will when he would have slept, or else oftentimes of himself he fell into such deep thoughts of this enterprise, casting in his mind all the dangers that might happen. (iii, 193)

Brutus is not only psychologically complex: he is a Roman with a complex heritage, who is descended from tyrannicides, and is forced to play a part in a 'modern' Rome in which he is uncomfortable and historically out of place. There is perhaps a trace of metatheatrical convenience behind this: Elizabethan actors would find it easier to act ancient Romans who were not quite comfortable with the idea that they were ancient Romans than they would acting unselfconsciously ancient Romans. But the effect of this experiment with staging Plutarchan inwardness is in Brutus the creation of a character who is repeatedly changing and improvising the relationship between his inner thoughts and his actions, and who is continually attempting to realign himself against different versions of his nation's past.

The patrician conspirators in *Julius Caesar* are similarly not fixed embodiments of Roman virtue. They are torn between dimly remembered ideas of Stoic constancy and the radical competitiveness ascribed by Plutarch to his Romans. They are also haunted by the past, even driven by it. So, in Act 1 Scene 2, Cassius tempts Brutus to join the conspiracy against Caesar. Meanwhile, in the background, it seems as though the Roman republic is coming to an end, as Caesar is offered the crown of Rome. Cassius's argument to Brutus chiefly rests on the fact that Caesar is just another man and so cannot deserve sole supremacy in the state: 'I was born free as Caesar, so were you. | We both have fed as well, and we can both | Endure the winter's cold as well as he' (1.2.99–101). But he goes on to relate—in a passage that has no foundations in Plutarch—how 'once' on a winter's day Caesar challenged him to a swimming competition in the Tiber:

> But ere we could arrive the point proposed,
> Caesar cried 'Help me, Cassius, or I sink!'
> Ay, as Aeneas our great ancestor
> Did from the flames of Troy upon his shoulder
> The old Anchises bear, so from the waves of Tiber
> Did I the tirèd Caesar. And this man
> Is now become a god ... (1.2.112–18)

A commonplace of Latin literature and historiography is the myth that Rome was founded by tough men, who could endure any degree of hardship in order to graft a living out of a harsh landscape. They lived a simple and austere life. This went along with the belief that this 'prisca virtus', or ancient virtue, was followed by a softening of physique and a corresponding moral decline into soft and pampered ease. Cassius exploits that myth of ancient Rome in order to win

Brutus to his cause. He and Caesar, he suggests, were in the old days as tough as the toughest Romans from the ancient republic. They could swim in the Tiber on the coldest of winter days and endure unimaginable hardships. But that *modern* man, Caesar the future king, was weaker than Cassius. Cassius caps this point by an allusion to the very earliest period of Rome's existence—the moment when the mythical founder of Rome, Aeneas, had to carry his father Anchises from the flames of Troy in order to set out to establish the Roman nation. His claim is that Caesar is fallible, but also that he, Cassius, is a more perfect example of ancient Roman virtue than Caesar.

Yet what he says is also laden with the irony that comes from seeking analogies between past and present, and by the unsettling effects that follow from creating, as it were, parallel lives between ancient Rome and the Rome of the present. If Cassius's rescuing of Caesar from the Tiber is like Aeneas carrying Anchises from the flames of Troy, then is Cassius implicitly the single great Roman hero, the proto-king of Rome? Does this imply he sees *himself* as a king rather than Caesar? The example of Aeneas also introduces the awkward notion that Cassius imagines Caesar as his father. Aeneas, of course, rescued Anchises from death in the flames of Troy rather than killing him on the Capitol, as every schoolboy, Roman as well as Elizabethan, would know. As Sir Philip Sidney put it, 'who readeth Aeneas carrying old Anchises on his back, that wisheth not it were his fortune to perform so excellent an act?'[17] Is the ancient example of Aeneas in this respect functioning as a rebuke to Cassius? Does it suggest that he is a parricide and traitor rather than man of *pietas*?[18] Or does it indicate, as he himself would like it to, that he is a re-founder of Rome, a new Aeneas? The idea of ancient Rome seems to have a life of its own in *Julius Caesar*. It almost possesses an independent agency that can conflict with the attempts of the characters in the play to use it for their own purposes.

People who read about ancient Rome in the Elizabethan period were supposed to draw from it just the kind of exemplary authority which Cassius finds in his ancient Roman past. An ability to do as the Romans do was one of the principles which were supposed to follow from the classical education which Shakespeare and his contemporaries received in grammar school, and which was described in

Chapter 1. But what *Julius Caesar* does not imply—indeed, it strikingly does not do so—is that exemplary re-enactment of the past is a straightforwardly good thing. Rather, the use of past example to sanction present action seems a perplexing and misleading process. We can see this again when Brutus receives a letter urging him to act against Caesar on behalf of Rome. This supposedly represents the anonymous voice of the Roman people, although we know that actually it was forged by Cassius. Brutus reflects:

> My ancestors did from the streets of Rome
> The Tarquin drive when he was called a king. (2.1.53–4)

Ancient Rome is a moral *exemplum* for imitation in the present, it appears. But this moment is not simple. What disturbs the modern Brutus's exemplary reading of the earlier Roman hero Brutus's action in exiling the Tarquin kings from Rome after the rape of Lucretia is the way that the old exemplary story is combined with pressing demands for political action which he reads about in a string of letters which his audience knows to be forged. The historical sources and paradigms for his action, the witnesses to whose evidence he attaches weight, are substantially false. We might again recall Plutarch's delicately sceptical manipulation of sources, his fascination with 'reports' and testimonies, and his willingness to entertain multiple versions of Rome's foundation. Stories about ancient Rome are not simply true and to be imitated in this play: they are acts of persuasion, and those acts of persuasion can derive from either good or bad motives.

There has been a great deal of debate about the extent to which *Julius Caesar* might be associated with an anti-monarchical or republican movement or moment in late Elizabethan England. Critics have sometimes found in it advanced political views similar to those of the circle of the rebellious Earl of Essex, where there were clear signs of an interest in republican forms of government, in republican historiography, and in alternatives to hereditary monarchy.[19] The layered treatment of ancient Rome's own attitudes to antiquity in *Julius Caesar* points in a much more complex, though perhaps also politically more conservative, direction: it suggests that ancient Romans who acted on the example of early Rome consistently risked being misled by historical examples which were put together by unreliable witnesses in order to manipulate those who read them. That does not give a simple positive precedent to English Elizabethan readers who might seek to alter their own constitution because of their devotion to the ancient Roman example, any more than the play's highly 'contemporary' crowd scenes unequivocally invite its audience to identify with them: identification with the past is a threatening and disturbing matter in this play. And the idea of the Roman past might provide a stimulus to action; but this is a play written very shortly before *Hamlet*, in which all stimuli to action come under pressured investigation, and in which each stimulus is matched by a counter-stimulus to create not a single motive for action, but a blur of multiple motives. A desire to relive the past is no guarantee of moral probity, and can indeed be a mask for deception or self-deception.

Rome in *Julius Caesar* is, then, presented as a partially distinct cultural field, with its own characteristic kinds of moral language, and its own idea of the past. Rome in this play, though, manifests another aspect of 'antiquity'. The Rome of *Julius Caesar*, like Plutarch's Rome, often seems like another country, battered by events and forces which to Elizabethan audiences would seem archaic, terrifying, and uncontrollable. It is in particular a place awash with blood. Blood falls from the skies, stains the hands of the conspirators, inspires popular revulsion against them, and is eventually shed from the conspirators themselves as they seek a Roman death by suicide once their cause has failed. It is extraordinarily unsettling that a play so full of cautious, self-controlling moral rhetoric should also contain phrases like Antony's 'farewell, thou bleeding piece of earth', and have 'Fierce fiery warriors fight upon the clouds, | In ranks and squadrons and right form of war, | Which drizzled blood upon the Capitol' (2.2.19–21). Blood and supernatural beings sit in *Julius Caesar* at the same table as honour, constancy, and Roman virtue. This can create some moments of deeply unsettling drama. Brutus's wife Portia asks him to tell her what he is going to do, and reminds him that she is the daughter of Cato, that model of ancient Roman constancy. To prove that she comes from this ancient Roman bloodline, she says: 'I have made strong proof of my constancy, | Giving myself a voluntary wound | Here in the thigh' (2.1.298–300). 'Constancy' is one of the key words of the Roman moral vocabulary, and a 'voluntary wound', though its metrical awkwardness hints at its unnaturalness, is a Roman sign of virtue; but the juxtaposition here of constancy with a bleeding wound concealed in the thigh is so unsettling that in performance the scene can appear simply embarrassing. This moment illustrates that Shakespeare's ancient Rome is 'ancient' in at least two respects. It has its own moral language of Stoic 'constancy'; but the Rome of *Julius Caesar*, like that of *Titus Andronicus*, is also bloody in its antiquity. Cassius tempts Brutus on by saying his name is equal in power to that of Caesar: both are capable of raising the dead: 'Conjure with 'em: | "Brutus" will start a spirit as soon as "Caesar"' (1.2.147–8). Seconds after Portia has shown her wound, these shadows of an uncanny antiquity grow longer. Ligarius, who is sick, enters to confirm that he will take part in the conspiracy. He declares:

> By all the gods that Romans bow before,
> I here discard my sickness. Soul of Rome,
> Brave son derived from honourable loins,
> Thou like an exorcist hast conjured up
> My mortifièd spirit. (2.1.318–22)

What he means is that the virtuous image of Brutus, full of ancient Roman blood, has revived him. But the language in which he makes this claim is extremely revealing about what Shakespeare is doing with the idea of Rome in this play. Brutus is like an 'exorcist'. This is the first cited usage in *OED* which has an exorcist summoning up spirits rather than casting out devils. It is a slightly unnatural usage, which deprives the word of its purgative Christian associations, and which implies that Brutus's virtue has the power to make graves yawn and summon up the dead. It makes Ligarius speak as a dead spirit brought back from the afterlife by the conspiracy. Self-wounding, sacrificing, summoning up spirits, the Rome of *Julius Caesar* is a continual unsteady conjunction of high principle and bloody terror. Its moral ideals—which seem at once historically remote from the present and morally admirable—have as their almost indistinguishable twin another kind of antiquity which is savage and archaic. Ancient Rome is old not just because (as Plutarch put it) then 'valiantness was honoured in Rome above all other virtues' (ii, 144); it is also figured as antique in Shakespeare because it is a place in which uncanny and unnatural acts occur.

That archaic aspect of Rome is unmissable in the early scenes of *Julius Caesar*, with their portents, lions whelping in the streets, flashes of fire in the skies, the storms, comets, thunder, and shrieks of ghosts which reverberate through the first two acts of the play, all of which are distributed through those early scenes from a single passage of Plutarch:

For touching the fires in the element, and spirits running up and down in the night, and also these solitary birds to be seen at no one day's sitting in the great market place: are not all these signs perhaps worth the noting in such a wonderful chance as happened... Caesar's self also doing sacrifice unto the gods, found that one of the beasts which was sacrificed had no heart: and that was a strange thing in nature, how a beast could live without a heart. (v, 64)

It was probably Shakespeare's focus on these aspects of Rome that led him at a couple of points to write in a way that seems closer to Plutarch's words than either the humanistic translation of Amyot or North's faithful version of his French source.[20] When Caesar is killed, Plutarch describes him as being 'run through like some wild beast... for each person there needed to begin the sacrifice and taste of the slaughter'. This representation of the assassination as a sacrifice is present in Shakespeare's 'Let's be sacrificers but not butchers, Caius' (2.1.165). But North (following Amyot) simply says 'it was agreed among them, that every man should give him a wound, because all their parts should be in this murder' (v, 68).[21] This might be a sign that Shakespeare consulted a Latin version of Plutarch, but more probably it is an accidental consequence of his concentration on a Rome that kills and drizzles blood. The play seems to be driven by two forces which cannot quite look each other in the eye: the Roman heroes act like Roman heroes, founding their actions on the Roman past, and talking a moral language which tags them, from an Elizabethan perspective, as good old-fashioned Stoics. But *Julius Caesar* also creates a completely different kind of 'antiquity' which is alien to the regulated moral order which the Romans believe they inhabit. That is an antiquity of ghosts, spirits, blood, pollution, sacrifices, portents, and murder. This kind of 'antiquity' may owe something to Shakespeare's reading of Seneca's tragedies, in which hyper-real backgrounds of universal discord and disaster are routine companions of tragic events (see pp. 180–2 above), and it may also show traces of the violent world evoked in the early play *Titus Andronicus*. But unlike in Senecan drama, the Romans themselves consistently cannot interpret this backdrop of bloody portents. It is as though they simply cannot understand it within their restricted ethical vocabulary. Caesar himself is particularly prone to mishear the archaic voices in the play, and to translate them into a comfortable Roman moral language. So Caesar asks, before he sets off to the Capitol, 'What say the augurers?' (2.2.37). His servant replies:

> They would not have you to stir forth today.
> Plucking the entrails of an offering forth,
> They could not find a heart within the beast. (2.2.37–40)

Caesar takes the absence of a heart in the sacrifice (which again derives from that single passage in Plutarch on the omens at Rome) like this:

> The gods do this in shame of cowardice.
> Caesar should be a beast without a heart
> If he should stay at home today for fear. (2.2.41–3)

Caesar is deaf in one ear, and that is in various ways crucial to the play. His disability reminds us that this man who wants to be a monument and a king is mortal and frail, but also that the world is repeatedly telling him things which he simply cannot hear because he has an image of himself as constant, inflexible, perfect.

Just occasionally Caesar's own words suggest that he might be aware of the uncanny world which he persistently ignores. A little earlier in the same scene he insists to Calpurnia that 'Caesar shall forth. The things that threatened me | Ne'er looked but on my back; when they shall see | The face of Caesar, they are vanishèd' (2.2.10–12). The formality of the language here (Caesar habitually engages in what is called 'illeism': that is, he repeatedly refers to himself in the third person) suggests a military hero who turns to face his enemies and makes them flee in terror. But in this play so full of strange portents it's impossible to exclude the suspicion that these unspecified 'things that threatened me' are also imaginary fears, ghosts and bogeymen, which vanish when you turn to look at them. The Roman heroes of *Julius Caesar* are intent on separating the language of ancient Roman virtue from the world of archaic horror in which they find themselves. But Shakespeare insists that those two forms of antiquity live alongside each other, and only deafness like Caesar's, or thick sight like Cassius's, can fail to perceive that they are aspects of the same ancient world. The stories the Romans tell to encourage themselves and their rivals to act seem increasingly to be fictions on which they rely in order to keep out the dark that surrounds them.

### *Coriolanus*

Plutarch (and one could not quite say this about Virgil or Ovid) made Shakespeare think. It is often said that *Coriolanus* is closer to Plutarch's 'Life of Caius Martius Coriolanus' than any other of the Plutarchan plays are to their equivalent sources. That is true, but it is in many ways a misleading fact, since it might suggest that Shakespeare simply chopped and shaped the actions and speeches recorded in Plutarch's 'Life' of Coriolanus into theatrical form. This is not what he did with Plutarch here or elsewhere. He thought hard about the 'Life of Caius Martius Coriolanus', and, I will suggest, was particularly influenced by discursive passages in it which he could not directly dramatize. Those passages repeatedly feed the play's imagery and argument, and help create its picture of the very early Roman republic. Shakespeare may also, as will be argued at the very end of this chapter, have drawn on some elements in Plutarch which appear impossible to dramatize in order to develop some wider thoughts about the relationship between tragedy, the gods, and voluntary human actions.

These are large claims. The first thing to make clear in order to substantiate them is that Plutarch's 'Life of Coriolanus' contains not just a vivid biography of an early republican warrior. It also includes several passages in which Plutarch explains to his Greek audience the nature of Roman customs, and what were to him the slightly alien moral principles on which early Romans lived their lives. There is one very obvious example. When Caius Martius is given the title of 'Coriolanus', Plutarch painstakingly explains to his Greek audience how Romans came by their last names, their 'cognomens', or honorific surnames. These were acquired, he says, as a result of physical attributes or feats of arms, and were 'some addition given, either for some act or notable service, or for some mark on their face, or of some shape of their body, or else for some special virtue they had' (ii, 154–5). This passage on the customs of Rome sufficiently interested at least one early reader of Amyot's French text to make him underline it.[22] In a way Shakespeare underlines it too, although he was not ham-fisted enough to have attempted directly to dramatize this passage by (say) having a character come on and explain how Romans came by their surnames. Instead he attached enormous weight to names and name-giving throughout the play. 'Coriolanus' means 'the man who was victorious at Corioles', so the very title of the play suggests an equation between people's names and what they have done, and perhaps implies too that a person's identity is intimately connected with public recognition of their actions. The printed text of the play in the first Folio, which is thought to derive from an authorial draft, registers the significance of naming in ways which would be invisible in performance but highly visible (even to the point of being slightly confusing) to a reader: the central character's speech-headings change from 'Mar.' or 'Martius' to 'Corio.' or 'Cor.' once he has been given the honorific title 'Coriolanus' for his actions in the siege of Corioles. (This probably reflects the marginal notes to North's Plutarch rather than the text itself, since the former refer to him as 'Coriolanus' from this point onwards, while the latter carries on calling him 'Martius': Shakespeare even read Plutarch's margins carefully.) 'Welcome to Rome, renownèd Coriolanus'—the moment when the honorific name is used in public and at Rome—is the point that marks the change in speech-headings (2.1.164). Many editors mark the change from the moment the hero is acclaimed as 'Coriolanus' on the battlefield (1.10.64), despite the clear association in the Folio text between the honorific cognomen and the town of Rome. The concern with names also seeps out into the surrounding drama, and provides one of those little characterizing details which Plutarch himself had insisted were at the core of biographical history. So just a few stage moments after he has been offered the new name of Coriolanus, Caius Martius is so tired by his conquests that he is unable to remember the name of the Volscian who had given him hospitality, and whom he wishes to reward (1.9.89)—and that episode is made out of Plutarchan concerns with naming, but is not itself in Plutarch. Names become a theme of the play, at the end of which the hero 'forbade all names. | He was a kind of nothing, titleless, | Till he had forged himself a name o' the fire | Of burning Rome' (5.1.12–15). He seems, that is, to be seeking the new and terrifying cognomen of 'Romanus', the one who conquers Rome.[23] But of course, given the careful association the play has built up between such honorific names and formal welcomes by Rome, a man who destroys Rome almost by definition can never be given the name 'Romanus', since he will have destroyed the institution that would grant him that honorific title. As with *Antony and Cleopatra*, Shakespeare did not simply make a drama out of the actions related in the 'Life' of Coriolanus: he worked 'invisible' passages of exposition from his source into the theme and fabric of his play.

Shakespeare seems to have paid particularly close attention to his source at the moments when Plutarch's 'Life' presents Roman customs from the Greek historian's ethnographic perspective. When Coriolanus stands for public office, Plutarch writes as follows: 'For the custom of Rome was at that time, that such as did sue for any office should for certain days before be in the market place, only with a poor gown on their backs, and without any coat underneath, to pray the citizens to remember them at the day of election', so that 'they might show them their wounds they had gotten in the wars in the service of the commonwealth' (ii, 158). North's translation here was slightly wrong. The 'poor gown' was in both Plutarch and Amyot simply a toga, which was worn by candidates without a tunic beneath it so that they could readily show their wounds to their electorate. North's error prompts Shakespeare to invent a new garment, the 'napless vesture of humility' (2.1.231), the threadbare gown which Coriolanus wears when he appears before the plebeians to win their voices so that he can be elected consul. That chain of slight mistakes provides a good insight into the ways in which Shakespeare developed his conception of Rome with North's assistance. Plutarch explains a strange custom; North misunderstands and exaggerates its detail; Shakespeare responds by inventing a special early Roman costume worn by candidates for office.

He then feeds that 'Plutarchan' detail back into the drama. The scene in which Coriolanus puts on the vesture of humility in order to win the plebeians' 'voices' repeatedly draws attention to this 'custom': Coriolanus begs Menenius 'Let me o'erleap that custom' (2.2.137). Then when he does finally put on the napless vesture of humility he says, with heavy sarcasm reinforced by an ostentatiously bad rhyme, 'Custom calls me to't. | What custom wills, in all things should we do't' (2.3.117–18). Coriolanus at this point seems only partially assimilated to Roman practices, forced by 'custom' to do something which he cannot abide doing. As a result he seems almost a social anachronism, a patrician warrior who is living at a period in Rome's history when the Tribunes of the people and the plebeians themselves are dominating the republic, and who is provokingly at odds with the mood of his time. He is in a sense too ancient for early republican Rome.

It has been suggested that Shakespeare looked to Machiavelli or to other historians of Rome in order to understand the historical changes going on around Coriolanus.[24] This may be true, but Shakespeare could perfectly well have found within Plutarch a representation of Rome as a place of historical change, and perhaps also of decline. So Plutarch's description of electoral practices at Rome is followed by a passage explaining that candidates were compelled to dress without a tunic so that they could show their wounds, rather than to deprive them of hiding places for bags of money with which they could bribe the citizens to vote for them. 'It was but of late time, and long after this, that buying and selling fell out in election of officers, and that the voices of electors were bought for money' (ii, 158), he says. Plutarch's Rome has customs; it also changes and declines. As we have just seen, *Julius Caesar* represents a Rome which has various layers of history and a corresponding range of attitudes to virtue. *Coriolanus* is similar. Its hero only reluctantly adapts to the customs of his present, which are changing around him.

*Coriolanus*, a later, harder, and more uncompromising play than *Julius Caesar*, is, like its hero, difficult to like. That's partly because it attempts to evoke a much earlier Roman world than the earlier play. Towards the start of the 'Life' of Coriolanus, Plutarch states that Rome in this very early period of its history had a distinctive set of military and moral virtues: 'Now in those days, valiantness was honoured in Rome above all other virtues: which they called *Virtus*, by the name of virtue [it]self, as including in that general name all other special virtues besides. So that *Virtus* in the Latin, was as much as valiantness' (ii, 144). This passage is often quoted in relation to the play, but its most significant feature is sometimes overlooked: its tenses. They again show that Plutarch regarded Rome as an environment subject to change: 'in those days' points back to early republican Rome, but the final sentence suggests a much wider frame of reference, a Rome in which *virtus* meant 'valiantness' generally 'in the Latin'. And that slight slippage is very revealing about the perspective on Rome which Shakespeare took from Plutarch: it is a place in which ethical changes occur, even if the names by which it chooses to call virtue remain the same.

Shakespeare seems again to have virtually underlined this passage in Plutarch, since it surfaces at various points in *Coriolanus*. Cominius comes close to quoting Plutarch's remarks on 'valiantness' when he delivers his encomium of Coriolanus to the Roman people. In the mouth of Cominius, however, it becomes a statement not about 'old' Rome, but about the customs of the present moment, which is put into the present tense:

> It is held
> That valour is the chiefest virtue, and
> Most dignifies the haver. (2.2.83–6)

In its context, however, this is not a simple statement of fact about Rome, since it is positioned explicitly within a speech of advocacy: Cominius wants to persuade his audience that Coriolanus deserves public office, and throughout Shakespeare's Roman plays things that orators claim to be true tend not to be quite as true as they sound. The second time Plutarch's little bit of cultural history about early Roman virtue crops up in the play is slightly more unsettling. Shakespeare uses the word 'valiantness' for the only time in his career—and he must have learnt the word directly from North—when Volumnia, Coriolanus's mother, says to her son:

> Do as thou list.
> Thy valiantness was mine, thou sucked'st it from me,
> But owe thy pride thyself. (3.2.127–9)

The *really* antique Roman virtue is 'valiantness', martial energy. Volumnia identifies this not with an early stage in the Roman republic, but with the earliest stage of her son's life, and with her own milk. It is as though she is identifying herself and her own body with the most 'ancient' of all the ancient values of Rome. And that word 'ancient' in this play is only ever used in conjunction with abstract nouns for virtue or vice: so Coriolanus talks of his mother's 'ancient courage' (4.1.3); Sicinius refers to the 'ancient strength' of the plebeians (4.2.7). Sometimes the word means little more than 'long-standing' (Aufidius harbours 'ancient envy', 4.5.104, for Coriolanus which is matched by the 'ancient malice' felt towards him by plebeians and Aufidius alike, 2.1.225, 4.5.97); but in general 'ancient' in this play connotes 'old, constitutionally ingrained, part of the fabric of Rome' and it invites pairing with a term for antiquated virtue or a primal emotion.

These lexical details of the play are revealing about its overall structure and concerns. Coriolanus is represented as a social and historical throwback to ancient valiantness, who wishes to live in a world where this is all that you need. He is forced in the course of the play to compromise, with plebeians, with political structures, with Roman custom, and with his family. Volumnia's association between valiantness and her own maternal milk also suggests another vital aspect of the play. *Coriolanus* shares with *Julius Caesar* (and in many ways develops from it) a fascination with the unsettling relationship between abstract Roman virtues—constancy, courage—and physicality. *Coriolanus* is full of blood, nutritious milk, and perverse relationships between the two: warriors bleed so that the populace can live, 'tongues' are put into wounds (the populace votes for martial heroes), and the 'body politic' becomes a near-literal combination of different parts of the body in which some parts bleed or suffer for the others, and some parts starve to enable the others to live. Some of this comes from Plutarch, whose 'Life' does give plenty of food for writing about Roman virtue in relation to corporeality: towards its beginning it relates the fable of the belly and its relationship to the rest of the body, while at its end the Romans attacked by Caius Martius 'properly resembled the bodies paralytic and loosed of their limbs and members: as those which through the palsy have lost all their sense and feeling' (ii, 179).

But Shakespeare makes the interrelationship between blood and wounds and ancient Roman 'valiantness' in this play extremely complex, and it is made to vary between social groups and among different characters within those groups. Coriolanus perceives a relatively simple relationship between blood and virtue: 'valiantness' prompts military action, military action leads to wounds, and these wounds are visible testimonies to 'valiantness', which in turn should lead to both a reputation for virtue and to political office. Acquiring a name or a reputation therefore for him should be in principle akin to having deeds inscribed in your flesh: wounds show valour, valour guarantees greatness, so wounds guarantee greatness.

There are moments when some plebeians are willing to see the relationship between valiantness and high office in this way too. The third citizen says: 'if he show us his wounds and tell us his deeds, we are to put our tongues into those wounds and speak for them; so if he tell us his noble deeds we must also tell him our noble acceptance of them' (2.3.5–9). But other citizens tend to deny that there is a necessary relationship between wounds, virtue, and public recognition. They know that the movement from the wounds of a warrior to his being granted a role in the government of Rome is not inevitable. The citizens have to feel gratitude for the wounds before they vote for the man who bears them, and as a price of gratitude they require the humility of the person asking for their voices. They regard Coriolanus's belief that an entitlement to office can be derived necessarily from the presence of wounds on his body not as a truth about the Roman world, but as a sign of pride. As a result the play evokes a Rome in which the relationship between wounds and virtue matters to everyone, but in which everyone has a slightly different view of that relationship. And the more 'ancient', more uncompromisingly patrician and 'valiant' characters tend to see the relationship in simpler terms than the 'newer' men, such as the Tribunes or the people whom they represent. That is the chief means in this play by which Shakespeare creates the sense of a Roman polity which is at once unified and diverse, and which contains varied historical and social layers. He creates several different metaphorical economies which live uneasily side by side, with a thin cloak of custom to hold them together: everyone agrees that 'valiantness' is a social good of some kind, but patricians tend to see physical prowess as inevitably connected to political superiority, while plebeians tend to see that relationship as contingent. This gives as it were a mental grammar and set of intellectual dialects with which to complicate Plutarch's relatively simple vision of the Roman commonwealth as a state divided between the patricians and the commons. Patricians and plebeians share a tongue, as it were, or speak a similar language, which conjoins physical and spiritual realities—bodies, wounds, valiantness, votes, virtues. But these two groups, and indeed different characters within these two groups, see the nature of that conjunction in quite different ways. For Coriolanus in particular even to praise the actions which gave rise to wounds is a kind of insult to their moral eloquence, since for him they betoken virtue. As a result he needs no other men's tongues to display his political merit. When he is offered a financial reward for his military action, he refuses it as a 'bribe' (1.10.38), as though such a reward would anticipate that decadent future Rome which Plutarch had obliquely evoked in his description of Roman voting practices. He wishes to believe that action writes itself onto the body, and wounds simply embody virtue, and talking about them is a kind of decadence from ancient valiantness.

Coriolanus's mother Volumnia holds a particularly extreme version of the patrician view that there is a necessary correlation between blood (bleeding, but also making other people bleed) and virtue. In Plutarch, the uncontrolled irascibility of Coriolanus is ascribed to his upbringing by his mother: he 'being left an orphan by his father, was brought up under his mother, a widow, who taught us by experience, that orphanage bringeth many discommodities to a child, but doth not hinder him to become an honest man, and to excel in virtue above the common sort...For lack of education he was so choleric and impatient that he would yield to no living creature, which made him churlish, uncivil, and altogether unfit for any man's conversation' (ii, 144). The good Greek Plutarch believed that Coriolanus lacked the kind of philosophical and rhetorical training that went along with Greek education. Shakespeare, however, turns the relationship between mother and son into one which is intimately connected to the state of Rome. Volumnia is the focal point of the play because she, more than any other patrician figure, including her son, insists on the counter-intuitive correlation of blood with virtue, and does so in ways that are even by early-modern standards aesthetically unsettling. At the more gentle end of her rhetoric, she says of her son if he had died in battle, 'Then his good report should have been my son. I therein would have found issue' (1.3.20–1). This paradox is not too hard to swallow, since reputation is a live thing for Rome, and a child who has fame does in a sense have a future life even if he is literally dead. But elsewhere Volumnia creates particularly stark conjunctions between cool virtue and bleeding pieces of earth. In relishing her son's wounds, she declares 'The breasts of Hecuba | When she did suckle Hector looked not lovelier | Than Hector's forehead when it spit forth blood | At Grecian sword, contemning' (1.2.42–4). A breast that feeds and a brow that spits blood are both, according to her logic, 'lovely', markers of beauty and presumably also of virtue. This claim might have been less unsettling to early seventeenth-century ears than it is to ours, since maternal milk was regarded as a blanched form of blood in this period. But it is significant that Volumnia, who sees herself as a primal embodiment of tough ancient Roman virtue, whose very breasts drip 'valiantness', looks back to the ancient Greek examples of Hecuba and Hector here to articulate her peculiar view of the relationship between blood and virtue. She presents a view of the relationship between virtue and the body which seems shockingly old, and seems to predate even the early Roman equation of valiantness with wounds and of wounds with virtue, and which seems almost to place her in a mythical past.

This presentation of Volumnia goes beyond anything Shakespeare found in Plutarch. His massive expansion of her role and significance is nonetheless a consequence of the way that he read and responded to Plutarch. He seems to have constructed *Coriolanus* effectively by reading Plutarch's 'Life' backwards. That is, his transformation of Plutarch's 'Life of Caius Martius Coriolanus' is dominated by the need to motivate and explain its final scene. Plutarch's 'Life' ends with the hero's mother Volumnia urging the alienated hero not to attack Rome. He gives way to her supplication, and this more or less directly causes his death at the hands of his former allies the Volscians. It is quite likely that the theatrical potential of this scene was what first drew Shakespeare to this particular biographical history: Plutarch has Coriolanus on 'a chair of state, with all the honours of a general' (ii, 183), from which he descends when the Roman women enter, whereupon he 'kissed his mother, and embraced her a pretty while, then his wife and little children' (ii, 183), who then kneel before him. Martius raises them up in response to his mother's appeal, and makes peace with Rome. This is in Plutarch very much a 'scene' in a theatrical sense, in which (in the words of Shakespeare's own play) 'action is eloquence' (3.2.76).[25] It could readily be reconceived as a play, in which physical movements (kneeling, rising, embracing) carry a vast emotional charge. Shakespeare greatly extends this scene and runs it almost in slow motion, so as to allow it to dramatize a crisis within the hero and within a Roman conception of *pietas*, in which concern for family and parents overwhelms personal constancy. And the way he makes it work is by relentlessly associating Volumnia with 'ancient' virtue, with 'valiantness' that Coriolanus drank in her milk, which is at once a source of life and at the same time bloody and destructive. Coriolanus has been nurtured and fed on the notion that Rome drinks the blood of its heroes, and that loving and being killed in order to nourish someone are more or less the same. He dies as a sacrifice to that logic.

There are, however, some striking differences between Shakespeare's treatment of this climactic scene and Plutarch's. In Plutarch the embassy to Coriolanus by the women of Rome is preceded by a visit from the priests of Rome. North describes this embassy as consisting of 'all the bishops, priests, ministers of the gods, and keepers of holy things and all the augurs or soothsayers, which foreshow things to come by observation of the flying of birds' (ii, 179). The language here may explain why Shakespeare did not follow Plutarch at this point, and may also give a hint why Roman religion, with its augurs, soothsayers, and flamens, is rather less in evidence in this play than it is in *Julius Caesar*: North makes ancient Rome sound both ancient ('augurs and soothsayers') and disturbingly like early-modern Rome, a haunt of 'bishops, priests' and home to the Roman Catholic Church. Shakespeare substitutes for this embassy an attempt by Coriolanus's former friend and surrogate father Menenius to beg him to end the siege of Rome. This suits the tendency in the play as a whole to represent Rome as a kind of body, in which family and social ties are more significant than religion and the supernatural. The visit from the fatherly Menenius also fits into a fairly consistent treatment of Rome as the family from which Coriolanus is attempting to separate himself, 'As if a man were author of himself | And knew no other kin' (5.3.36–7). The fact that it was Menenius who delivered the fable of the belly to the plebeians in the first scene also makes him the obvious symbolic vehicle to illustrate Coriolanus's abjuration of his connection to the body politic, and his renunciation even of the names given to him by Rome.

That's the simple aspect of the way Plutarch is transformed here. But there are also deeper processes at work. After the visit of the priests, Plutarch inserts a long section of literary and philosophical speculation, in which he describes how Homer represents the gods' influence over the actions of men. He addresses one of the central questions provoked by the Homeric poems, and indeed one of the central questions for writers of tragedy in the Western tradition: are human beings driven to destruction by the gods, or do they destroy themselves by their own free will? Plutarch quotes a number of passages from Homer which apparently represent the gods compelling human beings to act, then he cites others which show men acting on the basis of their own deliberations. He concludes that there is no apparent conflict between these two apparently different perspectives:

> But in wondrous and extraordinary things, which are done by secret inspirations and motions, he [that is, Homer] doth not say that God taketh away from man his choice and freedom of will, but that he doth move it: neither that he doth work desire in us, but objecteth to our minds certain imaginations whereby we are led to desire, and thereby doth not make this our action forced, but openeth the way to our will, and addeth thereto courage, and hope of success. (ii, 181)

The gods, that is, do not move our limbs and constrain us to action as though we are puppets on strings, but they present us with objects that move our passions and prompt us freely to act in response to them. This passage from the 'Life of Caius Martius Coriolanus', which Shakespeare does not explicitly incorporate into his play about Coriolanus, is another piece of Plutarch which set him thinking. It was the most obvious place for him to have encountered discussion of the complex of free will and divine motivation which underlies much Greek tragedy.[26] The author of *Macbeth*, a play in which supernatural soliciting operates on the desires of the hero—and in which 'imagination' and 'desire' are key terms of moral psychology—must have found much on which to reflect in this passage, even if it did not lend itself to direct representation in dramatic form. Shakespeare may well have had 'less Greek', as Jonson claimed; he may well not have read Homer or Sophocles; and he may have only read some plays by Euripides in Latin translation; but he did have Plutarch to inform him of Homeric thinking about the relationship between the gods and human actions.

Plutarch's very Greek speculations about the nature of volition do feed into Shakespeare's Roman tragedy, but they do so in oblique ways. In Plutarch this long digression on moral philosophy is followed by a description of how Valeria, Publicola's sister, decides to visit Volumnia 'through the inspiration (as I take it) of some god above' (ii, 182) in order to persuade her to go and appeal to the obdurate Coriolanus. Shakespeare completely cuts this episode. His embassy from the Roman women does not originate in the divine prompting of Valeria. The women arrive suddenly and unexpectedly, heralded only by a 'shout within' (5.3.18, stage direction). At first glance that might appear to be all of a piece with Shakespeare's tendency in *Coriolanus* to downplay the importance of Roman religion, and to move Volumnia to its motive centre. But it does not indicate that Plutarch's complex piece of tragic argument struck him as an irrelevant piece of philosophizing which he could simply skip in reading and omit from his theatrical version. A ghost of it remains in the surviving text of the play. Among the embassy of mother, wife, and son that visits Coriolanus as he sits waiting to attack Rome is indeed Valeria. In a curious and unexplained moment Volumnia says: 'Do you know this lady?' and Coriolanus replies:

> The noble sister of Publicola,
> The moon of Rome, chaste as the icicle
> That's candied by the frost from purest snow
> And hangs on Dian's temple—dear Valeria! (5.3.64–8)

Valeria, who has a small speaking role elsewhere in the play, remains a mute throughout the scene. Editors and critics have puzzled over her significance. Why is she given such a fulsome greeting here?[27] She may just be a relic of the ancient source, or she might even conceivably be a relic of an earlier version of the play in which, as in Plutarch, Valeria prompted the delegation of Roman women. Certainly Valeria carries over onto the stage something of the uncanny power she has in Shakespeare's source: her theatrical charge, registered in Coriolanus's response to her, seems to exceed anything she says or does. And although the play tends to keep to the level of human drama, of the body, of the family and piety towards parents and kin, this scene does register a shadow of divine motivation inherited from Plutarch. As Coriolanus yields to his mother's persuasions in Plutarch he says:

> And with these words, herself, his wife and children, fell down upon their knees before him. Martius seeing that could refrain no longer, but went straight and lifted her up, crying out 'Oh mother, what have you done to me?' And holding her hard by the right hand, 'Oh mother,' said he, 'You have won a happy victory for your country, but mortal and unhappy for your son: for I see myself vanquished by you alone.' (ii, 186).

Shakespeare inserts a pause to let the hero's anguish show—to allow, as it were, the motivating passion so painstakingly described in his source silently to pull on his hero. Coriolanus then speaks:

> O mother, mother!
> What have you done? Behold, the heavens do ope,
> The gods look down, and this unnatural scene
> They laugh at. O my mother, mother, O!
> You have won a happy victory to Rome;
> But for your son, believe it, O believe it,
> Most dangerously you have with him prevailed,
> If not most mortal to him. (5.3.183–90)

These are the most memorable lines in the play. They derive directly from North's Plutarch, but they are made to resound far more widely than their equivalents in the source. It is so simple to omit the 'to me' from 'Oh mother, what have you done *to me*?' (and North here, via Amyot, accurately reflects Plutarch's Greek), but it reads like a radical transformation: the personal destruction of Coriolanus seems suddenly to expand outwards into a general tragedy. 'What have you done?' puts the stress on 'done', and on what has been done not just 'to me' but to the world. Then to bring in the gods as unmoved spectators of this 'unnatural scene' is simply amazing. It suddenly makes sense of the almost complete removal of references to Roman religious rites, practices, and portents in the play as a whole. In Plutarch the gods do not play with men like puppets, but they do provide objects and occasions which can move the passions, which can prompt human beings to act freely and of their own volition in response to a divine stimulus. In the Rome of *Coriolanus*, on the other hand, the gods seem to be an audience disengaged entirely from human emotions, who laugh at our tragedies. The play is relentlessly themed, and its vocabulary and imagery—right through its allusions to dragons and butterflies—seem to focus in violently on its central character: here the image of gods as spectators pulls together several references in the play to Coriolanus as a kind of actor ('Rather say I play | The man I am', 3.2.13–14). The whole 'unnatural scene', in which Coriolanus's love for his mother, an embodiment of simultaneously nutritious and murderous ancient Roman virtue, effectively causes his death, connects to the many associations between love and death in the play (as Aufidius says: 'Here I clip | The anvil of my sword, and do contest | As hotly and as nobly with thy love | As ever in ambitious strength I did | Contend against thy valour', 4.5.110–14). It also harks distantly back to Volumnia's unnatural preference for foreheads that spit blood over breasts that provide nutritious milk. Plutarch's gods, who motivate the female embassy to Coriolanus, which in turn moves the hero's passions, which in turn brings about his death, are transformed into cruel gods, who want to laugh at human tragedy and destruction. They are not the philosophically sophisticated gods of Homer or Sophocles or Plutarch, though the gods in Homer do often take the attitude of detached spectators to mortal actions. They are gods who are more akin to an Elizabethan audience, observing with a savage detachment the performance of an ancient Roman tragedy.

# *Conclusion*

When Thomas Heywood wrote his *Apology for Actors* shortly before Shakespeare's death, he began by considering the 'antiquity' of the theatre. Heywood wanted to make moralists and theologians, who were generally hostile to the stage, believe that it was 'antique' and therefore venerable and useful. Heywood went on to argue that plays could represent actions from classical antiquity so vividly that present-day audiences could learn from them how to reanimate the virtue of the past:

> To see a Hector all besmeared in blood, trampling upon the bulks of kings; a Troilus returning from the field in the sight of his father Priam as if man and horse even from the steed's rough fetlocks to the plume in the champion's helmet had been together plunged into a purple Ocean; to see a Pompey ride in triumph, then a Caesar conquer that Pompey; labouring Hannibal alive, hewing his passage through the Alps; to see, as I have seen, Hercules in his own shape hunting the boar, knocking down the bull, taming the hart, fighting with Hydra, murdering Geryon, slaughtering Diomed, wounding the Stymphalides, killing the centaurs, pashing the Lion, squeezing the dragon, dragging Cerberus in chains, and lastly, on his high pyramids writing *Nil ultra*: Oh these were sights to make an Alexander.[1]

'Oh these were sights to make an Alexander'—that phrase brings out one central aspect of early-modern attitudes to what we call 'the classics' on the stage. Bringing to life ancient heroes in the theatre could, in theory at least, have a moral effect on the present. It could even result in a kind of practical miniature 'renaissance', by reanimating the spirit of heroes like Alexander the Great among its audience.

Heywood should not be regarded as simply a spokesman for his age, however: he wrote a number of plays on classical themes, and was in this passage both blowing his own trumpet and defending his own profession against critical attacks from those who thought the theatre was a nursery of vice and idleness. But he does illustrate one of the themes of this book: that there were many layers to the concept of 'antiquity' in Shakespeare's period. 'Antiquity' could mean a distant past which might be studied in the way that anthropologists study alien cultures today, and in which ancient Romans display distinctively Roman 'valiantness'. 'Antiquity' could also be used to give a gloss of respectability to contemporary institutions such as the theatre. Or it could mean a pattern of moral or military excellence that might be revived by imitation, and which could influence the conduct of its audience.

The introduction to this book asked whether Shakespeare resembled the eighteenth-century art historian Johann Winckelmann in any way. Did he regard classical antiquity as a separate cultural field? Did he approach the classical past with the quasi-erotic longing with which Winckelmann described his love for the artworks of ancient Greece? This book has aimed to show that in a whole range of ways Shakespeare's engagement with classical antiquity could make him *appear to be* rather more like Winckelmann than he probably was. In the Roman plays he clearly was interested in the customs and distinctive behaviours of ancient Rome, though that came chiefly from Plutarch's curious Greek perspective on Roman culture and was by no means programmatically maintained in Shakespeare's plays. In his earlier writing, passages deriving from Ovid and Virgil are sometimes tagged as 'ancient' in their style or their setting in ways that make them sound as though they come from an earlier historical period. That was partly the consequence of the 'antiquity', relatively speaking, of English translations of those writers by the 1590s. Shakespeare was also in all probability looking back to his own grammar-school past to bring his knowledge of those works back to life. We also saw in Chapter 1 that an erotic, and sometimes a homoerotic, charge could surround the learning of classical texts in the early-modern classroom. All of these aspects of Shakespeare's response to classical antiquity make it in many ways more interesting than it would have been if he had had a clear sense of Graeco-Roman culture as a separate world, or if he had had a rigorously conceptualized understanding of what was involved in borrowing from or alluding to a classical author. He could make use of his classical reading so richly because he did not have a dogmatic or a programmatic attitude to it. Thomas M. Greene has seen a longing for a lost past as a characteristic feature of the Renaissance imagination.[2] Shakespeare did not directly articulate this longing, but he could often more or less accidentally sound as though he shared in it.

Shakespeare's *Sonnets* (which were printed in 1609, but which were probably written over quite a long period from the early 1590s up until some time close to their publication) provide particularly rich examples of the surprising and suggestive ways in which he could use his knowledge of and beliefs about classical antiquity. Many of the sonnets appear to be addressed to a young man, with whom the speaker seems to be in love. In the sonnets early in the printed sequence, in which the young man is urged to have children, he is potentially the source of a very literal kind of 'renaissance' or rebirth, in which his own beauty is reproduced in a son. He is also an object of some kind of desire. Curiously too he can be represented as something like a classical antiquity who is vividly alive in the present. According to the speaker of Sonnet 53, ancient and mythological beauties are not the archetypes of the young man's beauty, but instead are pale imitations of his loveliness:

> Describe Adonis, and the counterfeit
> Is poorly imitated after you.
> On Helen's cheek all art of beauty set,
> And you in Grecian tires are painted new. (53.5–8)

This seems to flip around Heywood's claim that seeing past heroes onstage could revive their virtues in the present. In the last two lines quoted here there is almost the suggestion of an impromptu androgynous piece of theatre, as the young man dresses himself as Helen of Troy 'painted new' in the sense of 'newly depicted' and also 'freshly made up and sexy in the here and now'. The 'ancient' world and the present are blended together along with the sexes in a way that is charged with eroticism and delight.

The sonnets are also much preoccupied with Time, who is urged 'O, carve not with thy hours my love's fair brow | Nor draw no lines there with thine antique pen' (19.9–10). That use of 'antique' is typical of Shakespeare: Time is crazy, a destructive fool. Like King Lear, he is an 'antic' in the sense of a madman as well as an old man. Perhaps Time is also imagined as someone who doodles what was known as 'antique work', or the swirling classical ornamentation of frown lines, over the lover's brow. The poet then says the young man should be preserved against the ravages of time, 'For beauty's pattern to succeeding men'. He is turned into an ideal for the future, a sort of modern 'antiquity' in the sense of a 'past object which invites wonder', who is preserved from the defacing 'antique pen' of Time by the modern pen of the poet. Sonnet 59 even represents the beloved as a contemporary wonder who surpasses those of antiquity:

> If there be nothing new, but that which is
> Hath been before, how are our brains beguiled,
> Which, labouring for invention, bear amiss
> The second burden of a former child!
> O that record could with a backward look
> Even of five hundred courses of the sun
> Show me your image in some antique book
> Since mind at first in character was done,
> That I might see what the old world could say
> To this composèd wonder of your frame;
> Whether we are mended, or whe'er better they,
> Or whether revolution be the same.
> O, sure I am the wits of former days
> To subjects worse have given admiring praise.

The antiquity imagined here is certainly associated with nostalgia and longing, but all of that nostalgia and longing seems to be turned the wrong way round. The speaker says, more or less, 'If all that we modern poets can bring forth is a version of what is old, then we are deluding ourselves if we think we can make new things. I want to look back at the past, and see if there was a parallel to your unsurpassable beauty in an ancient book. I would then be able to make a direct comparison between the poets of the present day and those of classical antiquity, and see how the ancients would fare when they wrote about you, and know whether we have an advantage over them simply as a result of your exceptional beauty, which we alone can represent, rather than our skill'. The longing for an 'antique book' is offset by an affection for modernity that is almost outrageous: the implication is that the object of his love is so superior to ancient beauties that all modern poems written about him must be better than their ancient rivals, and so the claim that modern poets can only reproduce old works is false. The young man makes it new.

As that example shows, Shakespeare's vision of 'antiquity' is very often just slightly out of step with orthodoxies, and is also often just slightly not what you would expect it to be. Why is 'record' asked to look back 'five hundred years'? A pedant would solemnly work out that this takes us to about 1100 (a date which probably had no literary significance for Shakespeare at all) rather than beyond that date to classical antiquity. That is a sign of how Shakespeare's conception of the 'antique' extends through the late medieval into what we now call 'classical antiquity'. There is a clear sense here of a past which is irrecoverably lost: 'record' *cannot* look back and find perfect beauty in the ancient archives, presumably because devouring time has done its work. The poet is therefore free to construct his own idealistic image of the young man afresh in the present. Shakespeare had a truncated view of the past similar to that which was articulated by Michel de Montaigne in one of his *Essays*. Montaigne (who was brought up speaking Latin as his first language) says that figures from the classical past were just as present to him as his own father, who had died only eighteen years before:

> I have more remembered and thought upon the fortunes and conditions of Lucullus, Metellus and Scipio, than of any of our countrymen. They are deceased, and so is my father, as fully as they: and is as distant from me and life in eighteen years as they were in sixteen hundred: whose memory, amity and society, I notwithstanding omit not to continue to embrace and converse withal, with a perfect and most lively union.[3]

There are two features of this passage that make it a particularly valuable aid for thinking about Shakespeare's relation to classical antiquity. Montaigne collapses time so that the ancient past and the recent past are both equally distant from the present. His father and Scipio are equally near or far. He also emphasizes the 'memory, amity and society' that link together the present, the recent past, and classical antiquity. The young man in Shakespeare's *Sonnets*, who surpasses the past, who is loved and described in the present, but who remains distant from the author and an unattainable object of desire, is very much a figure who embodies 'antiquity' in this range of senses: simultaneously distant and near, he is loved through being remembered and written about rather than through being present.

'Antiquity' also plays a part in the group of sonnets traditionally referred to as the 'rival poet' group. The identity of the 'rival' poet has been the subject of much inconclusive speculation: Marlowe or Chapman are the favourites, although it's more likely that he is an imagined composite figure.[4] The 'rival poet' is a young, modern, varied, changeful, rhetorically energetic poet against whom Shakespeare can define his own poetic identity. One aspect of that poetic identity is Shakespeare's own antiquity, both in the physical and the stylistic senses. Shakespeare's persona in the sequence, 'beated and chapped with tanned antiquity' (62.10) as he is, confesses that his style is antiquated in comparison to the poems written by his rivals:

> I never saw that you did painting need,
> And therefore to your fair no painting set.
> I found—or thought I found—you did exceed
> The barren tender of a poet's debt;
> And therefore have I slept in your report:
> That you yourself, being extant, might well show
> How far a modern quill doth come too short,
> Speaking of worth, what worth in you doth grow.
> This silence for my sin you did impute,
> Which shall be most my glory, being dumb;
> For I impair not beauty, being mute,
> When others would give life, and bring a tomb.
> There lives more life in one of your fair eyes
> Than both your poets can in praise devise. (Sonnet 83)

The contrast between the poet's plain, mute love and the 'painting' offered by the rival poet is clear enough. But here again part of the allure of the beloved comes from his association with antiquity: 'you yourself being *extant*' uses 'extant' in *OED* sense 4(b): 'Continuing to exist; that has escaped the ravages of time, still existing', and the word in that sense is often used of texts which have survived the destructive effects of time (Hamlet boasts that the Italian story of the murder of Gonzago is 'extant', 3.2.250). The young man, despite his resemblance to an ancient text, 'grows' and 'lives' in a way that cannot be replicated by a 'modern' quill—and here the word 'modern' exploits the recently emergent sense of 'now, as opposed to antiquity' and the equally recent sense 'up to the minute, fashionable'. The sonnet, though, gives to these meanings of 'modern' a negative charge. The young man is like an antiquity. His beauty is best served by an old, perhaps tired, perhaps dumb, poet, rather than some pedlar of modern nonsense. There is an implication here that Shakespeare's kind of 'antiquity'—being old-fashioned but being also associated with ancient simplicity—is different from the flashy modernity of his rivals.

Within a few years of his death Shakespeare had acquired a reputation for native skill. This very often carried with it the assumption that he lacked classical learning. As this book has shown, that assumption was not warranted. But it was a profound and long-standing consequence of the particular way in which Shakespeare presented 'antiquity' in his work. Bottom blunders his way through Ovid, in a fustian style that seems decades out of date. Hamlet stumbles his way through a passage that recalls Virgil's *Aeneid* in a style that again seems old. Tongue-tied, old-fashioned, blunt Shakespeare stands up against the flash modernity of the rival poet in the sonnets. In all these ways Shakespeare's own subtle, surprising, and immensely powerful uses of classical antiquity encouraged rival poets and successors, including Ben Jonson, to believe that he really knew very little at all about the classics.

They were wrong. Shakespeare learnt an enormous amount from classical comedy. His interest in the ways people deceive themselves and the role inference and imagination play in human life and in human loves in particular were substantially developed from his reading in Plautus and Terence. His ability to represent people apparently in the act of deliberation, to show them thinking, was grounded in his classical and rhetorical education and developed in part through his reading of Plutarch.

Jonson in his elegy on Shakespeare imagined Shakespearian tragedy being watched by an audience of Greek dramatists:

> call forth thundering Aeschylus,
> Euripides and Sophocles to us,
> Pacuvius, Accius, him of Cordova dead,
> To life again, to hear thy buskin tread
> And shake a stage...

Shakespeare almost certainly never read Sophocles or Euripides (let alone the much more difficult Aeschylus) in Greek, and yet he managed to write tragedies which invite comparison with those authors. He did so despite the limitations of his classical knowledge, and perhaps in part because of them. He read Plutarch in North's translation rather than reading Sophocles in Greek. This meant that he read (as the last chapter showed) a direct, clear statement about the relationship between divine promptings and human actions rather than plays in which complex thoughts about the interrelationship between human and divine agency were buried implicitly within a drama. Having 'less Greek' could therefore have enabled him to appear to understand more about Greek tragedy, and its complex minglings of voluntary actions and divine promptings, than he would have done if he had actually been able to work his way through Aeschylus and Euripides in the original.

In the course of this book we have seen the structural and stylistic debts Shakespeare owed to a whole range of classical writers and to their Elizabethan translators and imitators. We have seen him in his early career learning to sound Ovidian while trying very hard not to sound like a grammar-school boy who lacked a university degree. We have seen what he knew about Rome, how he represented the Roman world, and how his responses to and uses of Latin literature changed in the course of his career. He read new works, and learnt things from his contemporaries, and from himself and his collaborators. He also forgot things, and changed his approach to classical antiquity in a variety of ways. Along the way he got some things sublimely wrong. But one thing is absolutely clear: an engagement with classical antiquity was one of the central foundations of his writing.

# Notes

**NOTES TO INTRODUCTION**

1. Quotation from Martin Butler, Ian Donaldson, David Bevington (eds), *The Cambridge Edition of the Works of Ben Jonson*, 7 vols. (Cambridge: Cambridge University Press, 2012).
2. John Dryden, *Essays*, ed. W. P. Ker, 2 vols. (Oxford: Oxford University Press, 1900), ii, 18.
3. See Ian Donaldson, 'Looking Sideways: Jonson, Shakespeare, and the Myths of Envy', *Ben Jonson Journal* 8 (2001), 1–22, Brian Vickers (ed.), *English Renaissance Literary Criticism* (Oxford: Clarendon Press, 1999), p. 539, Lawrence Lipking, *The Life of the Poet: Beginning and Ending Poetic Careers* (Chicago and London: University of Chicago Press, 1981), pp. 140–4.
4. Francis Meres, *Palladis Tamia* (London: P. Short for C. Burbie, 1598), fol. 281[v].
5. Johann Joachim Winckelmann, *The History of Ancient Art*, 2 vols., trans. G. H. Lodge (London: Samson, Low, Marston, Searle and Rivington, 1881), ii, 364–5.
6. Patrick Cheney, *Shakespeare, National Poet-Playwright* (Cambridge: Cambridge University Press, 2004), pp. 49–73; Katherine Duncan-Jones, *Ungentle Shakespeare: Scenes from his Life* (London: Arden Shakespeare, 2001), p. 107; MacDonald P. Jackson, 'Francis Meres and the Cultural Contexts of Shakespeare's Rival Poet Sonnets', *Review of English Studies* 56 (2005), 224–46.
7. See Stephen Greenblatt, *The Swerve: How the Renaissance Began* (London: Bodley Head, 2011).
8. See Julia Haig Gaisser, *Catullus and his Renaissance Readers* (Oxford: Clarendon Press, 1993).
9. See Derek Attridge, *Well-Weighed Syllables: Elizabethan Verse in Classical Metres* (London: Cambridge University Press, 1974).
10. Samuel Daniel, *Poems and A Defence of Rhyme*, ed. A. C. Sprague (Chicago and London: Chicago University Press, 1965), p. 139.
11. Emrys Jones, *The Origins of Shakespeare* (Oxford: Clarendon Press, 1977), pp. 85–118.
12. Geoffrey Bullough, *Narrative and Dramatic Sources of Shakespeare*, 8 vols. (London: Routledge & Kegan Paul, 1957), viii, 169.

13. Mark Girouard, *Elizabethan Architecture: its Rise and Fall, 1540–1640* (New Haven and London: Yale University Press, 2009), p. 132.
14. John M. A. Charlton, *The Banqueting House, Whitehall* (London: HMSO, 1964), p. 20.

## NOTES TO CHAPTER 1

1. Richard Farmer, *An Essay on the Learning of Shakespeare* (Cambridge: J. Archdeacon, 1767), p. 49.
2. Thomas Cooper, *Thesaurus Linguae Romanae & Britannicae* (London: Henry Wykes, 1565), sig. I4[r].
3. See, notably, Peter Beal, 'Notions in Garrison: The Seventeenth-Century Commonplace Book', in W. S. Hill (ed.), *New Ways of Looking at Old Texts* (Binghampton, New York: Medieval and Renaissance Texts and Studies, 1993), pp. 131–47 and Anne Moss, *Printed Commonplace-Books and the Structuring of Renaissance Thought* (Oxford: Clarendon Press, 1996).
4. Grace Starry West, 'Going by the Book: Classical Allusions in Shakespeare's *Titus Andronicus*', *Studies in Philology* 79 (1982), 62–77 suggests the passage criticizes Roman education; Jonathan Bate, *Shakespeare and Ovid* (Oxford: Clarendon Press, 1993), pp. 107–9 more plausibly argues that Shakespeare is attacking Elizabethan education, in which it was possible to know the words of a text and learn nothing from its moral content.
5. Desiderius Erasmus, *Colloquies*, ed. C. R. Thompson, 2 vols., volumes 39–40 of the *Collected Works of Erasmus* (Toronto and London: University of Toronto Press, 1997), xl, 1097.
6. *Marcus Tullius Cicero, his Three Books of Duties to Marcus his Son*, trans. Nicholas Grimald (London: Thomas Este, 1556), sig. A8[v].
7. Johannes Sturm, *A Rich Storehouse or Treasure for Nobility and Gentlemen*, trans. T. Browne (London: Henry Denham, 1570), fol. 36[v].
8. Shakespeare may have known *A Rich Storehouse* as early as the mid 1590s, since T. W. Baldwin notes an 'amusing parallel' between Holofernes's use of the word 'peregrinate' to describe an imported word and Sturm's treatise: T. W. Baldwin, *William Shakspere's Small Latine and Lesse Greeke*, 2 vols. (Urbana, Ill.: University of Illinois Press, 1944), ii, 224. Its relation to *The Tempest* is discussed in Donna B. Hamilton, *Virgil and The Tempest: the Politics of Imitation* (Columbus: Ohio State University Press, 1990), pp. 13–19.
9. British Library, Harley MS 6018, fol. 149.
10. David McPherson, 'Ben Jonson's Library and Marginalia: An Annotated Catalogue', *Studies in Philology* 5 (1974), 1–106; 57 doubts that Jonson made the small number of underlinings in his copy of Pierre de La

Rovière, *Poetae Graeci Veteres, Tragici, Comici, Lyrici, Epigrammatarii* (Geneva: La Rovière, 1614), Cambridge University Library, shelf mark Adv.a.35.2.

11. The Montaigne is British Library shelf mark C.21.e.17. The Ovid is Bodleian Library, Oxford, shelf mark MS. Autogr. f. 1. See S. Schoenbaum, *William Shakespeare: Records and Images* (London: Scolar Press, 1981), pp. 100–4.
12. Marcus Tullius Cicero, *The Five Questions which Mark Tully Cicero Disputed in his Manor of Tusculanum*, trans. J. Dolman (London: Thomas Marshe, 1561), sig. E6$^{v}$, translating 1.67.
13. Patricia Parker, *Literary Fat Ladies: Rhetoric, Gender, Property* (London: Methuen, 1987), pp. 27–9.
14. Rosemary O'Day, *Education and Society 1500–1800: The Social Foundations of Education in Early Modern Britain* (London: Longman, 1982), pp. 185–90.
15. Heather James, 'Shakespeare's Learned Heroines in Ovid's Schoolroom', in C. Martindale and A. B. Taylor (eds), *Shakespeare and the Classics* (Cambridge: Cambridge University Press, 2004), pp. 66–85.
16. John Aubrey, *Brief Lives*, ed. A. Clark, 2 vols. (Oxford: Clarendon Press, 1898), i, 227. This is no more implausible than other claims about the 'lost' years: see Park Honan, *Shakespeare: a Life* (Oxford: Oxford University Press, 1998), p. 60.
17. O'Day, *Education and Society*, p. 61.
18. Dionysius Cato, *Cato Translated Grammatically*, trans. J. Brinsley (London: H.L. for T. Man, 1612), fol. 37$^{v}$.
19. Polonius's advice also parodies the traditional genre of advice to a son, which included a work supposedly by Aristotle. For early-modern versions of this tradition, see Louis B. Wright, *Advice to a Son: Precepts of Lord Burghley, Sir Walter Raleigh, and Francis Osborne* (Ithaca, N.Y.: Cornell University Press, 1962).
20. Baldwin, *Small Latine*, ii, 617–61. On early-modern Greek learning more generally, see Paul Botley, *Learning Greek in Western Europe, 1396–1529: Grammars, Lexica, and Classroom Texts* (Philadelphia, PA: American Philosophical Society, 2010).
21. John Brinsley, *Ludus Literarius: or, The Grammar School* (London: for T. Man, 1612), p. 229.
22. Homer, *Achilles' Shield. Translated as the other Seven Bookes of Homer, out of his Eighteenth Book of Iliads*, trans. G. Chapman (London: J. Windet, 1598), sig. A2$^{v}$.
23. Walter J. Ong, 'Latin Language Study as a Renaissance Pubery Rite', *Studies in Philology* 56 (1959), 103–24 may overstate the case, but there is a case to make.

24. Elizabeth D. Harvey, *Ventriloquized Voices: Feminist Theory and English Renaissance Texts* (London: Routledge, 1995); Lynn Enterline, *Rhetoric of the Body from Ovid to Shakespeare* (Cambridge: Cambridge University Press, 2000); Lynn Enterline, 'Rhetoric, Discipline, and the Theatricality of Everyday Life in Elizabethan Grammar Schools', in P. Holland and S. Orgel (eds), *From Performance to Print in Shakespeare's England: Redefining British Theatre History* (Basingstoke: Palgrave, 2006), pp. 173–90 and Lynn Enterline, *Shakespeare's Schoolroom: Rhetoric, Discipline, Emotion* (Philadelphia: University of Pennsylvania Press, 2012).
25. Roger Ascham, *English Works: Toxophilus; Report of the Affaires and State of Germany; The Scholemaster*, ed. W. A. Wright (Cambridge: Cambridge University Press, 1904), p. 183.
26. Ibid., p. 183.
27. Sturm, *Storehouse*, fol. 32ᵛ.
28. William Kempe, *The Education of Children* (London: Thomas Orwin for John Porter, 1588), sig. F2ʳ.
29. Joel B. Altman, *The Tudor Play of Mind: Rhetorical Inquiry and the Development of Elizabethan Drama* (Berkeley and London: University of California Press, 1978).
30. Aphthonius, *Aphthonii Sophistae Progymnasmata*, ed. R. Agricola, G. M. Cattaneo and R. Lorichius (London: Thomas Marsh, 1580), p. 187ʳ.
31. Mathurin Cordier, *Cato Construed* (London: Andrew Maunsell, 1584), sig. H8ᵛ.
32. Gabriel Harvey, *Four Letters, and Certain Sonnets Especially Touching Robert Greene* (London: J. Wolfe, 1592), p. 29.
33. Thomas Wilson, *The Art of Rhetoric for the Use of Such as are Studious of Eloquence* (London: George Robinson, 1585), p. 207.
34. Wilfrid R. Prest, *The Inns of Court under Elizabeth I and the Early Stuarts, 1590–1640* (London: Longman, 1972).
35. John Manningham, *The Diary of John Manningham of the Middle Temple, 1602–1603*, ed. R. P. Sorlien (Hanover, NH: New England University Press, 1976), p. 48.

#### NOTES TO CHAPTER 2

1. David Scott Wilson-Okamura, *Virgil in the Renaissance* (Cambridge: Cambridge University Press, 2010), p. 21.
2. Charles Martindale and Michelle Martindale, *Shakespeare and the Uses of Antiquity: an Introductory Essay* (London and New York: Routledge, 1990), p. 53.

3. Charles Martindale, 'Shakespeare and Virgil', in C. Martindale and A. B. Taylor (eds), *Shakespeare and the Classics* (Cambridge: Cambridge University Press, 2004), pp. 89–106; pp. 89–90.
4. Philipp Melanchthon and Stephan Reich, *In M. Fabij Quintiliani Institutionum librum decimum, doctissimorum virorum annotationes* (Leipzig, 1570), p. 134.
5. *Opera P. Virgilii Maronis. Pauli Manutii annotationes Brevissimae in margine adscriptae. Homeri loca magis insignia, quae Virgilius imitatus est.* The edition was first printed in 1570. The reference to the imitations of Homer on the title page was first made in the edition of 1576, although the commentary remained exactly the same.
6. For Virgil as a poet who wrote in order to be a school text, see Andrew Wallace, *Virgil's Schoolboys: the Poetics of Pedagogy in Renaissance England* (Oxford: Oxford University Press, 2010).
7. For wider discussion of Shakespeare's relation to the *Georgics*, particularly in relation to the history plays and the theme of government, see James C. Bulman, 'Shakespeare's Georgic Histories', *Shakespeare Survey* 38 (1985), 37–47 and Dermot Cavanagh, 'Georgic Sovereignty in *Henry V*', *Shakespeare Survey* 63 (2010), 114–26.
8. William Fitzgerald, 'Vergil in Music', in J. Farrell and M. C. J. Putnam (eds), *A Companion to Vergil's Aeneid and Its Tradition* (Chichester: Wiley-Blackwell, 2010), pp. 341–52.
9. See Victoria Moul, 'Ben Jonson's *Poetaster*: Classical Translation and the Location of Cultural Authority', *Translation and Literature* 15 (2006), 21–50.
10. Margaret Tudeau-Clayton, *Jonson, Shakespeare and Early Modern Virgil* (Cambridge: Cambridge UP, 1998), Heather James, *Shakespeare's Troy* (Cambridge: Cambridge University Press, 1997).
11. On this part of the poem and its influence on Shakespeare, see Heather James, 'Dido's Ear: Tragedy and the Politics of Response', *Shakespeare Quarterly* 52 (2001), 360–82.
12. William S. Anderson, *The Art of the 'Aeneid'* (Englewood Cliffs: Prentice-Hall, 1969), pp. 42–3.
13. There is some circularity to Baldwin's claim: 'I believe it is clear that in some way Shakspere had acquired a firm and lasting knowledge of at least the first two, the fourth, and the sixth books of the *Aeneid*... Intensive drill in grammar school was probably upon these first six books', T. W. Baldwin, *William Shakspere's Small Latine and Lesse Greeke*, 2 vols. (Urbana, Ill.: University of Illinois Press, 1944), ii, 495. A sixteenth-century reader of Theodore Pulman's 1580 edition of Virgil made extensive interlinear notes on *Aeneid* II, 35–225 (Cambridge University Library, shelf mark Pet. O.2.7) and very much sparser notes elsewhere: selective reading was not unusual.

14. At 1.3.158 I adopt 'sighs' from the Quarto rather than 'kisses' favoured by Wells and Taylor.
15. For links with the *Aeneid*, see John M. Major, 'Desdemona and Dido', *Shakespeare Quarterly* 10 (1959), 123–5, James, 'Dido's Ear', Sarah Dewar-Watson, 'Othello, Virgil, and Montaigne', *Notes and Queries* 57 (2010), 384–5.
16. John Manningham, *The Diary of John Manningham of the Middle Temple, 1602–1603*, ed. R. P. Sorlien (Hanover, NH: New England University Press, 1976), p. 202.
17. See the classic account by Harry Levin, *The Question of Hamlet* (Oxford: Oxford University Press, 1959), pp. 138–64. Emrys Jones, *The Origins of Shakespeare* (Oxford: Clarendon Press, 1977), pp. 275–7 suggests the passage is a pastiche of Lucan. Joseph Loewenstein, 'Plays Agonistic and Competitive: the Textual Approach to Elsinore', *Renaissance Drama* 19 (1988), 63–96 finds it 'Jonsonian in its slavish neoclassicism' (p. 75), but embeds the speech within arguments over the relationship between literary imitation of the classics and plagiarism of playbooks. Andrew Wallace, '"What's Hecuba to Him?": Pain, Privacy, and the Ancient Text', in D. Beecher and G. Williams (eds), *Ars Reminiscendi: Mind and Memory in Renaissance Culture* (Toronto: Centre for Reformation and Renaissance Studies, 2009), pp. 231–43 relates its combination of memory and consolation to schoolroom practices.
18. Gabriel Harvey, *Gabriel Harvey's Marginalia*, ed. G. C. M. Smith (Stratford-upon-Avon: Shakespeare Head Press, 1913), p. 232.
19. Aphthonius, *Aphthonii sophistae Progymnasmata*, ed. R. Agricola, G. M. Cattaneo and R. Lorichius (London: Thomas Marsh, 1580), p. 177; Richard Rainolde, *A Book Called the Foundation of Rhetoric* (London: John Kingston, 1563), fol. 50[v].
20. *Aeneid* 4.367, in which Dido compares Aeneas to the offspring of these savage creatures, was also echoed in Marlowe's version, 5.1.159, but he says 'Tygers of *Hircania* gave thee sucke' rather than using 'Hircanian'. The more usual form of the adjective was 'Hyrcan', which was used by Samuel Daniel in 1594 and by William Painter in 1566, both of whose works Shakespeare knew.
21. John Kerrigan, 'Hieronimo, Hamlet and Remembrance', *Essays in Criticism* 31 (1981), 105–26.
22. John Dryden, *The Works*, ed. E. N. Hooker, H. T. Swedenberg and V. A. Dearing, 20 vols. (Berkeley: University of California Press, 1956–2000), xiii, 244.
23. Margaret Tudeau-Clayton, 'Scenes of Translation in Jonson and Shakespeare: *Poetaster*, *Hamlet*, and *A Midsummer Night's Dream*',

*Translation and Literature* 11 (2002), 1–23; George L. Geckle, 'The Wind or the Wound: Marlowe's *Dido Queen of Carthage*, II.1, 253–254', *Papers of the Bibliographical Society of America* 71 (1977), 194–9; James Black, 'Hamlet Hears Marlowe: Shakespeare Reads Virgil', *Renaissance and Reformation* 30 (1994), 17–28.

24. On Shakespeare and Phaer, see Baldwin, *Small Latine*, ii, 463–4, 479–81.
25. Virgil, *The Thirteen Books of Aeneidos*, trans. T. Phaer and T. Twyne (London: Thomas Creede, 1600), sig. D2[v].
26. Robert Greene and Henry Chettle, *Greene's Groatsworth of Wit, Bought with a Million of Repentance* (London: [J. Wolfe and J. Danter] for William Wright, 1592), sig. F1[v].
27. See James S. Shapiro, *1599: A Year in the Life of William Shakespeare* (London: Faber and Faber, 2005).
28. Robert S. Miola, 'Vergil in Shakespeare', in J. D. Bernard (ed.), *Vergil at 2000: Commemorative Essays on the Poet and his Influence* (New York: AMS Press, 1986), pp. 241–58.
29. See James P. Bednarz, *Shakespeare and the Poets' War* (New York: Columbia University Press, 2001) and James Shapiro, *Rival Playwrights: Marlowe, Jonson, Shakespeare* (New York: Columbia UP, 1991).
30. For *Aeneid*, 6.853 see Thomas Dekker, *The Whole Magnificent Entertainment* (London: E. Allde for T. Man the younger, 1604), sig. C2[v].
31. Ibid., sig. B1[r].
32. See Lisa Hopkins, *The Cultural Uses of the Caesars on the English Renaissance Stage* (Aldershot: Ashgate, 2008), pp. 16–22.
33. Nicholas Moscovakis, 'Partial Views: Literary Allusion, Teleological Form, and Contingent Readings in *Hamlet*', in S. Cohen (ed.), *Shakespeare and Historical Formalism* (Aldershot: Ashgate, 2007), pp. 147–75 also detects a Virgilian teleological plot in *Hamlet*.
34. See Barbara Bono, *Literary Transvaluation: From Vergilian Epic to Shakespearean Tragicomedy* (Berkeley, Los Angeles and London: University of California Press, 1984) and Miola, 'Vergil in Shakespeare', p. 254: 'The play rewrites the fourth *Aeneid* and reverses its values.' On Aeneases in epic romances who cannot leave their Didos, see Colin Burrow, *Epic Romance: Homer to Milton* (Oxford: Clarendon Press, 1993).
35. Earlier studies tend to simplify the relationship: see Robert Wiltenburg, 'The *Aeneid* in *The Tempest*', *Shakespeare Survey* 39 (1986), 159–68 and J. M. Nosworthy, 'The Narrative Sources of *The Tempest*', *Review of English Studies* 24 (1948), 281–94. More recent work allows greater sophistication to the allusions, e.g. Donna B. Hamilton, *Virgil and The Tempest: the Politics of Imitation* (Columbus: Ohio State University Press, 1990), John Pitcher, 'A Theatre of the Future: The *Aeneid* and *The Tempest*',

*Essays in Criticism* 34 (1984), 193–215, and David Scott Wilson-Okamura, 'Virgilian Models of Colonization in Shakespeare's *Tempest*', *ELH* 70 (2003), 709–37, as well as several essays in Peter Hulme and William H. Sherman (ed.), *The Tempest and its Travels* (London: Reaktion, 2000), notably those by Donna Hamilton and Barbara Mowat.

36. Jan Kott, 'The *Aeneid* and *The Tempest*', *Arion* N.S. 3 (1976), 424–51, Nosworthy, 'Narrative Sources', 293. For a summary of previous views and a suggestion that Montaigne holds the key, see Gail K. Paster, 'Montaigne, Dido, and *The Tempest*: "How Came that Widow in?"', *Shakespeare Quarterly* 35 (1984), 91–4. It was not very common to refer to Dido as a 'widow', though she is called that by Phaer in his general summary of the *Aeneid*, Virgil, *The Thirteen Books of Aeneidos*, sig. A8$^{r}$.
37. Raphael Holinshed, *The Second Volume of Chronicles: Containing the Description, Conquest, Inhabitation, and Troublesome Estate of Ireland* (London: G. Bishop, R. Newberie, H. Denham, 1587), p. 25. See Hamilton, *Politics of Imitation*, pp. 59–60, Wilson-Okamura, 'Colonization', 717.
38. See variously Hamilton, *Politics of Imitation*, p. xi (the play 'constructed an argument for constitutionalism'); James, *Shakespeare's Troy*, p. 221: 'Emphatically not seditious in its themes, the play nonetheless aligns the theater with constitutional theory that derives the royal authority from the people'; Tudeau-Clayton, *Jonson, Shakespeare and Early Modern Virgil*, pp. 194–244.
39. See John E. Curran, *Roman Invasions: The British History, Protestant anti-Romanism, and the Historical Imagination in England, 1530–1660* (Newark and London: Associated University Presses, 2002), and Hopkins, *Caesars*, pp. 114–18.
40. William Camden, *Britain, or a Chorographical Description of England, Scotland, and Ireland*, trans. P. Holland (London: George Bishop and John Norton. 1610), pp. 8–9.
41. Ibid., p. 88.
42. Shakespeare can be forgiven for failing to create a clear chronology from Holinshed: 'This Brutus . . . was the son of Silvius, the son of Ascanius, the son of Aeneas the Trojan, begotten of his wife Creusa, and born in Troy, before the city was destroyed. But as other do take it, the author of that book (whatsoever he was) and such other as follow him, are deceived only in this point, mistaking the matter, in that Posthumus the son of Aeneas (begotten of his wife Lavinia, and born after his father's decease in Italy) was called Ascanius, who had issue a son named Julius, who (as these others do conjecture) was the father of Brutus, that noble chieftain and adventurous leader of those people, which being descended (for the more part in the fourth generation) from those Trojans that escaped with life, when that royal city was destroyed by the Greeks, got possession of

this worthy and most famous isle.' Raphael Holinshed, *The First Volume of the Chronicles of England, Scotland, and Ireland* (London: Henry Bynnemen for George Bishop, 1577), fol. 9[r].

43. William Shakespeare, *Cymbeline*, ed. M. Butler (Cambridge: Cambridge University Press, 2005), p. 216.
44. Cf. the use of fourteeners and poulter's measure (twelve-syllable lines alternating with fourteeners) in *Timon of Athens*, 5.5.71–8, which reproduces North's translation of Timon's two epitaphs.
45. On dreams and oracles in the Greek romances, see Shadi Bartsch, *Decoding the Ancient Novel: the Reader and the Role of Description in Heliodorus and Achilles Tatius* (Princeton: Princeton University Press, 1989), pp. 80–108. Cf. the Pythian oracle in Heliodorus's *Ethiopean History*, 2.35.5; cf. Brutus's dream in which Diana promises him a British kingdom in Geoffrey of Monmouth, *The History of the Kings of Britain*, ed. M. D. Reeve and N. Wright (Woodbridge: Boydell Press, 2007), p. 20, and the long and opaque prophecies of Merlin, pp. 144–5.
46. Patricia Parker, 'Romance and Empire: Anachronistic *Cymbeline*', in G. M. Logan and G. Teskey (eds), *Unfolded Tales: Essays on Renaissance Romance* (Ithaca: Cornell University Press, 1989), pp. 189–207, James, *Shakespeare's Troy*, p. 152.

## NOTES TO CHAPTER 3

1. See Katharina Volk, *Ovid* (Oxford: Wiley-Blackwell, 2010), pp. 20–34; Niklas Holzberg in Peter E. Knox (ed.), *Oxford Readings in Ovid* (Oxford: Oxford University Press, 2006), pp. 51–68.
2. Jonathan Bate, *Shakespeare and Ovid* (Oxford: Clarendon Press, 1993), p. 167 finds traces of the exile poetry in *Richard II*, 1.3.204, 258, 261.
3. Jennifer Ingleheart (ed.), *Two Thousand Years of Solitude: Exile after Ovid* (Oxford: Oxford University Press, 2011); A. Bartlett Giamatti, *Exile and Change in Renaissance Literature* (New Haven and London: Yale University Press, 1984), pp. 12–32; P. A. Rosenmeyer, 'Ovid's *Heroides* and *Tristia*: Voices from Exile', *Ramus* 26 (1997), 29–56; Stephen Hinds, 'Booking the Return Trip: Ovid and *Tristia* 1', *Proceedings of the Cambridge Philological Society* 31 (1985), 13–32, reprinted in Knox, *Oxford Readings in Ovid*, pp. 415–40.
4. See Joachim du Bellay, *The Regrets; with The Antiquities of Rome, Three Latin Elegies, and The Defense and Enrichment of the French Language*, ed. R. Helgerson (Philadelphia: University of Pennsylvania Press, 2006).
5. A. Kent Hieatt, 'The Genesis of Shakespeare's Sonnets: *Spenser's Ruines of Rome: By Bellay*', *PMLA* 98 (1983), 800–14.

6. See Philip R. Hardie, *Ovid's Poetics of Illusion* (Cambridge: Cambridge University Press, 2002), pp. 106–42, Gareth D. Williams, *Banished Voices: Readings in Ovid's Exile Poetry* (Cambridge: Cambridge University Press, 1994), and Joseph Farrell, 'Reading and Writing in the *Heroides*', *Harvard Studies in Classical Philology* 98 (1998), 307–38.
7. J. R. Dasent (ed.), *Acts of the Privy Council, 1542–1631* (London: HMSO, 1890–1964), xiii, 389–90.
8. See Adam G. Hooks, 'Shakespeare at the White Greyhound', *Shakespeare Survey* 64 (2011), 260–75 and M. L. Stapleton, 'Venus as Praeceptor: The *Ars Amatoria* in *Venus and Adonis*', in P. C. Kolin (ed.), *Venus and Adonis: Critical Essays* (New York: Garland, 1997), pp. 309–21.
9. Cf. *Twelfth Night*, 4.2.50–1, in which Feste taunts Malvolio by asking him 'what is the opinion of Pythagoras concerning wildfowl?'; *As You Like It*, 3.2.172–3, where Rosalind jests that 'I was never so berhymed since Pythagoras' time that I was an Irish rat'; and *Merchant of Venice*, 4.1.129–37, where Graziano imagines Shylock to be the reincarnation of a wolf.
10. Joseph Farrell, 'The Ovidian *Corpus*: Poetic Body and Poetic Text', in P. Hardie, A. Barchiesi, and S. Hinds (eds), *Ovidian Transformations. Essays on Ovid's Metamorphoses and its Reception* (Cambridge: Cambridge Philological Society, 1999), pp. 127–41.
11. *Ovid's Metamorphoses Translated by Arthur Golding*, ed. M. Forey (London: Penguin, 2002), p. 463. All quotations from Golding are from this edition.
12. See David Armitage, 'The Dismemberment of Orpheus: Mythic Elements in Shakespeare's Romances', *Shakespeare Survey* 39 (1987), 123–33.
13. Joseph B. Solodow, *The World of Ovid's Metamorphoses* (Chapel Hill, N.C., and London: University of North Carolina Press, 1988), pp. 215–19.
14. Francis Beaumont, *Salmacis and Hermaphroditus* (London: For John Hodgets, 1602), sig. A4r.
15. Francis Meres, *Palladis Tamia* (London: P. Short for C. Burbie, 1598), fol. 281v. See note 9.
16. For the play as an indictment of Roman education, see Grace Starry West, 'Going by the Book: Classical Allusions in Shakespeare's *Titus Andronicus*', *Studies in Philology* 79 (1982), 62–77; Bate, *Shakespeare and Ovid*, pp. 101–17 more plausibly relates the play's interest in schoolroom learning to early-modern humanism, and Vernon Guy Dickson, '"A pattern, precedent, and lively warrant": Emulation, Rhetoric, and Cruel Propriety in *Titus Andronicus*', *Renaissance Quarterly* 62 (2009), 376–409 argues the play resists the notion that England should emulate Rome.

17. See the classic essay by Eugene M. Waith, 'The Metamorphosis of Violence in *Titus Andronicus*', *Shakespeare Survey* 10 (1957), 39–49.
18. Thomas Cooper, *Thesaurus Linguae Romanae & Britannicae* (London: Henry Wykes, 1565), s.v. 'barbarus'.
19. Forey emends to 'pinions'. 'Pinsons' is a northern dialect word for pincers.
20. Frank Kermode, *Shakespeare's Language* (New York: Farrar Straus and Giroux, 2000), pp. 7–11.
21. Kim Solga, 'Rape's Metatheatrical Return: Rehearsing Sexual Violence among the Early Moderns', *Theatre Journal* 58 (2006), 53–72; Liz Oakley-Brown, *Ovid and the Cultural Politics of Translation in Early Modern England* (Aldershot: Ashgate, 2006), pp. 23–43.
22. Brian Vickers, *Shakespeare, Co-author: a Historical Sudy of Five Collaborative Plays* (Oxford: Oxford University Press, 2002), pp. 148–243.
23. See Ian Donaldson, *The Rapes of Lucretia: a Myth and its Transformations* (Oxford: Clarendon Press, 1982); for Shakespeare as a republican, see Andrew Hadfield, 'Tarquin's Everlasting Banishment: Republicanism and Constitutionalism in *The Rape of Lucrece* and *Titus Andronicus*', *Parergon* 19 (2002), 77–104 and Andrew Hadfield, *Shakespeare and Republicanism* (Cambridge: Cambridge University Press, 2005).
24. See William Shakespeare, *The Complete Sonnets and Poems*, ed. C. Burrow (Oxford: Oxford University Press, 2002), pp. 48–50 and T. W. Baldwin, *On the Literary Genetics of Shakspere's Poems and Sonnets* (Urbana: University of Illinois Press, 1950), pp. 108–53.
25. The opposition between Livy as 'political' history and Ovid as 'emotional' history is by no means absolute: some early-modern editions categorized Lucretia's speech after her rape in Livy as a 'querela', or complaint, and marked it as 'lamentatio Lucretiae ad virum, patrem, & amicos, de violatione' (the lamentation of Lucretia for her rape to her husband, father, and friends) Titus Livy, *Historiae Romanae Principis Decades Tres* (Paris: Michel de Vascosan, 1552), sig. C1$^{r}$.
26. See A. B. Taylor, 'Golding's Ovid, Shakespeare's "Small Latin", and the Real Object of Mockery in "Pyramus and Thisbe"', *Shakespeare Survey* 42 (1990), 53–64, Madeleine Forey, '"Bless thee, Bottom, Bless thee! Thou art Translated!": Ovid, Golding, and *A Midsummer Night's Dream*', *Modern Language Review* 93 (1998), 321–9, Margaret Tudeau-Clayton, 'Scenes of Translation in Jonson and Shakespeare: *Poetaster*, *Hamlet*, and *A Midsummer Night's Dream*', *Translation and Literature* 11 (2002), 1–23.
27. Peter Holland, 'Theseus' Shadows in *A Midsummer Night's Dream*', *Shakespeare Survey* 47 (1994), 139–51.
28. Bate, *Shakespeare and Ovid*, p. 131.

29. Ovid, *Fabularum Ouidii Interpretatio, Ethica, Physica, et Historica*, ed. G. Sabinus (Cambridge: Thomas Thomas, 1584), p. 234.
30. On this scene, see Leonard Barkan, '"Living Sculptures": Ovid, Michelangelo, and *The Winter's Tale*', *ELH* 48 (1981), 639–67, Bate, *Shakespeare and Ovid*, pp. 219–39, A. D. Nuttall, '*The Winter's Tale*: Ovid Transformed', in A. B. Taylor (ed.), *Shakespeare's Ovid* (Cambridge: Cambridge University Press, 2000), pp. 135–49, Hardie, *Ovid's Poetics*, pp. 193–206.
31. Barkan, '"Living Sculptures"', 663. See also Nevill Coghill, 'Six Points of Stage-craft in *The Winter's Tale*', *Shakespeare Survey* 11 (1958), 31–41.
32. See Richard Meek, 'Ekphrasis in *The Rape of Lucrece* and *The Winter's Tale*', *Studies in English Literature, 1500–1900* 46 (2006), 389–414.
33. Charles Martindale and Michelle Martindale, *Shakespeare and the Uses of Antiquity: an Introductory Essay* (London and New York: Routledge, 1990), p. 23; cf. Raphael Lyne, 'Ovid, Golding, and the "Rough Magic" of *The Tempest*', in A. B. Taylor (ed.), *Shakespeare's Ovid* (Cambridge: Cambridge University Press, 2000), pp. 150–64, p. 160, who finds in it 'a combination of discernible allusion and awkwardly irrelevant intertextuality'. Cf. Bate, *Shakespeare and Ovid*, pp. 249–54.
34. Sarah Annes Brown, *The Metamorphosis of Ovid: from Chaucer to Ted Hughes* (London: Duckworth, 1999), pp. 72–6.
35. William Lily, *A Short Introduction of Grammar* (Geneva: C. Bade, 1557), p. 8.

### NOTES TO CHAPTER 4

1. Francis Meres, *Palladis Tamia* (London: P. Short for C. Burbie, 1598), p. 282.
2. Erich Segal, *Roman Laughter: the Comedy of Plautus* (Oxford: Oxford University Press, 1987), p. 40.
3. Alison Sharrock, *Reading Roman Comedy: Poetics and Playfulness in Plautus and Terence* (Cambridge: Cambridge University Press, 2009), p. 12.
4. Ibid., p. 140.
5. Charles Hoole, *A New Discovery of the Old Art of Teaching School* (London: H. T. for Andrew Crook, 1659), p. 122. Hoole is describing practices which were followed well before the date his treatise was published.
6. Desiderius Erasmus, *Collected Works of Erasmus 24: Literary and Educational Writings 2: De Copia/De Ratione Studii*, ed. C. R. Thompson (Toronto, Buffalo, London: University of Toronto Press, 1978), p. 669.

7. Mathurin Cordier, *Corderius' Dialogues Translated Grammatically*, trans. J. Brinsley (London: Anne Griffin, 1636), pp. 30–1. The Latin text first appeared in 1564 and was widely used in schools, although probably not until shortly after Shakespeare left school.
8. Gabriel Harvey, *Pierce's Supererogation, or a New Praise of the Old Ass* (London: J. Wolfe, 1593), p. 157.
9. Terence, *Flowers or Eloquent Phrases of the Latin Speech*, ed. N. Udall and J. Higgins (London: Thomas Marshe, 1575), sig. Y8$^{v}$.
10. Translation from Joel B. Altman, *The Tudor Play of Mind: Rhetorical Inquiry and the Development of Elizabethan Drama* (Berkeley and London: University of California Press, 1978), p. 133.
11. On the development of comic theory through editions of Terence, see T. W. Baldwin, *Shakspere's Five-act Structure: Shakspere's Early Plays on the Background of Renaissance Theories of Five-act Structure from 1470* (Urbana: The University of Illinois Press, 1947), Marvin T. Herrick, *Italian Comedy in the Renaissance* (Urbana: University of Illinois Press, 1960), and Altman, *Tudor Play of Mind*, pp. 130–47. See also the sophisticated analysis in Lorna Hutson, *The Invention of Suspicion: Law and Mimesis in Shakespeare and Renaissance Drama* (Oxford: Oxford University Press, 2007).
12. See James Shapiro, *Rival Playwrights: Marlowe, Jonson, Shakespeare* (New York: Columbia University Press, 1991).
13. Robert Greene and Henry Chettle, *Greene's Groatsworth of Wit, Bought with a Million of Repentance* (London: [J. Wolfe and J. Danter] for William Wright, 1592), sig. F1$^{v}$.
14. Geoffrey Chaucer, *The Works of our Ancient and Learned English Poet, Geoffrey Chaucer, Newly Printed*, ed. T. Speght (London: George Bishop, 1598), sig. a4$^{v}$.
15. Robert S. Miola, *Shakespeare and Classical Comedy: the Influence of Plautus and Terence* (Oxford: Clarendon Press, 1994), p. 22 finds seventeen confusions in *Menaechmi* and fifty in *Errors*.
16. Wolfgang Riehle, *Shakespeare, Plautus, and the Humanist Tradition* (Cambridge: D. S. Brewer, 1990), pp. 36–43.
17. A strong statement of this view is in William Shakespeare, *The Comedy of Errors*, ed. R. A. Foakes (London: Methuen, 1962), pp. xxxiv–ix.
18. Thomas Goodwin, *Romanae Historiae Anthologia: An English Exposition of the Roman Antiquities, Wherein Many Roman and English Offices are Paralleled and Divers Obscure Phrases Explained* (Oxford: Printed by Joseph Barnes, 1614), p. 15. The distinction is made by Servius in his commentary on Virgil's *Georgics* 3.22–5 and is noted by Abraham Fleming in his translation of the *Georgics* in 1589, so was available to Shakespeare

before the 1590s, although the use of rotating scenery in the early-modern stage appears not to have been common before Jonson's *Masque of Queens* of 1609. The ancient use of revolving scenes is also discussed in Vitruvius, *De Architectura*, 5.6.8. See William E. Miller, 'Periaktoi in the Old Blackfriars', *Modern Language Notes* 74 (1959), 1–3.

19. See, e.g., Germaine Greer, *Shakespeare's Wife* (London: Bloomsbury, 2007).
20. R. L. Hunter, *The New Comedy of Greece and Rome* (Cambridge: Cambridge University Press, 1985), p. 92.
21. Titus Maccius Plautus, *Menaechmi*, ed. A. S. Gratwick (Cambridge: Cambridge University Press, 1993), p. 29.
22. Miola, *Shakespeare and Classical Comedy*, pp. 29–30.
23. Introductions are in Subha Mukherji and Raphael Lyne (eds), *Early Modern Tragicomedy* (Woodbridge: D. S. Brewer, 2007), Marvin T. Herrick, *Tragicomedy: its Origin and Development in Italy, France, and England* (Urbana: University of Illinois Press, 1955).
24. Notably Altman, *Tudor Play of Mind*, Hutson, *Invention of Suspicion*, and most recently Joel B. Altman, *The Improbability of Othello: Rhetorical Anthropology and Shakespearean Selfhood* (Chicago and London: University of Chicago Press, 2010).

## NOTES TO CHAPTER 5

1. T. W. Baldwin, *William Shakspere's Small Latine and Lesse Greeke*, 2 vols. (Urbana: University of Illinois Press, 1944), ii, 553–61.
2. For enthusiastic lists of parallels, see John William Cunliffe, *The Influence of Seneca on Elizabethan Tragedy: an Essay* (London: Macmillan and Co., 1893); for an excessively categorical rejection of them, see G. K. Hunter, *Dramatic Identities and Cultural Tradition: Studies in Shakespeare and his Contemporaries: Critical Essays* (Liverpool: Liverpool University Press, 1978), pp. 159–73.
3. Gordon Braden, *Renaissance Tragedy and the Senecan Tradition: Anger's Privilege* (New Haven and London: Yale University Press, 1985); Robert S. Miola, *Shakespeare and Classical Tragedy: the Influence of Seneca* (Oxford: Clarendon Press, 1992).
4. Lucius Annaeus Seneca, *Phaedra*, ed. M. Coffey and R. Mayer (Cambridge: Cambridge University Press, 1990), p. 38.
5. Lucius Annaeus Seneca, *Seneca: His Ten Tragedies*, ed. T. Newton and T. S. Eliot, 2 vols. (London and New York: Constable and Co. Ltd.; A.A. Knopf, 1927), i, xii: Seneca's tragedies are not just poor Greek tragedies, but 'belong to a different race'.

6. Lucius Annaeus Seneca, *Lucii Annei Senecæ Tragedia Prima quæ Inscribitur Hercules Furens, nuper recogn. & in Angl. metrum conversa per I. Heywodum*, trans. J. Heywood (London: H. Sutton, 1561), title page.
7. Charles Hoole, *A New Discovery of the Old Art of Teaching Schoole* (London: H. T. for Andrew Crook, 1659), p. 198.
8. Richard Tottel, *Tottel's Miscellany (1557–1587)*, ed. H. E. Rollins, 2 vols. (Cambridge, MA: Harvard University Press, 1928), poem 118 from *Thyestes* and 210, from *Hippolytus*.
9. See John G. Fitch, 'Playing Seneca', in George William Mallory Harrison (ed.), *Seneca in Performance* (London: Duckworth, 2000), p. 9.
10. Howard Baker, *Induction to Tragedy: a Study in a Development of Form in Gorboduc, The Spanish Tragedy and Titus Andronicus* (University, Louisiana: Louisiana State University Press, 1939), pp. 121–39 insists on the irrelevance of Seneca; but see Alessandro Schiesaro, *The Passions in Play: Thyestes and the Dynamics of Senecan Drama* (Cambridge: Cambridge University Press, 2003), pp. 70–85.
11. *Epistulae Morales*, 84.7.
12. Hugh Parry, 'Ovid's *Metamorphoses*: Violence in a Pastoral Landscape', *Transactions and Proceedings of the American Philological Association* 95 (1964), 268–82.
13. MacDonald P. Jackson, *Studies in Attribution: Middleton and Shakespeare* (Salzburg: Institut für Anglistik und Amerikanistik, Universität Salzburg, 1979), pp. 148–58; Brian Vickers, *Shakespeare, Co-author: a Historical Sudy of Five Collaborative Plays* (Oxford: Oxford University Press, 2002), pp. 148–243, esp. p. 179 for echoes of Peele in 2.2. Jonathan Bate (who is sceptical about Peele's authorship and the Senecan influence on Shakespeare) has this scene as the start of Act 2 in his Arden 3 edition.
14. See further Braden, *Anger's Privilege*, and, for the prose, Miriam T. Griffin, *Seneca: a Philosopher in Politics* (Oxford: Clarendon Press, 1992). Reassessments of Nero include Edward Champlin, *Nero* (Cambridge, MA and London: Belknap, 2003) and Melissa Barden Dowling, *Clemency and Cruelty in the Roman World* (Ann Arbor: University of Michigan Press, 2006).
15. Braden, *Anger's Privilege*.
16. Michel de Montaigne, *The Essays or Moral, Politic and Military Discourses*, trans. J. Florio (London: Valentine Sims for Edward Blunt, 1603), p. 595.
17. *L. Annaei Senecæ opera, per Das. Erasmum Roterod. emendata. Adiecta sunt eiusdem scholia nonulla*, ed. D. Erasmus (Basel: Froben, 1529), sig. a6[r].
18. *Decem tragœdiæ quæ Lucio Annæo Senecæ tribuuntur, operâ F. Raphelengii, ope I. Lipsii emendatores*, ed. F. Raphelengius (Leiden: Franciscus Raphelengius,

1589), p. 387; see Mayer Roland, 'Personata Stoa: Neostoicism and Senecan Tragedy', *Journal of the Warburg and Courtauld Institutes* 57 (1994), 151–74.

19. Lucius Annaeus Seneca, *Octavia*, ed. A. J. Boyle (Oxford: Oxford University Press, 2008), p. 175 notes that this is 'an allusion to the "renascent Rome" which followed the death of Nero'.
20. On literary self-consciousness generally in Seneca, see Schiesaro, *Passions in Play*, esp. pp. 221–4, and C. A. J. Littlewood, *Self-Representation and Illusion in Senecan Tragedy* (Oxford: Oxford University Press, 2004).
21. Seneca, eds. Newton and Eliot, *Seneca: His Ten Tragedies*, ii, 27.
22. Lucius Annaeus Seneca, *The Second Tragedy of Seneca Entitled Thyestes Faithfully Englished by Jasper Heywood Fellow of All Souls College in Oxford*, trans. J. Heywood (London: Thomas Berthelette, 1560), sig. $4^{*}3^{v}$.
23. Thomas Nashe, *Works*, ed. R. B. McKerrow and F. P. Wilson, 4 vols. (Oxford: Blackwell, 1958), iii, 315–16.
24. *Gabriel Harvey's Marginalia*, ed. G. C. M. Smith (Stratford-upon-Avon: Shakespeare Head Press, 1913), p. 232.
25. See C. J. Herington, 'Senecan Tragedy', *Arion* 5 (1966), 422–71, Thomas G. Rosenmeyer, *Senecan Drama and Stoic Cosmology* (Berkeley: University of California Press, 1989) and Braden, *Anger's Privilege*.
26. See David E. Hahm, *The Origins of Stoic Cosmology* ([Columbus]: Ohio State University Press, 1977), p. 163 and the useful summary in Michael J. White, 'Stoic Natural Philosophy (Physics and Cosmology)', in B. Inwood (ed.), *The Cambridge Companion to the Stoics* (Cambridge: Cambridge University Press, 2003), pp. 124–52.
27. Michael Lapidge, 'Stoic Cosmology', in J. M. Rist (ed.), *The Stoics* (Berkeley, Los Angeles, and London: University of California Press, 1978), pp. 161–85.
28. A. J. Boyle, *Tragic Seneca: an Essay in the Theatrical Tradition* (London and New York: Routledge, 1997), p. 59: 'analogies between Phaedra and her mother, Pasiphae, between Hippolytus and the bull that Pasiphae loved, and between the Minotaur and the bull from the sea . . . seem to assert the imperatives of history, the dispassionate cyclic order of things, the circle of fate, fortune, nature.'
29. Rosenmeyer, *Senecan Drama*, p. 182.
30. Miola, *Seneca*, p. 14.
31. Peter Holland, 'Theseus' Shadows in *A Midsummer Night's Dream*', *Shakespeare Survey* 47 (1994), 139–51.
32. William Shakespeare, *A Midsummer Night's Dream*, ed. H. F. Brooks (London: Methuen, 1979), pp. lxii–lxiii.
33. Seneca, eds. Coffey and Mayer, *Phaedra*, p. 131.

34. Harry Berger, Jr., *Imaginary Audition: Shakespeare on Stage and Page* (Berkeley and Los Angeles: University of California Press, 1989); Lukas Erne, *Shakespeare as Literary Dramatist* (Cambridge: Cambridge University Press, 2003).
35. Emrys Jones, *Scenic Form in Shakespeare* (Oxford: Clarendon Press, 1971).
36. J. H. M. Salmon, 'Stoicism and Roman Example: Seneca and Tacitus in Jacobean England', *Journal of the History of Ideas* 50 (1989), 199–225.
37. Cunliffe, *Seneca*, p. 25. Miola, *Seneca*, p. 93.
38. Cunliffe, *Seneca*, p. 82.
39. Cf. ibid., p. 84 and *Hercules Furens*, 1330–6.
40. Inga-Stina Ewbank, 'The Fiend-Like Queen: A Note on *Macbeth* and Seneca's *Medea*', *Shakespeare Survey* 19 (1966), 82–94; 85.
41. *Seneca: His Ten Tragedies*, ii, 90.
42. William Camden, *Britain, or a Chorographical Description of England, Scotland, and Ireland*, trans. P. Holland (London: George Bishop and John Norton, 1610), p. 88.
43. Cunliffe, *Seneca*, p. 85; William Shakespeare, *King Lear*, ed. R. A. Foakes (Walton-on-Thames: Nelson, 1997), p. 107.
44. John M. Wallace, '*Timon of Athens* and the Three Graces: Shakespeare's Senecan Study', *Modern Philology* 83 (1986), 349–63 and John M. Wallace, 'The Senecan Context of *Coriolanus*', *Modern Philology* 90 (1993), 465–78.

## NOTES TO CHAPTER 6

1. Plutarch, *Plutarch's Lives of the Noble Grecians and Romans*, ed. G. Wyndham, 6 vols. (London: D. Nutt, 1895), i, 7. All subsequent quotations are from this edition, to which references are given in parentheses in the text.
2. William Shakespeare, *A Midsummer Night's Dream*, ed. P. Holland (Oxford: Clarendon Press, 1994), pp. 53–4.
3. E. A. J. Honigmann, 'Shakespeare's Plutarch', *Shakespeare Quarterly* 10 (1959), 25–33; for the wider diffusion of Plutarchan thinking in Shakespeare, see Judith Mossman, '*Henry V* and Plutarch's *Alexander*', *Shakespeare Quarterly* 45 (1994), 57–73 and Judith Mossman, 'Plutarch and Shakespeare's *Henry IV Parts 1 and 2*', *Poetica* 48 (1997), 99–117.
4. Simon Swain, *Hellenism and Empire: Language, Classicism, and Power in the Greek World, AD 50–250* (Oxford: Clarendon Press, 1996), pp. 135–86.
5. Plutarch, *Life of Antony*, ed. C. B. R. Pelling (Cambridge: Cambridge University Press, 1988), p. 7.
6. Paul A. Cantor, 'Shakespeare's Parallel Lives: Plutarch and the Roman Plays', *Poetica* 48 (1997), 69–81.

7. Earlier critics tended to assume that Shakespeare read the lives and not the comparisons between them. That orthodoxy was questioned by Honigmann, 'Shakespeare's Plutarch', whose argument was further developed by Cantor, 'Shakespeare's Parallel Lives'.
8. Thucydides is critical of using poets as historical evidence in *History of the Peloponnesian War*, 1.21.1. The study of Greek historians' use of literary forms and literary evidence is a growth area: see Simon Hornblower, 'Narratology and Narrative Techniques in Thucydides', in S. Hornblower (ed.), *Greek Historiography* (Oxford: Oxford University Press, 1994), pp. 131–66; C. B. R. Pelling, *Literary Texts and the Greek Historian* (London: Routledge, 2000); Jonas Grethlein, *The Greeks and Their Past: Poetry, Oratory and History in the Fifth Century BCE* (Cambridge: Cambridge University Press, 2010).
9. Tim Duff, *Plutarch's Lives: Exploring Virtue and Vice* (Oxford and New York: Clarendon Press, 1999), p. 15.
10. Cicero, *Three Books of Duties to Marcus his Son*, trans. N. Grimald (London: Richard Tottel, 1574), sig. B2$^{r}$. For those with 'small Latin', Grimald's translation faces a Latin text. Editions survive from 1553, 1556, 1558, 1568, 1574, 1583, 1596, 1600.
11. See further Geoffrey Miles, *Shakespeare and the Constant Romans* (Oxford: Clarendon Press, 1996), ch. 1.
12. Michel de Montaigne, *The Essays or Moral, Politic and Military Discourses*, trans. J. Florio (London: Valentine Sims for Edward Blount, 1603), p. 67.
13. Sir Thomas Smith, *De Republica Anglorum*, ed. M. Dewar (Cambridge: Cambridge University Press, 1982), p. 57.
14. See Annabel M. Patterson, *Reading Holinshed's Chronicles* (Chicago: University of Chicago Press, 1994).
15. E. K. Chambers, *William Shakespeare: A Study of Facts and Problems*, 2 vols. (Oxford: Clarendon Press, 1930), i, 399.
16. William Shakespeare, *Julius Caesar*, ed. D. Daniell (Walton-on-Thames: Nelson, 1998), p. 60.
17. Sir Philip Sidney, *An Apology for Poetry or the Defence of Poesy*, ed. G. Shepherd (Manchester: Manchester University Press, 1973), p. 114.
18. Cf. Robert S. Miola, *Shakespeare's Rome* (Cambridge: Cambridge University Press, 1983), pp. 82–5, who sees Cassius as repudiating the Roman virtue of *pietas*. Coppélia Kahn, *Roman Shakespeare: Warriors, Wounds, and Women* (London: Routledge, 1997), pp. 88–9 perceptively relates this passage to the foundational role of male emulation within the Roman republic.

19. Andrew Hadfield, *Shakespeare and Republicanism* (Cambridge: Cambridge University Press, 2005). James S. Shapiro, *1599: A Year in the Life of William Shakespeare* (London: Faber and Faber, 2005), pp. 133–92.
20. Stuart Gillespie, *English Translation and Classical Reception: Towards a New Literary History* (Oxford: Wiley-Blackwell, 2011) trenchantly argues against those who want Shakespeare to reach back through North to Plutarch's Greek, but there are times when this is what he seems to do.
21. Plutarch, *Caesar*, ed. C. B. R. Pelling (Oxford: Oxford University Press, 2011), p. 65.
22. Plutarch, *Les Vies Des Hommes Illustres, Grecs et Romains, Comparées l'une avec l'autre*, trans. J. Amyot (Paris: Jacques du Puys, 1572), p. 127 (All Souls College Library, shelf mark SR.9.P).
23. Kenneth Burke, '*Coriolanus*—and the Delights of Faction', *The Hudson Review* 19 (1966), 185–202; 197.
24. Anne Barton, *Essays, Mainly Shakespearean* (Cambridge: Cambridge University Press, 1994), pp. 136–60.
25. On the theatricality of Plutarch and Shakespeare's development of Volumnia, see C. B. R. Pelling, *Plutarch and History: Eighteen Studies* (Swansea: Classical Press of Wales and Duckworth, 2002), pp. 387–411.
26. See Cynthia Marshall, 'Shakespearc, Crossing the Rubicon', *Shakespeare Survey* 53 (2000), 73–88, which presents this aspect of Plutarch as pivotal to Shakespeare's career and to his representation of character. Stuart Gillespie, *English Translation*, pp. 47–59 gives a more sceptical account.
27. Adrian Poole, *Coriolanus* (New York and London: Harvester Wheatsheaf, 1988), p. 102 puzzles over this 'astonishingly operatic address'.

## NOTES TO CONCLUSION

1. Thomas Heywood, *An Apology for Actors* (London: Nicholas Okes, 1612), sigs. B3$^{v}$–B4$^{r}$.
2. Thomas M. Greene, *The Light in Troy: Imitation and Discovery in Renaissance Poetry* (New Haven and London: Yale University Press 1982).
3. Michel de Montaigne, *The Essays or Moral, Politic and Military Discourses* (London: Valentine Sims for Edward Blount, 1603), p. 596 (3.9).
4. MacDonald P. Jackson, 'Francis Meres and the Cultural Contexts of Shakespeare's Rival Poet Sonnets', *Review of English Studies* 56 (2005), 224–46.

# *Further Reading*

GENERAL STUDIES

T. W. Baldwin, *William Shakspere's Small Latine and Lesse Greeke*, 2 vols. (Urbana, IL: University of Illinois Press, 1944) remains the standard account of what Shakespeare knew about the classics. Baldwin is prone to overestimate the quality of Shakespeare's education and to downplay the influence of any work which he might have encountered outside school. Charles Martindale and Michelle Martindale, *Shakespeare and the Uses of Antiquity: an Introductory Essay* (London and New York: Routledge, 1990) provide a good general introduction, while Charles Martindale and A. B. Taylor (eds), *Shakespeare and the Classics* (Cambridge: Cambridge University Press, 2004) includes essays on most aspects of Shakespeare's classicism. The now dated J. A. K. Thomson, *Shakespeare and the Classics* (London: Allen and Unwin, 1952) is generally sceptical about the extent of Shakespeare's knowledge and is of historical interest. A conservative selection of Shakespeare's more obvious classical (and other) sources is in Geoffrey Bullough (ed.), *Narrative and Dramatic Sources of Shakespeare*, 8 vols. (London: Routledge and Kegan Paul, 1957–75). Shakespeare's reading is exhaustively considered in Stuart Gillespie, *Shakespeare's Books: A Dictionary of Shakespeare's Sources* (London and New Brunswick, NJ: The Athlone Press, 2001), which includes helpful discussion both of individual authors and Shakespeare's view of them, as well as valuable bibliographies. For earlier bibliography, John W. Velz, *Shakespeare and the Classical Tradition: a Critical Guide to Commentary, 1660–1960* (Minneapolis: University of Minnesota Press, 1968) remains helpful. Stuart Gillespie, *English Translation and Classical Reception: Towards a New Literary History* (Oxford: Wiley-Blackwell, 2011) offers a wider perspective on English literature and classical reception, which supplements older but still valuable studies, including Thomas M. Greene, *The Light in Troy: Imitation and Discovery in Renaissance Poetry* (New Haven and London: Yale University Press, 1982) and G. W. Pigman, 'Versions of Imitation in the Renaissance', *Renaissance Quarterly* 33 (1980), 1–32. For specific Shakespearian debts to classical authors it is always helpful to read the introductions to editions of the plays and poems in the Oxford, New Cambridge, and Arden 2 and 3 series, although editors are increasingly prone to downplay classical influences, perhaps because they and their readers lack the necessary antennae to detect them. Volumes in the *Cambridge Companions* series generally provide the most approachable introductions to the major classical authors, and most include at least one chapter on reception, which does finally seem to be recognized as a valuable way of studying classical literatures by all but the most stubborn reactionaries in classics departments. Three of my own articles develop arguments similar to that of the book as a whole: Colin Burrow, 'Shakespeare and Humanistic Culture', in C. Martindale and A. B. Taylor (eds), *Shakespeare and the Classics* (Cambridge: Cambridge University Press, 2004), pp. 9–27, 'Shakespeare' in *The Oxford History of Classical Reception*, ed. Philip Hardie and Patrick Cheney (Oxford: Oxford University Press, forthcoming), and 'Classical Influences' in *The Oxford Handbook of Shakespeare's Poetry*, ed. Jonathan Post (Oxford: Oxford University Press, forthcoming).

## LEARNING FROM THE PAST

On sixteenth-century education, Rosemary O'Day, *Education and Society 1500–1800: The Social Foundations of Education in Early Modern Britain* (London: Longman, 1982) and David Cressy, *Education in Tudor and Stuart England* (London: E. Arnold, 1975) provide useful background. Valuable exposition and analysis of the rhetorical tradition, with some consideration of Shakespeare, is in Peter Mack, *Elizabethan Rhetoric: Theory and Practice* (Cambridge: Cambridge University Press, 2002), which supplements Baldwin's *Small Latine and Lesse Greeke*. Scholars since at least Joel B. Altman, *The Tudor Play of Mind: Rhetorical Inquiry and the Development of Elizabethan Drama* (Berkeley and London: University of California Press, 1978) and Emrys Jones, *The Origins of Shakespeare* (Oxford: Clarendon Press, 1977) have appreciated the significance of schoolroom practices for sixteenth-century drama, and pedagogy has increasingly been related to larger questions about relations to sexuality and to authority figures in the period in more recent criticism, including Rebecca W. Bushnell, *A Culture of Teaching: Early Modern Humanism in Theory and Practice* (Ithaca, NY: Cornell University Press, 1996), Jeffrey A. Dolven, *Scenes of Instruction in Renaissance Romance* (Chicago and London: University of Chicago Press, 2007), Lynn Enterline, 'Rhetoric, Discipline, and the Theatricality of Everyday Life in Elizabethan Grammar Schools', in P. Holland and S. Orgel (eds), *From Performance to Print in Shakespeare's England: Redefining British Theatre History* (Basingstoke: Palgrave, 2006), pp. 173–90, Andrew Wallace, *Virgil's Schoolboys: the Poetics of Pedagogy in Renaissance England* (Oxford: Oxford University Press, 2010), and, most recently and most fully, Lynn Enterline, *Shakespeare's Schoolroom: Rhetoric, Discipline, Emotion* (Philadelphia: University of Pennsylvania Press, 2012).

**VIRGIL**

Charles Martindale (ed.), *The Cambridge Companion to Virgil* (Cambridge: Cambridge University Press, 1997) contains essays on most aspects of Virgil, while Philip Hardie's crisp *Virgil* (Oxford: Oxford University Press for the Classical Association, 1998) provides a masterly ultra-brief introduction to the *oeuvre*. There is no single book on Shakespeare and Virgil: studies tend to focus on individual plays. Heather James, *Shakespeare's Troy* (Cambridge: Cambridge University Press, 1997) provides thought-provoking analysis of the matter of Troy, while Margaret Tudeau-Clayton, *Jonson, Shakespeare and Early Modern Virgil* (Cambridge: Cambridge University Press, 1998) contrasts Shakespeare's treatment of Virgil with Jonson's more conservative approach. Robert S. Miola, 'Vergil in Shakespeare', in J. D. Bernard (ed.), *Vergil at 2000: Commemorative Essays on the Poet and his Influence* (New York: AMS Press, 1986), pp. 241–58 provides an overview, while Patricia Parker, 'Romance and Empire: Anachronistic *Cymbeline*', in G. M. Logan and G. Teskey (eds), *Unfolded Tales: Essays on Renaissance Romance* (Ithaca NY: Cornell University Press, 1989), pp. 189–207, extends Virgilian influences into the late plays. A. D. Nuttall, 'Shakespeare and Virgil', in C. Martindale (ed.), *Virgil and his Influence: Bimillennial Studies* (Bristol: Bristol Classical Press, 1984), pp. 71–93 considers resemblances rather than influences between the two writers, and Charles Martindale, 'Shakespeare and Virgil', in C. Martindale and A. B. Taylor (eds), *Shakespeare and the Classics* (Cambridge: 2004), pp. 89–106 is sceptical about the degree of influence. Suggestive discussion of *The Tempest* is in David Scott Wilson-Okamura, 'Virgilian Models of Colonization in Shakespeare's *Tempest*', *ELH* 70 (2003), 709–37 and in Donna B. Hamilton, *Virgil and The Tempest: the Politics of Imitation* (Columbus: Ohio State University Press, 1990), while Barbara Bono, *Literary Transvaluation: From Vergilian Epic to Shakespearean Tragicomedy* (Berkeley, Los Angeles, and London: University of California Press, 1984), although it concentrates chiefly on *Antony and Cleopatra*, offers valuable thoughts on more general relationships between the two authors. Virgil's position in the pedagogic tradition is considered in Andrew Wallace, *Virgil's Schoolboys: The Poetics of Pedagogy in Renaissance England* (Oxford: Oxford University Press, 2010) and more widely in David Scott Wilson-Okamura, *Virgil in the Renaissance* (Cambridge: Cambridge University Press, 2010). The niche topic of the *Georgics* in Shakespeare is discussed in James C. Bulman, 'Shakespeare's Georgic Histories', *Shakespeare Survey* 38 (1985), 37–47 and Dermot Cavanagh, 'Georgic Sovereignty in *Henry V*', *Shakespeare Survey* 63 (2010), 114–26. The best single essay on the emotional and political impact of Virgil's *Aeneid* on Shakespeare's conception of tragedy, audiences, and compassion is

Heather James, 'Dido's Ear: Tragedy and the Politics of Response', *Shakespeare Quarterly* 52 (2001), 360–82, which has implications far beyond its title.

**OVID**

The best starting points for study of Ovid himself are Philip Hardie (ed.), *The Cambridge Companion to Ovid* (Cambridge: Cambridge University Press, 2002), followed by Philip Hardie, *Ovid's Poetics of Illusion* (Cambridge: Cambridge University Press, 2002). Katharina Volk's *Ovid* (Oxford: Wiley-Blackwell, 2010) is also lively and helpful, and can be supplemented by classic studies such as L. P. Wilkinson, *Ovid Recalled* (Cambridge: Cambridge University Press, 1955), Karl Galinsky, *Ovid's Metamorphoses: an Introduction to the Basic Aspects* (Oxford: Basil Blackwell, 1975), and Joseph B. Solodow, *The World of Ovid's Metamorphoses* (Chapel Hill, NC, and London: University of North Carolina Press, 1988), as well as more politically inflected work such as Alessandro Barchiesi, *The Poet and the Prince: Ovid and Augustan Discourse* (Berkeley and London: University of California Press, 1997) and Karl Galinsky, *Augustan Culture: an Interpretive Introduction* (Princeton, NJ: Princeton University Press, 1996). Peter E. Knox (ed.), *Oxford Readings in Ovid* (Oxford: Oxford University Press, 2006) gathers a good collection of essays, and Peter E. Knox (ed.), *A Companion to Ovid* (Chichester and Malden, MA: Wiley-Blackwell, 2009) includes authoritative overviews (among which Gordon Braden, 'Ovid and Shakespeare', is a particular highlight). Jonathan Bate, *Shakespeare and Ovid* (Oxford: Clarendon Press, 1993) provides a vivid and readable account of Ovid's influence on Shakespeare, while more detailed studies of particular aspects of the relationship can be found in A. B. Taylor (ed.), *Shakespeare's Ovid: the 'Metamorphoses' in the Plays and Poems* (Cambridge: Cambridge University Press, 2000) and in Charles Martindale and A. B. Taylor (eds), *Shakespeare and the Classics* (Cambridge: Cambridge University Press, 2004). On Ovid's presence in early-modern culture, Richard A. Lanham, *The Motives of Eloquence: Literary Rhetoric in the Renaissance* (New Haven and London: Yale University Press, 1976) and Leonard Barkan, *The Gods Made Flesh: Metamorphosis and the Pursuit of Paganism* (New Haven and London: Yale University Press, 1986) remain informative and imaginative, while more recent studies with psychoanalytic and theoretical ambitions include Lynn Enterline, *Rhetoric of the Body from Ovid to Shakespeare* (Cambridge: Cambridge University Press, 2000) and Goran V. Stanivukovic, *Ovid and the Renaissance Body* (Toronto and London: University of Toronto Press, 2001). *Ovid's Metamorphoses Translated by Arthur Golding*, ed. M. Forey (London: Penguin, 2002) presents a modernized text of Golding's translation, one of several English versions discussed in Raphael Lyne, *Ovid's Changing Worlds: English Metamorphoses, 1567–1632* (Oxford: Oxford University Press, 2001).

## ROMAN COMEDY

R. L. Hunter, *The New Comedy of Greece and Rome* (Cambridge: Cambridge University Press, 1985) remains a reliable guide to ancient comedy in general, supplemented by the more recent Marianne McDonald and J. Michael Walton (eds), *The Cambridge Companion to Greek and Roman Theatre* (Cambridge: Cambridge University Press, 2007). Alison Sharrock, *Reading Roman Comedy: Poetics and Playfulness in Plautus and Terence* (Cambridge: Cambridge University Press, 2009) is sharp on the self-consciousness of the Roman playwrights. On Plautus, Erich Segal, *Roman Laughter: the Comedy of Plautus* (Oxford: Oxford University Press, 1987) emphasizes 'festive comic' elements, while Niall W. Slater, *Plautus in Performance: the Theatre of the Mind* (Princeton: Princeton University Press, 1985) is suggestive for thinking about Shakespearian illusion-making. Eduard Fraenkel, *Plautine Elements in Plautus* (Oxford: Oxford University Press, 2007) is the classic study, and is not quite as German as its title makes it sound. The recent revised Loeb Classical Library edition, ed. Wofgang de Melo (Harvard: Harvard University Press, 2011) has an extremely helpful introduction. On Terence, Sander M. Goldberg, *Understanding Terence* (Princeton: Princeton University Press, 1986) provides a clear and reliable introduction. The special issue of *Ramus* 33 (2004) contains some valuable material (notably John Henderson's aggressively anti-humanistic reading and Emily Gowers's fine discussion of the prologues). Shakespeare's reading in comic theory is outlined in T. W. Baldwin, *Shakspere's Five-act Structure* (Urbana: The University of Illinois Press, 1947), while his general debt to different comic traditions, classical and Italian, is clearly set out in Leo Salingar, *Shakespeare and the Traditions of Comedy* (Cambridge: Cambridge University Press, 1974). Robert S. Miola, *Shakespeare and Classical Comedy: the Influence of Plautus and Terence* (Oxford: Clarendon Press, 1994) suggests debts to Roman comedy extend even into *King Lear*, while Wolfgang Riehle, *Shakespeare, Plautus, and the Humanist Tradition* (Cambridge: D.S. Brewer, 1990) focuses more narrowly on the earlier plays. By far the most wide-ranging and thought-provoking recent study of this topic (although its title shows that it covers other areas too) is Lorna Hutson, *The Invention of Suspicion: Law and Mimesis in Shakespeare and Renaissance Drama* (Oxford: Oxford University Press, 2007).

## SENECA

T. S. Eliot's classic introduction to the 1927 edition of Newton's 1581 volume (*Seneca: His Ten Tragedies*, ed. T. Newton and T. S. Eliot, 2 vols. (London and New York: Constable and Co. Ltd.; A.A. Knopf, 1927)) is a provocative starting point, while C. J. Herington, 'Senecan Tragedy', *Arion* 5 (1966), 422–71 remains a—probably indeed *the*—outstanding critical study. More recent work on the dynamics and literary relationships of Senecan drama is in Alessandro Schiesaro, *The Passions in Play: Thyestes and the Dynamics of Senecan Drama* (Cambridge: Cambridge University Press, 2003). A. J. Boyle, *Tragic Seneca: an Essay in the Theatrical Tradition* (London and New York: Routledge, 1997) provides vivid contextualization and a concluding survey of Seneca's Renaissance influence, while the essays collected in John G. Fitch (ed.), *Seneca* (Oxford: Oxford University Press, 2008) give much local insight. Most recent discussion of relationships to Shakespeare tends to start by resisting the largely negative view of the matter in G. K. Hunter, *Dramatic Identities and Cultural Tradition: Studies in Shakespeare and his Contemporaries: Critical Essays* (Liverpool: Liverpool University Press, 1978), pp. 159–213 (anticipated by F. L. Lucas, *Seneca and Elizabethan Tragedy* (Cambridge: Cambridge University Press, 1922), pp. 117–23), which in turn was prompted by John William Cunliffe, *The Influence of Seneca on Elizabethan Tragedy: an Essay* (London: Macmillan & Co., 1893), who achieved the rare but not unprecedented feat of being both implausible in overall argument and drily empirical in method. Gordon Braden, *Renaissance Tragedy and the Senecan Tradition: Anger's Privilege* (New Haven and London: Yale University Press, 1985) remains the most intellectually ambitious and stimulating account of Seneca's drama and its impact on Shakespeare, and ranges well beyond England, while Robert S. Miola, *Shakespeare and Classical Tragedy: the Influence of Seneca* (Oxford: Clarendon Press, 1992) explores the influence in impressive detail throughout the canon. The best study of the role of Stoic philosophy in Shakespeare is Geoffrey Miles, *Shakespeare and the Constant Romans* (Oxford: Clarendon Press, 1996). Tough meat, although immensely nourishing, is Mayer Roland, 'Personata Stoa: Neostoicism and Senecan Tragedy', *Journal of the Warburg and Courtauld Institutes* 57 (1994), 151–74.

## PLUTARCH

Tim Duff, *Plutarch's Lives: Exploring Virtue and Vice* (Oxford: Clarendon Press, 1999) is the most approachable introduction to the *Lives*, and presents Plutarch as a sophisticated 'literary' historian who has much in common with

Shakespeare. Significant but sometimes technical revaluations of his work and working practices are collected in C. B. R. Pelling, *Plutarch and History: Eighteen Studies* (Swansea: Classical Press of Wales and Duckworth, 2002), and Pelling's selection, *Rome in Crisis: Nine Lives by Plutarch*, ed. I. Scott-Kilvert and C. B. R. Pelling (London: Penguin, 2010), though it does not include all the Roman lives used by Shakespeare, has a very valuable introduction, as does Plutarch, *Life of Antony*, ed. C. B. R. Pelling (Cambridge: Cambridge University Press, 1988), and Plutarch, *Caesar*, ed. C. B. R. Pelling (Oxford: Oxford University Press, 2011), each of which includes discussion of Shakespeare. The special issue of *Poetica* 48 (1997), ed. Mary Ann McGrail contains a number of essays on relationships between Shakespeare and Plutarch. Mungo William MacCallum, *Shakespeare's Roman Plays and Their Background* (London: Macmillan, 1910), though now a little quaint, still has value as a careful and learned study. On the Roman plays in general, see Reuben A. Brower, *Hero and Saint: Shakespeare and the Graeco-Roman Heroic Tradition* (Oxford: Clarendon Press, 1971), Paul A. Cantor, *Shakespeare's Rome: Republic and Empire* (Ithaca: Cornell University Press, 1976), Coppélia Kahn, *Roman Shakespeare: Warriors, Wounds, and Women* (London: Routledge, 1997), Geoffrey Miles, *Shakespeare and the Constant Romans* (Oxford: Clarendon Press, 1996), and Robert S. Miola, *Shakespeare's Rome* (Cambridge: Cambridge University Press, 1983). The tendency to exaggerate the coherence of the group is on display in John W. Velz, 'The Ancient World in Shakespeare: Authenticity or Anachronism? A Retrospect', *Shakespeare Survey* (1978), 1–12, along with a useful overview of past criticism. On *Antony and Cleopatra*, Barbara Bono, *Literary Transvaluation: From Vergilian Epic to Shakespearean Tragicomedy* (Berkeley, Los Angeles, and London: University of California Press, 1984) and Janet Adelman, *The Common Liar: an Essay on Antony and Cleopatra* (New Haven: Yale University Press, 1973) remain helpful, while on *Coriolanus*, stimulating critical points of departure are the essay on the play in Stanley Cavell, *Disowning Knowledge in Seven Plays of Shakespeare* (Cambridge: Cambridge University Press, 2003), pp. 143 ff., and Janet Adelman, *Suffocating Mothers: Fantasies of Maternal Origin in Shakespeare's Plays, Hamlet to The Tempest* (New York and London: 1992), pp. 146–64, as well as Adrian Poole, *Coriolanus* (New York and London: Harvester Wheatsheaf, 1988). Excellent on Shakespeare's debts to Plutarchan psychology is Cynthia Marshall, 'Shakespeare, Crossing the Rubicon', *Shakespeare Survey* 53 (2000), 73–88.

# Index